SOCIAL NETWORKING
FOR SCHOOLS

SOCIAL NETWORKING FOR SCHOOLS

Steven M. Baule and Julie E. Lewis

 LINWORTH

AN IMPRINT OF ABC-CLIO, LLC
Santa Barbara, California • Denver, Colorado • Oxford, England

Library of Congress Cataloging-in-Publication Data

Baule, Steven M., 1966– author.
  Social networking for schools / Steven M. Baule and Julie E. Lewis.
     pages cm
  Includes bibliographical references and index.
     ISBN 978–1–58683–537–8 (hardcopy : alk. paper) — ISBN 978–1–58683–538–5 (ebook)
  1. Education—Effect of technological innovations on. 2. Educational technology—Social aspects. 3. Students—Social networks. I. Lewis, Julie E. author. II. Title.
  LB1028.3.B384 2012
  371.33—dc23   2012014933

ISBN: 978–1–58683–537–8
EISBN: 978–1–58683–538–5

16 15 14 13 12   1 2 3 4 5

This book is also available on the World Wide Web as an eBook.
Visit www.abc-clio.com for details.

Linworth
An Imprint of ABC-CLIO, LLC

ABC-CLIO, LLC
130 Cremona Drive, P.O. Box 1911
Santa Barbara, California 93116-1911

This book is printed on acid-free paper ∞

Manufactured in the United States of America

CONTENTS

CHAPTER 1

Overview of Social Media Tools

According to some futurists, handheld devices will replace desktop and laptop computers by 2020 as the most common method of interacting on the Internet. Smart phones are now outselling other types of cellular phones. Smart phones and tablets have outpaced computer sales in the last 12 months. The world is becoming increasingly digital and mobile. For instance, the print newspaper, which has historically been a hallmark of democratic societies serving information to the masses, is dying. Readership is down by seven million people in the last 25 years, and small papers are closing daily. Are those former newspaper readers simply going without? No, they are moving to digital formats. Websites, wikis, and blogs are replacing traditional news services. Information is more fractured and multi-faceted, and the 30-second web video is replacing the three- to five-page news magazine article. With over a billion web pages to go to, how does one even find the best sources of information? Well, one checks out what their friends are reading by checking Facebook. Then check Delicious to see what is popular, or just try StumbleUpon.

The *Chicago Tribune* joined the social networking movement when it created Triblocal.com, sites where individuals are able to post news articles about the happenings in their specific neighborhood or suburb. The best of these are then published weekly. It has generated additional readership and revenue in an otherwise gloomy publishing market.

Barack Obama raised $55 million in one month during the 2008 presidential election campaign through social networking and without a single traditional fund-raiser the same month. Social networking properly used is able to reach a tremendous amount of people in an extremely short period of time. Over 10 percent of available graduate programs are online programs, according to the listings of GradeSchools.com.

More than five million people follow Lady Gaga on Twitter. Similar numbers follow Ashton Kutcher and Britney Spears. One teacher decided to capitalize on her students' love for Twitter and sends out tweets to remind students to come to class and be prepared for the assignments that are due. She claims that tweets have increased success in the classroom by 35 percent.

Ninety-three percent of adult Americans own a cell phone. Over 53 percent of adults in the United States now have a social media account of one type or another. However, about two-thirds of public schools ban cell phone use. Since most students already have cell phones by ninth grade, schools could save money by allowing cell phone use and not purchasing student response systems, but using the cell phones for that purpose.

It seems clear to almost all that social networking and digital realities are converging on all aspects of modern life. Schools and educators need to adapt them for student learning and engagement. In order to incorporate social networking tools into schools, the first step is to understand what social networks are. However, there are a wide range of definitions being used to define social networking and social networking tools. The term social networking can conjure up a wide range of images; a business woman using LinkedIn to make new sales contacts, Katy Perry posting a sample of a new video to her Facebook page, three middle school students texting about basketball, a school principal tweeting a reminder about parent-teacher conferences, or a librarian posting a review of the most recent book she read are all examples of social networking. The Social Media Buying Guide (www.socialmediabuyingguide. org/community/glossary.htm) may have one of the best definitions for social networking as "the assembly, or coming together of individuals in specific groups or communities. Although social networking is possible in person, especially in schools or in the workplace, it is most popular online." Doug Williams SEO Services (www.dougwilliams.com/blog/blogging-terms/web -20-terms.php) defines social networking as "linking people to each other in some way. Social networking sites bring people together who people interested in a particular subject." However, this definition does stop short of what educators are often hoping for. Wikipedia (which may be the most commonly used social network tool in schools—often to the chagrin of teachers and librarians) explains social networks in the following way:

> A *social networking service* is an online service, platform, or site that focuses on building and reflecting of social networks or social relations among people, e.g., who share interests and/or activities. A social network service essentially consists of a representation of each user (often a profile), his/her social links, and a variety of additional services. Most social network services are web based and provide means for users to interact over the internet, such as e-mail and instant messaging,

although online community services are sometimes considered as a social network service. In a broader sense, social network service usually means an individual-centered service whereas online community services are group-centered. Social networking sites allow users to share ideas, activities, events, and interests within their individual networks. (Wikipedia, 2012)

The Young Adult Library Service Association (YALSA, 2010) defines social networking in the online world as "the ability to connect with people through websites and other technologies like discussion boards."

For the purposes of this text, the focus will be on those communities that are either partially or entirely virtual. Educators want to take social networking one step further and not simply link people, but link them in ways that will facilitate and support learning. The concept is that social networking is more than simple access to Web 2.0 functionality. At its most basic, social networking allows individuals to become part of a community. Simply being able to post a comment to another's blog doesn't make someone truly part of a social community. The purpose of this text is to provide guidance and examples on how to effectively use online social networking to support the goals of education.

A question that often comes up is: Why should schools embrace social networking? Many people who grew up before the digital revolution see MySpace, Twitter, and other social networking services as nothing more than a waste of time in front of a keyboard. Actress and octogenarian Betty White had the following to say about social networking when she appeared on *Saturday Night Live* in May 2010:

> I really have to thank Facebook ... I didn't know what Facebook was, and now that I do know what it is, I have to say, it sounds like a huge waste of time. I would never say the people on it are losers, but that's only because I'm polite. People say "But Betty, Facebook is a great way to connect with old friends." Well at my age, if I wanna connect with old friends, I need a Ouija Board. Needless to say, we didn't have Facebook when I was growing up. We had phonebooks, but you wouldn't waste an afternoon with it. (Betty White's *Saturday Night Live* monologue, http://www.hulu.com/watch/147966/saturday-night-live-betty-white-monologue [accessed April 6, 2012])

Although White was saying this in the context of a Facebook campaign to get her to host *SNL*, the sentiments expressed are often expressed by the pre-digital generations. So, why would one want to "waste time" on social networking in schools? Primarily, in order to be successful, schools have to be a reflection of society. The ultimate goal of education is to prepare children for the world into which they will graduate. So, schools must embrace the technologies that are being used in the society in which children will gradu-ate. Social networks are growing at an incredible rate. Currently, if Face-book were a country, it would now be the third-most populous in the world behind only China and India. A year ago, it was the sixth-more popu-lous country. At press time, 7.5 Facebook users are added every second. China's birthrate is approximately 1.7 people per second and India's 1.2 people per second. Facebook is clearly a global phenomenon, but it is by no means a unique service.

Many students are already using Facebook and similar sites on the web. According to the National School Board Association (NSBA, 2007), 81 per-cent of students between the ages of 9 and 17 use social networking sites, and 71 percent use them at least weekly. In some ways, not addressing social networking is no less reasonable than if schools would choose to eliminate driver education. The argument might go something like this: "Just because students drive when they aren't in school doesn't mean that we have to em-brace cars and teach students how to use them in school." Of course, most states require driver education courses. Some few are beginning to require some type of Internet safety training, which often requires some exposure to social networking. Many schools didn't create driver education courses until there was either a state requirement or a perceived need due to traffic safety issues in the community. In many ways, social networks are currently ignored as not being a "legitimate educational topic or tool," but social net-works can be legitimate education tools. Cars however, are no more than a way to transport students to and from school.

Why some educators continue to ignore the true potential of technology in education is frustrating and shortsighted. There is no large industry besides education that isn't embracing technology to improve itself. Ron Paige, at the time U.S. secretary of education, stated the following in 2002.

> But to a large extent, schools have been an exception to this informa-tion revolution. Indeed, education is the only business still debating the usefulness of technology. Schools remain unchanged for the most part despite numerous reforms and increased investments in computers and networks. The way we organize schools and provide instruction is essentially the same as it was when our Founding Fathers went to school. Put another way, we still educate our students based on an agricultural timetable, in an industrial setting, yet tell students they live in a digital age.

Education needs to embrace new methods and tools in order to continue to complete in a much smaller world. According to the NBSA (2007), 60 per-cent of school-aged children and young adults using social networks discuss school-related topics and 50 percent use social networks to communicate about schoolwork. There is no one right answer to solve all of the issues in education. Social networking tools are simply another set of tools to use to try to engage students, to support learning for both students and staff, and to communicate the successes and needs of the school with stakeholder and the larger community. This text will attempt to provide the reader with a basic understanding of existing and emerging social networking services and how they can be harnessed to assist schools.

A potential reason for the lack of use of social networks is that the users of social networking sites tend to be younger than the average faculty member. One educational blogger noted schools don't use social media because "their leaders don't understand social media. Too many of them think that social media tools are just about sharing what you had for breakfast (BTW, I had oatmeal) or sharing pictures from parties" (Byrne, 2010).

Of the major social networking sites, only LinkedIn, which focuses on business relationships, Flickr, a photo-sharing site and Classmates, which focuses on reunion type relationships, have a majority of users over 34 years old. Only LinkedIn has more than two-thirds of its members in an age category of 35 or older (Jordan, 2012). Educators are much less likely to be using social networking than their students. In Pingdom's recent survey (2010), a full 25 percent of all social network users were between the ages of 35 and 44. Forty-two percent of all social network users were under 35.

WEB 2.0 SERVICES

The term Web 2.0 is generally used to identify tools and technologies created around the idea that the people who use the web shouldn't passively absorb what's available; rather, they should be active contributors, helping customize media and technology for their own purposes as well as those of their communities. Instant messaging, chat, blogs, social networking services, and video-sharing services are all examples of Web 2.0 technologies.

In many ways, it is difficult to clearly differentiate between the web, Web 2.0 services, and social networking services. World Wide Web inventor Tim Berners-Lee called the term Web 2.0 a "piece of jargon," precisely because he intended the web in his vision to be "a collaborative medium, a place where we all meet and read and write" (Lawson, 2005). Berners-Lee's point is that the web has always been intended as a way to share information. The tools available simply make it easier to do so than those tools previously available. So, in fact, Web 2.0 is really more like Web 1.1; an upgrade to existing services and not a new version. Web 2.0 will most likely remain in the vernacular to mean an interactive website or service.

Social networking services are a subset of Web 2.0 services that not only allow for customization and user definition, but that allow for the ability to foster collaboration and community. Twenty-one percent of students in 2007 (NSBA, 2007) were creating or editing online content each week beyond the simple exchange or posting of music, photos, and/or videos. That number is almost certainly higher today.

One area of concern is that students who admit to not following common Internet safety rules, such as not sharing personal information, representing themselves as someone else, or posting inappropriate pictures, are also more likely to use social networking services to organize events, promote new sites, or influence their peers to specific brands or services. There is clearly a need for these students to receive guidance and direction on how to use social networks safely and potentially with greater effectiveness. As of 2007, about 80 percent of school districts have some prohibitions about on-line chat and instant messaging. More than 50 percent prohibited any access to social networking in 2007 (NSBA, 2007). Sixty-nine percent of school districts ban cell phone use. However, nearly two-thirds of students in such schools report that they use their phones during the school day anyway. The average high school student sends about 400 text messages a week, and 100 of those are while sitting in a classroom (Lenhart, et al., 2010).

As part of the report on Online Social Networking (2007), the NSBA made the following recommendations regarding social networking:

- Consider using social networking for staff communications and pro-fessional development
- Find ways to harness the educational value of social networking
- Ensure equitable access
- Pay attention to the nonconformists
- Reexamine social networking policies
- Encourage social networking companies to increase educational value.

The specific recommendation regarding nonconformists is because the study found them to be much more engaged and influential in social networking but only lukewarm about schooling in its traditional format. The NSBA feels that social networking will be an important way to engage some segments of students moving forward.

BASIC SOCIAL NETWORKING SERVICES

What are those social networking services? Social networking services provide three basic functions; connect, share and publish.

Connecting is the basic function of most social network services. A user creates a profile and then connects to others. Profile information varies greatly among the various services. Most systems allow for some images and videos to be posted as part of a profile. Profiles can be created for indi-viduals as well as for organizations and products. Connections can come from a variety of directions. Most sites will gather contact information from a person's e-mail account(s) and search to see if those people have profiles and then auto-generate invitations to make connections. A teacher could simply send a connection link to parents or ask students to connect to her site.

Many sites also allow for groups of like-minded people to be established. Some of these may be geographical, tied to the region where the user lives or to their alma mater. Groups can focus on hobbies or other interests as well. History teachers and baseball coaches might each form a group. Usually members can join multiple groups.

Most social network sites allow for some type of connections to other users. Sites like LinkedIn see connecting as the key function of the site—in this case, so professionals can continue to stay in touch even when they change positions or companies without having to rebuild a Rolodex. In fact, one communications director identified LinkedIn as the Rolodex of social networks.

Once a member has connected, they can usually share information with other members. *Sharing* is the second basic function. This can be as simple as commenting about others' profiles or posting a picture to connected members. It can be as complicated as sharing multipart multimedia presentations and videos. Teachers can share videos with students or parents, principals can post welcome videos, etc. Edmodo allows teachers to provide a library of materials for students. Some schools post video announcements each day. Sharing is generally limited to those people who are connected together via the social network site. This allows one to share pictures with friends, coworkers, or classmates but not necessarily with everyone on the web. The privacy settings of most sites allow a user to determine with how wide of a group they wish to share materials. Sharing can also take the form of e-mail, comments on profile pages, or an announcement of one's current location or relationship status. CourseCracker.com provides links to external sites for most of its subject areas as well.

Publishing is the third basic function of social networking services. Publishing is in many ways simply sharing to a much larger audience. Instead of limiting access to one's contacts, published materials are available to everyone on the web, or at least everyone with an account on the site in question. Videos, blog entries, white papers, and multimedia presentations are all publishable on the web via social networks. Some sites, like YouTube and TeacherTube are much more interested in sharing and distributing content then in connecting users. Although users can comment on videos, for instance in YouTube, comments often are recorded for only a small fraction of the views recorded for a video selection. If one wants a rap video to help students learn the original 13 colonies or a puppet video on test anxiety, one will be able to find them on TeacherTube. Other sites are set up to share favorite websites, favorite restaurants, etc. Student publishing gives an entire new set of audience options for students producing project work in schools.

Blogs are a good example of a service in which publishing is the primary focus. Privacy and safety considerations are considerable in determining whether to share or publish student work in many cases.

Core to all three of these functions is for a user to have a *profile* that allows them to connect with other users. The profile is the core building block of the social network. Users enter basic information, such as their location, age, gender, marital status, and level of education. Many also ask several "favorite" questions; for instance, what is your favorite book, song movie, actor/actress, or television series? Some services allow the user to greatly personalize the look of the profile page. Some third parties even provide profile page templates for some sites. Some examples include MySpace Pimper (www.myspacepimper.com), PageRage (www.pagerage.com) and Webfetti (www.webfetti.com).

Once a user's profile has been created, the user can look for *friends*, or connections, to other members of the network. Some users will try to have a huge number of friends. Others will be more selective about whom they befriend. This is particularly important in educational circles, where teachers and administrators are often held to a higher standard than others in the community. Teachers and library media specialists may want to be careful about whom they friend. Even if the school or district one works for doesn't prohibit *friending* students, one should weigh the advantages and disadvantages of doing so. Most systems then allow the user to determine with whom they want to share their profile and related material. Many systems base sharing levels on three tiers:

1. A user's friends or direct connections (most restrictive)
2. Friends of friends or indirect connections (restrictive)
3. Access to any registered user (less restrictive)

Some systems also allow guests to view materials without registering, effectively making materials available to anyone with web access. A good example of how to manage privacy settings for Facebook is Alison Driscoll's *Facebook Fail: How to Use Facebook Privacy Settings and Avoid Disaster*, available at http://mashable.com/2009/04/28/facebook-privacy-settings/. The concepts that she articulates are readily adaptable to other social networks as well.

Users can also gather connections by joining interest groups or forums within a social network. Commonly referred to in nearly all systems as *groups*, this makes it easy for new users to find other users with similar interests. Yahoo, for instance, has over 900 groups dedicated to animal topics, including Holistictoller to discuss holistic heath care for our Nova Scotia Duck Tolling Retrievers and SkunkInfo, which is more self-explanatory. Over 39,000 groups cover topics on games and gaming from bingo to video game development.

For good sets of step-by-step instructions on how to start building a social networking presence, check out the following, websites:

About.com—How to Get Started with Social Networking: http://webtrends.about.com/od/socialnetworking/a/socialnetwork_h.htm
Edutopia.com—How to Use Social-Networking Technology for Learning: www.edutopia.org/how-use-social-networking-technology
PLCMC's Learning 2.0—Web 2.0 23 Step Tutorial: http://plcmcl2-things.blogspot.com

The PLCMC site offers an excellent step-by-step introduction for those interested in getting more hands-on experience with social media and Web 2.0 tools in general. It is an excellent way to provide basic familiarity for hesitant users who don't know how to start exploring social networking.

A secondary function of many social networking services is linking two or more parties to external content or secondary services outside of its scope. Facebook does this with a wide variety of applications. These "apps" are often provided for some commercial purpose, either directly or indirectly. Games like FarmVille, Mafia Wars, and CityVille by Zynga are linked through Facebook and MySpace. Nearly 60 million people are active users of FarmVille according to Zynga's own website. Currently, there aren't many such apps that have direct educational value.

REASONS TO USE SOCIAL NETWORKING

Educators will often ask, "Why use social networks? It is just one more thing for me to worry about, and I already have enough on my plate."

Although many reasons are articulated for embracing social networking with students, those reasons tend to fall into four general categories: social networking is a significant portion of the world into which students will graduate; schools need to instruct students on how to use social networks safely; social networking builds collaboration skills that students will need in the workplace; and students are enthusiastic about social networking technologies, and schools should capitalize on that enthusiasm.

Currently social networks are one of the fastest-growing segments of the economy. For schools to ignore the impact of social networks on society would go against one of the basic premises of education's role—to prepare students for the society in which they will live and work as adults. Social networks allow members to communicate effectively throughout the electronic global environment. William Gibson spoke to the ubiquitous nature of electronic networks when he stated, "One of the things our grandchildren will find quaintest about is that we distinguish the digital from the real; the virtual from the real. In the future, that will become literally impossible."

Today's virtual social networks are as real and vital in today's society as country clubs were in the 1960s, or veterans' organizations were immediately after the Civil War or World War II. Professionals use social networks to expand their connections beyond the campus or corporations. Parents stay in contact with children. Former classmates reconnect, and artists promote their work.

Working with social networks does have its downside, as critics will happily point out. It is important that students learn how to work appropriately and safely in this environment. Schools are the best place to teach students how to navigate the vast electronic environments of the world. The world has always been a dangerous place, but one of the difficulties of electronic media in general is the difficulty in distinguishing the real from the digital. A saying from the early days of the Internet was "on the Internet, no one knows you are a dog." Similarly, teens often don't understand that not everyone on the Internet is completely honest and straightforward. The opportunity to expose students to social networking in the supervised setting of school is one that educators shouldn't let pass by. There are many education-oriented social networking options, most of which are free and greatly reduce many of the concerns often identified around student use of social networks. School attorneys listed student and employee misuse of the Internet as one of the top 10 legal concerns of 2010 (Stover, 2010). Some of the specific concerns raised by utilizing social networks are addressed in the next section of the text.

Social networks are an excellent way for students to get experience in a collaborative environment. Collaboration has been identified for the last several decades as an important workplace skill for students to learn. Cooperative learning pedagogy has been put into place in nearly all schools to support this need for better collaborative skills among students. The ability of workers to collaborate is considered a primary skill for success in the twenty-first-century workplace. The Partnership for 21st Century Skills lists the following collaboration skills as essential:

- Demonstrate ability to work effectively and respectfully with diverse teams
- Exercise flexibility and willingness to be helpful in making necessary compromises to accomplish a common goal
- Assume shared responsibility for collaborative work, and value the individual contributions made by each team member

Educators who don't feel that social networking should be embraced simply because the rest of the world, from General Electric to the U.S. Navy, has embraced them, may consider the specific collaborative skills students can learn from social networking experiences that will transfer to other school and work environments. One unintended consequence of social network use by students is that use breaks down the barriers among school cliques. Students seem to be more willing to work with others outside of their normal social circles online. Perhaps this is because online relationships can remove many of the inherent stereotypes teens perceive in their real-world interactions.

The last of the reasons to utilize social networking for students is that current adolescents and young adults are truly enthusiastic about social networking. They use it in all aspects of their lives. As the NSBA (2007) survey mentioned above, nearly three-quarters of children between the ages of 9 and 17 are using social networks at least once a week. The American Association of School Administrators (AASA) executive director, Dan Domenech (2010), recently encouraged superintendents and administrators to support the use of technology in order to harness the enthusiasm that students show for technology and in turn to get students more engaged in their learning. Since the first days of research on educational technology, one of the key findings uncovered was that children and teens were excited about using technology. The corollary to that finding is that students will spend more time on educational tasks when those tasks involve technology. Where students spend more time on a task, they tend to learn more. Utilizing social network technologies will engage students who are not engaged using traditional methods.

Tied to the engagement issue for students is that the effective use of technology can be used to expand the school day and even the school year. Discussions that used to be limited to a 50-minute class period in which only a few students could actually contribute can now expand to allow all students to contribute, and the discussion can take place over several days. Summer reading lists can be fostered with the development of a book discussion site so students can discuss books as they read them and not have to wait until August or September. Science lab results can be discussed in the same way. Role-playing simulations that are often not used due to a lack of time can now be managed with little instructional time being taken up, as much discussion can be done online. These types of interaction effectively allow schools to support 24/7 learning in the ways that ATMs and online banking have made banks into 24/7 institutions.

SOCIAL NETWORKING FOR PROFESSIONAL DEVELOPMENT

Providing professional development for educators is a constant struggle. Current budgets are stretched to the limit in many, if not all situations.

Besides the dollar cost of providing staff with excellent staff development options, there is a time factor. Taking teachers out of the classroom is another issue that schools deal with. Substitutes often are not able to instruct at the same level as regular staff, if at all. Professional development workshops in schools historically have often been one-shot affairs dealing with whatever the hot topic of the day was. With the changes in education requiring more data-driven accountability, such one-shot, fire-and-forget type of workshops are needing to be replaced with long-term commitment to capacity building among the staff. Another real area of concern in many districts is the ability to provide useful staff development for the low-incident professionals within the school. These are the professionals who don't have many, if any other, colleagues performing the same function within the building or district. These range from library media specialists and technology facilitators to occupational therapists and social workers. Many schools and districts have few professionals in these roles, and providing effective staff development for these categories of professionals is a constant challenge. It is rare for the needs of these specialists to be addressed at in-service days, where, except in the largest districts, the focus is generally on the needs of the classroom teacher.

As mentioned earlier, a significant portion of graduate study is available online. Many educators are used to using online engines as part of their learning, so the learning curve that existed at the turn of the twenty-first century isn't as high as it used to be. Most educators are becoming familiar with how to engage in online collaboration, particularly at the classroom level.

Social networking can address all of these concerns to at least some level. Online professional development is often less expensive than traditional workshops and conferences. Even if the cost of the workshop itself is the same, the cost of travel, lodging, and food is eliminated if not greatly reduced. This allows schools to spend more of their limited funding on professional development content. Some of these workshops are asynchronous, which provides for even more flexibility for staffing.

Online professional development is often accompanied by ongoing support for participant networking through a ning, a wiki, or some other interactive service. This allows participants to continue the conversations from a workshop into the future as they return to their schools and put into practice what they learned during training. In the 1990s, the last few minutes of a conference presentation were devoted to questions. Then e-mail arrived and allowed participants to communicate one to one with the presenter for weeks afterward. Now, social networks allow for robust interaction between the presenters and all of the participants, which can add great value to the initial presentation. This is especially true for those staff in low-incident positions such as library media specialists and many of the student service specialists.

An important side effect of these social networks is that instead of workshops being a one-and-done type of situation, presenters and other experts often now provide some level of ongoing support to participants. This allows for the true capacity building that should be the goal of effective professional development.

One of the major reasons for attending professional conferences is the networking opportunities that the social events at those conferences provide. Social networks, often established through professional organizations, allow for the type of networking that previously required significant time and travel. Some of the first of these types of resource- and expertise-sharing networks were established as listservs, LM_NET and EDTECH being excellent examples. However, social networks allow even greater connectivity and interaction between individuals. Social networking can further enhance the effectiveness of a school or district's professional learning communities and can create a virtual professional learning environment for those who don't have a supportive environment in their own building.

One effective use of social networking tools on the immediate horizon is the wider implementation of personal learning networks (PLNs) for individual educators. Using personal learning environments (PLE), which can be based on something as simple as using iGoogle, to create a basic website from which to work or a much more complicated commercial site, educators can control their own learning as to scope, pace, and methods of instruction. (See the image illustrating a sample iGoogle home page.) They can then link their PLE with other users (both fellow learners and experts) and expand the PLE into a PLN. The user can link to online course content, documents, government regulations and other materials, image archives, and more. Similar use of technology for personal learning development can be done with students from the middle school level forward.

Sample igoogle page

Creating Your Personalized iGoogle Home Page

1. Create a Google account if you don't already have one.

2. After creating an account, go to www.igoogle.com. If you haven't previously set up an iGoogle page, you should encounter the following page.

    a. Select your interests (you will be able to change them later).

    b. Select a theme.

    c. Enter your location and ZIP code.

    d. Select See Your Page.

3. A new home page should appear that will allow you to easily continue to modify it.

A menu along the left can help you navigate.

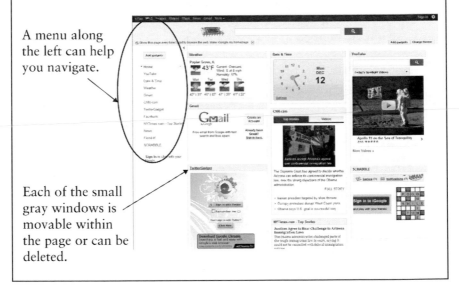

Each of the small gray windows is movable within the page or can be deleted.

4. Click on any "Gadget bar" to
see a simple menu Select Delete
This Gadget to remove the
gadget, etc. Minimizing the
gadget will show only the bar.
Maximizing the gadget will
make it take up the entire window.
Click, hold, and drag on any bar
to move the gadget to another
location in the window.

5. To add additional gadgets, select the Add Gadgets button at the top
left of the navigation menu. A gadget menu that allows you to search
for and select additional items for your iGoogle page will appear.

Adding RSS feeds to the page can let you read your favorite blog without
having to go to another page. Your e-mail can also be added in through
Gmail. Gadgets exist for Facebook, Twitter, and other popular social
media as well.

SOCIAL NETWORKS FOR SCHOOLS
AS ORGANIZATIONS

From the simple issue of providing homework reminders to middle school
parents as a safeguard to the occasionally fuzzy memories of seventh graders, to providing data to community members on an upcoming referendum,
social networks need to be used as a communication tool for the school
organization.

Schools as businesses cannot ignore social networking for public relations and human resource functions. Currently, Facebook is the number-one destination on the Internet, even surpassing Google. The advertisement and communication opportunities of social networking cannot be ignored by any level of a school's organization. The library media center, individual schools, and the district as a whole can all take advantage of social networks to promote the organization's message and goals and build support among stakeholders. As schools and districts face financial issues, the ability to communicate the issues and concerns of the organization are greatly enhanced by the effective use of social media. Twitter and similar services can assist districts in reminding parents and the greater community about upcoming events, deadlines, etc.

School human resource officials also need to take advantage of social networking to communicate job openings, attract candidates, and review applicants. It is common for universities to search social networking sites for information about potential student applicants. Schools should consider similar research in the hiring process.

IMPLEMENTING THE USE OF SOCIAL NETWORKING

Once a school has determined to use social networking, there are several basic things that the organization can do to support its development:

- Provide a reliable technology infrastructure
- Have the school's leadership model the importance of social networking
- Update the district's technology-use policy to encompass social networking issues
- Develop the necessary staff development to ensure staff understands how to use social networking to support learning
- Provide instruction to students to ensure they have all the tools to be safe users of social networks
- Communicate to parents about how social networks are being used
- Establish methods for ongoing monitoring of social networking and other technologies to ensure staff and students are safe and appropriate

The primary need in successfully implementing any educational technology, social networking included, is to ensure that the school or district has a robust and redundant technology infrastructure. If the district's technology resources are not reliable, then teachers and other staff will not plan to integrate technology within their instruction. Although things like redundant power supplies, backup systems, and hardware rotation plans are not sexy, they are essential in order for technology to be embraced by school staff. If staff are required to constantly have a set of backup lesson plans every time they are going to use technology, they are not going to use it.

Once the school or district has the necessary infrastructure in place, school leaders must be supportive of the use of social networks. This can be done in several ways. The simplest is for the school or district to establish social network profiles for the school itself. This sends a message about the legitimacy of the medium as well as a proactive method of communicating in the new medium. Announce the profiles to the entire staff and ask them to connect to the profile with their own professional profiles. Where leaders can provide models of professional learning environments, blogs, etc., staff will be more eager to embrace the same technologies.

Ensure that the organization's technology use policies are up to date and inclusive of the newer technology issues that arise with the use of social networks. Clearly articulate what is appropriate and unacceptable use of such technologies for students and staff. Put in place safeguards to retard cyberbullying, risky sexual behavior, and the disclosure of personal information. Provide systems for reporting predatory or dangerous behavior. Ensure that filters in place allow teachers and students to have access to the necessary tools they need in the classroom, library, or lab without creating extra hurdles for them to jump through.

Develop staff education programs so that the staff is made aware of how to utilize social networks in the instructional process. One of the easiest ways to provide training on social networks is to get the staff to use some of the more common social networking tools. Use the training to model an environment that embraces cooperation and collaboration. More detail about using social networking for professional development will be provided in a later chapter.

Provide students with the necessary instruction in order to use social networks responsibly both in and outside of educational settings. Education about student responsibilities and online safety is an important aspect of successful implementation of social networks within the school. Teachers and library media specialists must provide instruction on Internet safety that covers the following items:

- How to develop profiles and avoid disclosure of personal information
- Risky behaviors and addictions
- Cyberbullying—how to react, and how to report any dangerous behaviors
- Introduction to basic social networking tools
- Clear guidelines about potential penalties for misuse

After the educators and students have been trained, schools must educate parents on their role in supporting social networking. Providing this training is the most difficult, as parents can't be required to attend training in most settings. However, it may also be the most important way to establish a safe learning culture for students. Some of the ways in which parents and the wider community can be educated include: Creating brochures in print and online explaining the basics of social networks and what to watch for in their children's Internet use; distributing these to parent-teacher conferences, open houses, and other school events; and conducting parent workshops in conjunction with the PTA/PTO or other parent organizations that address Internet safety and the basics of social networking.

When possible, parent and community education should be done in collaboration with local law enforcement agencies, and potentially in league with the local public library as well. This will reinforce to parents and others the seriousness in which the school and law enforcement view cyberbullying and other unsafe behavior. A wide number of parent information sites exist on the web from which to develop one's own materials. Below are some examples:

- FBI's Parent Guide to Internet Safety: www.fbi.gov/stats-services/ publications/parent-guide/parent-guide
- i-SAFE's iParent Program: www.isafe.org/
- iKeepSafe's Parent Information Center: www.ikeepsafe.org/parents
- National Center for Missing and Exploited Children: www .missingkids.com
- NetCetera's Chatting with Kids about Being Online: www .onguardonline.gov/topics/net-cetera.aspx
- The Children's Partnership—A Parent's Guide to Kids Online: www.childrenspartnership.org
- Microsoft's Safe Kids Initiative Resources: www.microsoft.com/ presspass/safekids/initiatives.htm

In addition, many state's attorneys general and local law enforcement agencies have additional Internet safety resources that they will be willing to share with the school in organizing parent training.

- Illinois Attorney General's Cyberbullying site: http://illinoisattorney general.gov/cyberbullying/
- Iowa Attorney General's Cyberbullying information: http://secure online.iowa.gov/docs/cyberbullies.pdf
- New Jersey's Cyberbullying site: www.njbullying.org/Cyber bullying.htm
- Forest Ridge SD 142 (Illinois) Internet Safety Wiki: http://d142 .wikispaces.com/Internet+Safety

The last piece of implementation is the need for ongoing monitoring of the school's technology infrastructure. The school must provide the necessary resources to be able to detect predatory and/or unsafe technology use. The school must make sure that the processes taught to students as to how to report unsafe conduct are viable and that any reported conduct is properly investigated. Where possible, collaboration with local law enforcement agencies will reinforce the significance and potential consequences of unsafe behavior to both students and parents.

BARRIERS TO IMPLEMENTATION

The primary barrier to implementation of social networks in education is the lack of understanding of what social networks can do for education. In addition, the perception that social networks are time-wasting activities for teens and for those who are 30+ and still living in their parents' basements is real in many communities among some decision makers, and is a true barrier to successfully using social networks in schools. The most significant barrier is the need to address the legitimate concerns of those worried about student safety on social networks.

The safety issue is most likely the most significant barrier that educators will experience in trying to integrate effective social networking into instruction. In order to use social networks, schools should address student safety in a variety of ways as already outlined above. The school needs to have a clear technology-use policy in place for students and staff. Specifics about policy development are provided in the final chapter of this text, but the policy must clearly establish that the Internet is a learning tool to be used for the completion of class work and individual learning goals. It is not a tool for bullying, harassment, or virtual activities that wouldn't be allowed in the school building in a nondigital environment. Similarly, the student training outlined above is essential to successfully combating safety concerns.

SOCIAL NETWORKING OPTIONS FOR SCHOOLS

The social networking landscape is incredibly fluid. The industry leader of 2009 was MySpace. In 2011, Facebook has taken the lead. It could easily be something else in 2012, as of this writing. Universities, corporations, and even individuals working in their dorm rooms and garages are currently working to develop the next generation of interactive social networking tools. However, there are a number of core applications and network services which will likely be around for some time.

General Social Networking Services

These are the common general-use services that most people identify as social networks. They are commonly referred to in the media. The most common sites include:

- Bebo: www.bebo.com
- Facebook: www.facebook.com

- LinkedIn: www.linkedin.com
- MyLife: www.mylife.com
- MySpace: www.myspace.com
- Xanga: www.xanga.com

Educational Social Networks

These are fully functional social networks focused on the academic and education markets. Many are limited to educational users.

- Academia.edu: www.academia.edu
- eChalk: www.echalk.com
- Edmodo: www.edmodo.com
- Elgg: elgg.com
- ePals: www.epals.com
- Gaggle: www.gaggle.net
- LibraryThing: www.librarything.com
- Student.com: www.student.com

For instance, Gaggle includes safe teacher-student texting and other on-line learning tools including e-mail and blogs. Parent accounts in Gaggle can view their own children's accounts and communicate with their children's teachers, but cannot contact other children.

Blogs

The ability to self-publish directly to the web is supported by a variety of specialty applications. It is also supported in Microsoft Office 2007 and newer versions. SharePoint and other groupware applications also allow for individual blogs to be set up. Some of the most common blog sites include:

- Blogger: www.blogger.com
- LiveJournal: www.livejournal.com
- tBlog: www.tblog.com
- TypePad: www.typepad.com
- WordPress: www.wordpress.com

Microblogs

These are essentially blog services that allow for smaller blog entries. Twitter limits its blogs to 140 characters. Twitter is the king of microblogging, with millions of active users.

- Plurk: www.plurk.com
- Twitter: www.twitter.com
- Tumblr: www.tumblr.com

Discussion Groups

These allow users to send e-mails, share data, take polls, etc. They are similar to the older listserv technology but allow for more functionality than simple e-mail. The easiest way to set up a discussion group would be using one of the following free services:

- BigTent: www.bigtent.com
- Google Groups: groups.google.com
- MSN Groups: groups.msn.com
- Yahoo Groups: groups.yahoo.com

Image-Sharing Sites

These sites, amazingly enough, allow users to share images on the web. Some allow for uploading of images, while other focus on marking and organizing web-based images.

- Flickr: www.flickr.com
- Imgur: www.imgur.com
- Photobucket: photobucket.com

News Commentary/Rating Sites

These are sites that allow users to comment and vote on the relative value of news articles. These sites are important in some circles for rating the popularity of sites on the web. The following are a few sample sites of this genre:

- Digg: www.digg.com/news
- Fark: www.fark.com
- Newsvine: www.newsvine.com
- Reddit: www.reddit.com

Ning

Ning (www.ning.com) is a service allowing for the easy development of unique user-directed social networks. It is currently a pay service after a 30-day free trial. However, a classroom ning can be set up for about $20 a year. SocialGo (www.socialgo.com) is a similar service hosted in the UK; it remains free. Ning is not readily searchable using standard search engines. BuddyPress (www.buddypress.com) is another free social network engine that can easily be used by schools.

RSS Feeds

RSS stands for Really Simple Syndication. It allows one to disseminate web content to multiple users. Normally, the feed alerts a subscribed user to new content being posted via either a text message or an e-mail. Many schools use RSS feeds tied to blogs to announce whenever a new entry is posted. Some listings of RSS feeds can be found at:

- AOL Feeds Directory: http://m.aol.com/portal/directory.do ?tab=Directory&icid=tb_dir
- Feedage: www.feedage.com
- RSS Network: www.rss-network.com

Social Bookmarking or Tagging Sites

These sites allow one to identify things that one likes on the web and then share those with other users. They also allow random users to search sites that have been tagged without being connected to another user. One of the more simple uses of tagging sites is to allow one to share a set of bookmarks (Netscape term) or favorites (Internet Explorer term) via the web with others. Some of the more common tagging sites include:

- BlinkList: www.blinklist.com
- Delicious: www.delicious.com
- Mr. Wong: www.mister-wong.com
- StumbleUpon: www.stumbleupon.com

Survey Engines

These allow one to create and distribute surveys to specific user groups or make surveys available on a specific website. These can be used for simple classroom surveys or more complex organizational or parent surveys. These sites generally have both a free version and a more robust fee-based version.

- BooRoo: www.booroo.com
- Survey Monkey: www.surveymonkey.com
- Surveys Engine: www.surveys-engine.com

Video-Sharing Services

These services provide video sharing to either registered users or all web users. YouTube is the largest and most popular of these services. Some others include:

- Khan Academy: www.khanacademy.org
- SchoolTube: www.schooltube.com
- ScienceStage: sciencestage.com
- TeacherTube: www.teachertube.com
- YouTube–Education: www.youtube.com/edu

Virtual Bookshelves

These provide users the ability to share, recommend and review books.

- Goodreads: www.goodreads.com
- LibraryThing: www.librarything.com
- Revish: www.revish.com
- Shelfari: www.shelfari.com

Wikis

Wikis provide an interactive collaborative setting for users to share. Effectively, a wiki is a set of web pages that can be edited by anyone viewing the page. The most famous wiki is almost certainly Wikipedia, which is an attempt to create an authoritative encyclopedia online built from the submissions of users. An excellent (and potentially overwhelming) list of wiki engines is available at C2.com (c2.com/cgi/wiki?WikiEngines). A good comparison of wiki engine options is available at WikiMatrix (www.wikimatrix .org). Another set of wiki comparisons is available at Benedict Herold's blog (www.benh.org/techblog/2007/08/top-5-open-source-wiki-engines).

Some sample wikis include:

- Ballotpedia (ballotpedia.org), a political almanac
- Wikipedia (en.wikipedia.com), an encyclopedia
- Wiktionary (en.wiktionary.org), a dictionary
- Wikimapia (wikimapia.org), an atlas/ gazetteer
- Wikiquote (en.wikiquote.org), a collection of quotations

The following are some good annotated lists of educational related web applications and sites:

Allie Gray's 100 Apps for Tech-Savvy Teachers: www.rasmussen.edu/student-life/blogs/main/100-apps-for-teachers

Library Junction, 50 Apps for Tech Savvy Teachers: www.libraryjunction.net/blogs/item/50-apps-for-tech-savvy-teachers

The Teaching Box's Best Online Apps and Programs for Teachers: www.theteachingbox.com/the-best-online-apps-programs-for-teachers/

100 Best Blogs for Tech-Savvy Teachers: www.onlinecollegecourses.com/2009/09/13/100-best-blogs-for-tech-savvy-teachers/

OEDb's 101 Web 2.0 Teaching Tools: http://oedb.org/library/features/101-web-20-teaching-tools

77 Web Resources for Teachers to Try This Summer: http://issuu.com/richardbyrne/docs/77thingsforteacherstotrythissummer/1

Free Technology for Teachers Blog: www.freetech4teachers.com; regular listings of free Web 2.0 tools

Edudemic's 35 Best Web 2.0 Classroom Tools: http://edudemic.com/2010/07/the-35-best-web-2-0-classroom-tools-chosen-by-you/

Top 50 iPhone Apps for Educators: http://oedb.org/library/features/top_50_iphones_for_educators

Apps in Education (iPad): http://appsineducation.blogspot.com/2011/06/apps-for-teachers.html

CHAPTER 2

Social Media for Communications

Communications and public relations is one facet of a strong social media or social networking policy, but it is one of the most important for a school or district to embrace in order to be effective communicators in today's world. As the 24-hour news cycle continues to morph the methods in which school stakeholders obtain information and news, the ability for school leaders to effectively use social media for communications is imperative.

Media outlets are changing dramatically in the face of social media and Internet news sources in general. Newspaper readership is down significantly according to several sources, including the Pew Resource Center. Historically, local newspapers are where most school news has been covered in depth. As readership declines for print media, it makes effective communication even more difficult for schools. Currency is another hurdle for print media. Many local papers that devote significant ink to school news are not daily papers. The lead time to get news into print in weekly or biweekly papers makes using them as a conduit for important time-sensitive news and information less impactful.

Social media is changing the way that all strata of people communicate. Today, over 400 million people use Facebook (www.facebook.com). More than 26 million people have accounts on microblog site Twitter (www .twitter.com). Seven million people are using StumbleUpon (www .stumbleupon.com) a web-based bookmarking site that calls itself a "social discovery network." More than one million people use LinkedIn (www .linkedin.com). Those aren't the numbers of passing fads. The interactive social websites that make up what many call Web 2.0 are growing exponentially and are a mainstream force in modern society. Over

50 percent of students using social media stated in a recent National School Board Association poll that they use social media to help complete their schoolwork.

Schools should take advantage of these relatively easy and inexpensive media to improve communications and professional development for their organization. Accurate communication and rumor control have historically been time-consuming and expensive tasks for schools. Social media is an inexpensive and efficient way for a school to effectively communicate with its parents and the wider stakeholder community.

School districts have generally relied on mailings home to provide breaking or important news to parents. However, beyond the elementary-level "backpack mail," such communication generally requires schools to pay for a direct mailing to parents. Secondarily, schools often send out press releases or work with the local media to communicate with the public.

Postal mailings are generally expensive ventures when staff time, materials costs, and postage are considered. A school should consider the alternative of posting a brief summary of the issue on Twitter or another blog and linking that notification to a letter or news release on the school's website. If a district can embrace social media and get its parents and other stakeholders to sign up for notifications via e-mail or text, the school will be more effective and timely in communication and will save money as well.

Mailings are the other traditional communications tool that schools have used to inform the public. Mailings to all postal patrons are generally expensive for even the smallest districts, and often such mailings are recycled before they are opened. With the cash-strapped situation so many schools are in due to the economy, large mailings and mailing school newsletters to all stakeholders are often being eliminated because of budget constraints.

Teachers, principals, librarians, and others can inexpensively reach large audiences of stakeholders and the wider community when they utilize social networking effectively. Social networking allows for communicating with three primary stakeholder groups: parents, alumni, and the wider community. Historically, parents are the easiest group to communicate with because of the direct connection parents have with the school through their children. Sending materials home with students generally works through the elementary years. However, once students enter middle school and high school, parents and schools cannot always rely on students to carry information home in a timely manner.

Blogs are an easy way to communicate with parents and remind them of upcoming events on a daily basis. Posting the school's daily announcements to a blog or to Facebook can help parents work as partners to ensure that students are prepared for picture day, final exams, or a guest speaker. Although simple, this is an excellent way to keep parents in the loop on what is happening in the school without any additional cost and nearly no additional effort on the part of school staff (assuming that the daily announcements are printed somewhere). Social networks are inexpensive ways to send reminders about where to look for school closing information, parent-teacher conferences, that grades are forthcoming, etc. This can help parents and schools work more effectively together. Posting to social networks can also assist in making sure that noncustodial parents receive the same information that custodial parents receive without additional cost to the district.

Alumni are one of the most difficult groups for many schools to communicate with and gather information from. Social media are almost tailor-made to help schools keep in contact with alumni. Setting up a basic LinkedIn profile and a Facebook page for a school allows former students to "Like" their school and connect. Once this connection is established, one can use it to communicate happenings to the alumni as well as solicit information and survey alumni as to their thoughts and perspectives on their preparation. Reunion information can easily be distributed, and alumni are an excellent potential source of fund-raising for many schools. The wider "networking" aspects of many social networking sites can help schools track down more elusive alumni who have moved from the area or who haven't regularly updated address information with the district. Overall, social networking is an excellent vehicle for connecting schools and their former students.

Social networking is also a good way to communicate with the wider community beyond current parents. Blogs, tweets, Facebook updates, etc., are all useful ways to keep the wider community up to date as to what is going on in the school. The traditional quarterly or semiannual district newsletter is becoming extremely expensive. Postage alone is an expensive proposition for many schools. Where districts can continue to publish a newsletter, the blog feeds, etc., can deal with the day-to-day issues in a much more timely and current way than a printed newsletter can. The printed newsletter can then be used to delve into greater depth on one or two main issues.

Connecting with other community groups, parent and booster organizations, and other local governments can help to create a positive, supportive culture for the school online as well as in the schools and at school events. Announcing fund-raising events, student performances, and athletic contests via social media can assist in raising attendance and increasing funds generated via donations and gate receipts, as well as enhancing the standing of the activities in question. Well-established, credible social media sources that provide information about a school can be invaluable when a crisis arises or when it's time to pass a referendum. Elections and other high-profile events, such as the hiring of a superintendent or the closing of a school, often bring out a number of bloggers or others who take to the Internet to deliver their messages. If the school already has a strong social media communications structure in place, it is much easier for the school to provide accurate information and combat disinformation and rumors that often arise in such situations.

The obvious downside to such Internet-based electronic communication is that some families simply don't have access to those resources. In the registration process, schools need to allow families the ability to indicate that they don't have access to the Internet and would prefer hard copies of announcements and other key communications from the district. This type of safety net will ensure that those without access to the Internet aren't left out. Even in those schools or districts where only a minority of the stakeholders has access to social media, some of the families will have access. It is important to begin to build a social media communication structure as noted above, before the school or district needs it. The growth of social media communications tools is such that even in the most extreme circumstances, at least some of the families are in tune with social media communications channels.

ANNOUNCEMENTS

Social network tools are an increasingly effective and efficient method for communicating with a school or district's stakeholders. From messages about registration dates and school closings to birth announcements and homework reminders, social networks are increasingly used for communication by educators at all levels. One of the most basic ways to use social networks is to communicate announcements.

Twitter (a microblog) is one of the easiest ways to send out announcements. In the summer of 2011, Twitter accounts belonging to schools, districts, and individual educators announced the availability of public swimming pools and cooling centers while reminding readers to check on their elderly and infirm neighbors. Library tweets reminded students to read to keep their skills up over the summer and sent out brief reviews of books being read by the staff or students in summer reading programs.

Irving ISD @IrvingISD
> Football teams & marching bands start practicing next week ... but now is the time to help kids to start eating ... http://fb.me/1bVPziiM1

Northside ISD @NISD
> School starts in 4 weeks! All your back-to-school questions answered here: http://t.co/Y5wr9TF

sraslim @sraslim
> Troy High School Library Facebook is now defunct. Keeping it up for old news.

dcfireems @dcfireems
> DC Cooling Centers - Rec Centers, Libraries, Sr Wellness Centers - DC Rec pools are a great way to stay cool outdoors (some indoors)

Barrington 220 @barrington220
   Watch this great video and vote for Station Middle School's effort to enhance its Library Media programs for students.

During the school year, tweets and blogs remind students about upcoming events, and parents about open houses, report card pickup, and early-release days. Coaches blog about how the team did at its last game and what to prepare for the next practice. Kindergarten teachers explain what is happening during this week of school and how parents can prepare their children for what they will be learning next.

One key set of items to make sure to announce are any grants or awards the organization wins. It is a good way both to gather positive news for the district and to thank the organization(s) who helped make the grant or award possible.

Two of the most difficult decisions for educators are: where to start; and how social networking tools can be used to communicate effectively. If nothing else, start with a Twitter account for important communications. Sign up at http://twitter.com. Twitter limits messages to 140 characters, so most messages will be short. However, even without being a confirmed minimalist, one can provide informative tweets and often link them to more complete information in a blog, a press release, or a short video clip. From a straightforward communication perspective, it isn't necessary for a communication-focused account to follow any other tweeters, and in some cases, it might even be counterproductive. As the Belvidere, Glenbrook North, and Sarasota District screen shots illustrate, some districts are effectively utilizing Twitter to communicate with their communities.

Belvidere D100 Twitter screen shot

Sarasota Twitter screen shot

Glenbrook North HS screen shot

TWITTER ALTERNATIVES

Instead of Twitter, which is definitely the king of microblogs, an individual educator, school, or district may wish to use one of the following microblogs for announcements. This is particularly true if the community in which one works tends toward conservative views and links Twitter too directly with Lady Gaga and similar pop-culture icons.

Plurk (www.plurk.com) is a microblog that shares much of Twitter's feel. However, it is based in Taiwan, and over 40 percent of its users are Taiwanese. Plurk is exceptionally easy to use.

Posterous (https://posterous.com) is a microblog that allows for individual or group postings. The site allows for video and images to be uploaded, after which they are integrated into the site. The end user doesn't have to do more than upload the desired file(s). Posterous also allows integration with Twitter and Facebook. Posterous has been purchased by Twitter and will likely soon be absorbed by the more popular site.

Qaiku (www.qaiku.com) is another microblog in the same vein as Jaiku and Twitter. It was also developed in Finland and was intended to take over Jaiku's functions after Jaiku was purchased by Google. It has a multilingual focus, unlike Twitter, in that it is searchable by language.

Tumblr (www.tumblr.com) is another viable alternative to Twitter. Tumblr has a more flexible interface and allows for more types of information to be shared than is generally allowed on Twitter. It also allows for a private blog, meaning that one's posts would be available only to those invited.

VIDEO-BASED ANNOUNCEMENTS

Since there are so many video-sharing services, it isn't difficult to create video announcements or school "newscasts" and provide those to the wider community through YouTube, TeacherTube, or similar venues. It isn't difficult to embed such videos into an organization's existing website, but they can also be linked into Facebook, YouTube, and other video-sharing services. A few potential examples might include:

- A superintendent or principal's welcome message to the district or school
- A beginning of the year message about the year's academic or other focus
- Book talks for a summer reading list for incoming freshmen
- A request from a PTO officer as to why it would be important to join the organization
- A welcome video for incoming kindergarten parents
- A video introduction of a school's new teaching staff
- A clip from an author visit or other school assembly
- A summary of how the budget is developed in laymen's terms

EMERGENCY COMMUNICATION EFFORTS

When schools have to close due to inclement weather or some other disaster, social media becomes an easy way to communicate with a wide variety of stakeholders quickly. Some regions have created resources for emergency closings, such as Cancellations.com (www.cancellations.com), Weather Closings (www.weatherclosings.com) or The Emergency Closing Center in the greater Chicago area (www.emergencyclosingcenter.com). Other schools advertise that emergency closing information will be posted to the district's Twitter account, etc. When the Joplin Missouri School District had to cope with providing information in the aftermath of the destructive tornado that hit that community in 2011, Superintendent C. J. Huff stated, "Facebook was how we communicated with people. It was the primary tool for getting information. We used Facebook to help locate people who hadn't been accounted for" (Kennedy, 2011).

For instance, the Montgomery Public School District in Maryland provides text messages, e-mail, Twitter and web alerts in addition to traditional television and radio communication of school closings (www.montgomeryschools md.org/emergency) Unlike the traditional media formats, these emergency notifications can be accessed in six languages (English, Chinese, French, Korean, Spanish, and Vietnamese). The Anchorage, Alaska, School District provides emergency information via Twitter and Facebook as well as through traditional media and on its website. Anchorage provides a separate Twitter feed, @asd_closures, for emergency information (www.asdk12.org/aboutasd/closure.asp).

Often the telephony messaging systems that schools have been using for a decade can also integrate emergency closing information to other communication media besides telephones. As traditional telephone land lines are being replaced by mobile devices (not only phones, but tablets, etc.), these systems are eager to embrace social networking within their communications sphere. Examples include SchoolMessenger (www.schoolmessenger .com) that allows information to be sent via phone, e-mail, SMS, and Facebook. Emergency-Broadcasting.com (www.emergency-broadcasting.com) at this point provides only traditional voice and text messaging. DialMy-Calls (www.dialmycalls.com) provides phone, e-mail, and SMS notifications, but it is also working on an iPad app to receive notifications as well.

As the police, fire, and EMS dispatch traffic in a wide range of communities are now available to be listened to via the web, iPad, and Droid applications, it is more important to make sure that school stakeholders are given accurate and timely information about emergency calls to schools. When fire engines show up at the school, it might be important for the principal to tweet that it was only a false alarm or to let the community know that it was a minor fire in an electrical outlet. Realize that with the wide array of communications technology available to students particularly at the secondary level, even if fire engines are arriving for a drill, someone is probably texting *fire engs @ school*. Parents or others will pick that up and be increasingly concerned or worried until the school communicates that it was a false alarm, etc. One communications expert (Jaksec, 2011) suggests having the following announcement made in crisis situations over the public address system:

> There is a lot of misinformation on campus regarding the emergency call that occurred on campus this morning. We aren't able to provide all of the details at this time, but we shall release a statement shortly. Remember, you should not be texting or using your cell phone at this time.

CALENDAR INFORMATION

One of the most common reasons parents visit a school's website is to find calendar information. When is the school play? Is the band concert at 6:00 or

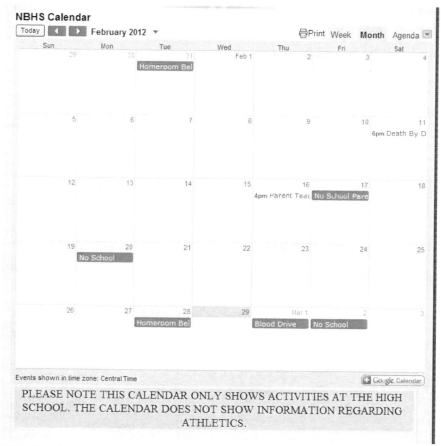

NBHS Calendar

Creating a Google Calendar for Homework Assignments

1. Log into Google.
2. Select Calendar.
3. Select New from My Calendars.

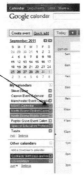

4. Fill out the Calendar Information.

  a. Title
  b. Description
  c. Sharing—must
     make this public

5. Select Create Calendar.

6. Select Settings and then select Sharing for Homework Calendar.

*You must make this
change to allow public
access.*

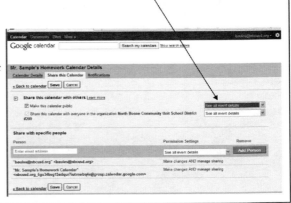

7. Click on the Save button.

   To enter items in the Calendar (while signed
   into Google):

1. Select the date for the assignment from the
   Calendar.

2. The Event Dialogue box should appear;
   select Edit Event.

3. Fill in the information and select Save.

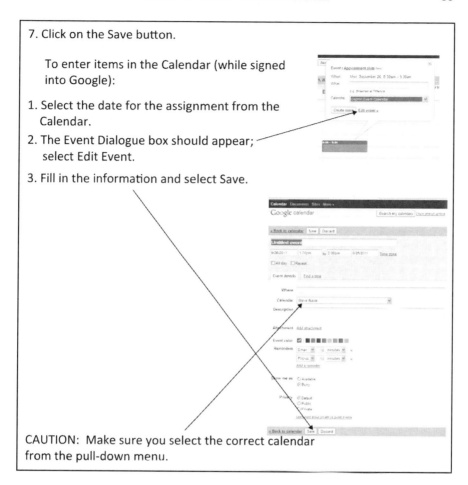

CAUTION: Make sure you select the correct calendar
from the pull-down menu.

7:00 p.m.? Are parent-teacher conferences on Tuesday or Thursday? As an
example, see the screen shot of the North Boone High School calendar.
These types of questions are common to anyone who ever answered the
phone in the school office as well. There are a number of good calendar programs as part of social media that can allow people to sign up for notifications and reminders about events as well as make school calendars more
easily accessible.

ALLOWING PEOPLE TO CONNECT

Although people can easily set up a Twitter account and follow a library,
school, or district, for some it is another step. Setting up fan pages in
Facebook, LinkedIn, MySpace, and other social networks is an easy way to

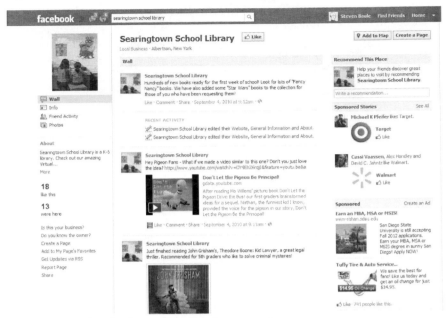

Searington School Library Facebook screen shot

broaden access to one's constituents. See the Searington School Library Facebook screen shot as an example.

It is relatively simple to create a Facebook account and then create an organization page for your school or library. Facebook doesn't allow you to create an account as an organization. They want users to create an account linked to an individual and then create an organizational page for your school, for instance. This allows users to "like" an organization instead of "friending" a person. However, the impact is the same. A Facebook or MySpace page allows a school, a library, or a teacher to provide more information than that allowed via Twitter in one sitting. However, simply setting up the account isn't the end of the work. MySpace works differently, as it assumes every account is a person and, oddly, school districts and libraries are listed with a gender and an age in most cases.

Once the Facebook page is set up, one has to advertise its presence. Some will choose to do this right away. Others might want the site to be up for a while and for people to find it on their own first. This will allow for more information to actually be available prior to a formal announcement. Once an organization is ready to make a formal announcement, let the local media know as well as post the new contact information on the district's website, including the information in newsletters, e-mails, etc. This should help grow a base group of constituents that will then help spread the word about the organization's new communication avenues.

One of the easiest things to post to Facebook and similar networks is a picture of an event. Whether they are pictures of an author visit, a poetry slam, or the last football game or wrestling meet, those pictures are sure to draw a crowd of virtual onlookers. One must make sure that such images are posted in accordance with the organization's policies on distributing images, particularly where students are involved.

Facebook apps have been designed to allow parents to see what their students are eating in the school cafeteria. A number of school districts began using such apps during the 2011–2012 school year (Zwang, July 2011). These apps not only allow parents to see what is available for lunch, but also to track their children's individual eating habits at school. These apps also provide nutritional information and provide up to data account information for parents.

- LunchPrepay.com: www.lunchprepay.com
- Meals Plus Facebook Site: www.facebook.com/MealsPlus

MORE COMPLETE INFORMATION

Although Twitter and its allies are excellent for providing short announcements and reminder type information, there are other social media that can be used in conjunction with a more complete plan to provide richer communications to parents and other stakeholders. Facebook and similar networks allow for much more information to be included within a single (wall entry on Facebook) communication.

Blogs are another excellent way to be able to put out a great deal of information for the public. For educational organizations, Goggle's Blogger (www.blogger.com) is an exceptional choice, because it can be managed through the same administrative tools that manage Google Apps, etc. This allows an organization to allow any and all of the organization's employees and even students to set up blogs with little overhead or cost. Blogs allow for a steady stream of information and commentary and allow educators to provide that information along with graphs, charts or other visuals, links to more information, and more.

A recent article in the *School Administrator* suggested using a district's website to rectify misperceptions within the community. A blog is an even better method, as it allows users to subscribe to the blog and get the updated information directly in their e-mail's inbox or in a variety of other ways. However, instead of allowing comments directly on the blog, which creates some potential legal issues (those will be addressed in Chapter 5), force those comments to be delivered as e-mail to the blogger. This will allow for some interactive communication without potentially sullying the blog as an information source for the community. See the screen shot of North Boone's district blog entries for a typical month.

BLOG ARCHIVE

▼ 2012 (20)

   ► February (7)

   ▼ January (13)

      Honoring Black Veterans during Black History Month...

      An opportunity to recognize our best teachers

      A message about the school breakfast program

      Evening Activities Canceled

      Internet Freedoms and the current Blackout

      Grading Practices Survey

      Workshop on e Readers to be held at NBHS

      Poison Control Initiative

      After School Activities and Contests Cancelled

      Community Resources Open House

      School Calendar Survey Results

      Congratulations to the NB Library Staff

      Grow America

   ► 2011 (75)

Simple template. Powered by Blogger.

NBHS Blog history screen shot

Many blog engines allow for a great deal of flexibility in this area. So, one could allow only a single person to post blog entries, but other staff members could still comment without opening the blog for general commentary. Alternatively, several members could be allowed to comment or post. In situations in which staff could comment on book lists or upcoming school events, this might allow for a more interesting blog. In situations in which the blog's focus is providing official information, it may be more appropriate for the blog to have a single voice. However, "guest bloggers" could always be brought in to speak about specific issues. Potentially, the business manager could speak about a budget issue, or the curriculum director could speak to an upcoming change in core curriculum. See Table 2.1 that shows a potential schedule for blog postings.

KEEPING INFORMATION UP TO DATE

Providing a steady flow of information is important. One of the worst things that can happen is for a school or district to set up social media communications tools and then forget about them. Leaving any of these items to go out to pasture is unwise. It is difficult to continue to control too many communications tools at once, so delete ones that are either redundant or no longer garner the necessary viewership in order to be effective communication tools. Social networking sites of almost any type are meant to be kept up to date. When they aren't regularly updated, they tend to give the impression that the user isn't entirely with it or the site has been abandoned. MySpace is a great place to go to find examples of the virtual ghost towns with tumbleweeds instead of up-to-date information. Many celebrities had MySpace pages, but have since migrated to Facebook, Twitter, and other venues. The MySpace sites remain, but often with a message that there has been no recent activity.

Table 2.1   Sample Blog Topics and Timelines

Staff Member	Frequency	Potential Topics
Superintendent	Weekly or Monthly	Overall district initiatives, budget issues, big-picture district concerns and information
Business Manager	Monthly	Financial updates, bond information, bid information, etc.
Curriculum Director	Weekly	Changes in curriculum, test scores, other assessment information, solicitation of parental input, grants received
Principal	Daily or Weekly	School-wide news, student activities and athletic updates, etc.
Librarian	Weekly	New materials, quick tips for parents on using resources with their children, book talks, technology info
Teacher	Daily or Weekly	Classroom news, homework information, event information, etc.

Similarly, don't allow a school or district to set up blogs for every employee just assuming that everyone will use them. After a workshop on how to set up a blog, one technology director created about 80 staff blogs. Only about 10 staff members were keeping those blogs up at the end of the school year, and an embarrassing number of staff hadn't posted anything since the sample "your first blog post" that was done in the workshop. It's embarrassing not necessarily because the staff members decided not to use it, but because parents and other community members found those blogs among the list of active blogs they could sign up to read regularly. When making these types of blogs easily accessible to the public, set clear expectations about how often they need to be updated before they will be removed or at least made nonpublic. Principals may decide that blogs need to be updated weekly and that such blogs can replace the weekly classroom newsletters that were previously sent.

When one isn't sure what to blog about, look to what others in similar roles are sharing with their readers. The examples of topic clouds or labels shown here come from a representative school library blog.

MANAGING THE STREAM OF INFORMATION

One of the ways to manage these multiple media is to use some additional application to gather the information from one site and post it to the others.

TOPIC CLOUD

AUP   collaboration

Education

Ethics **Libraries** Planning
PLN   Reading   Research
Social Media   SocialMedia

Technology Twitter
Uncategorized Web
Web2.0

School Library topic cloud

LABELS

Article   (22)   author
interview (3) Blog Award
(6) Blog Tour (4) Book
Blogger   Hop   (20)
Book   Preview   (6)

Book Review

(146) Book Trailer (1)
BzzAgent (8) Children

(3) Fiction (128)

Giveaway (9) Guest
Post (8) Kindle (1)
LibraryThing   (8)
Meme (47) Memoir
(5) Non-Fiction (27)
Other Blogs (42)
Outside   the
Library   (28)
Personal Note (13)
Product   Review   (6)
Short   Stories   (2)
Swagbucks (18) The
Sunday Salon (23)
Weekend Cooking (3)
Winner (1) Young Adult
(19)

School Library blog labels

For instance, if a small school wanted to manage a blog for newsletters and a Twitter account for announcements, they would have only two streams of information to manage. However, many parents and grandparents are on Facebook, and the school principal would like to take advantage of that fact to widen the scope of communication. This will reach more stakeholders, but will it require more work? Not necessarily. The Facebook page, after initial setup, can be fed its information from both Twitter and the blog by using a tool like RSS Graffiti (www.rssgraffiti.com) to populate the Facebook wall with the information posted to Twitter and from the blog. These applications can potentially manage a number of accounts both in and out, which can help with multiple communication streams. Other RSS feed builders or RSS feed burners can gather information from a variety of sources including websites, Twitter, blogs, etc. and post them to a wide variety of other resources. Search for "rss feed builder," "rss feed burner," or "rss feed generator" in order to find other examples on the web.

PRACTICALITIES OF MANAGING SOCIAL MEDIA COMMUNICATIONS

A key concept in effectively using social media is to ensure that the district's subscriptions are managed by the end users. The school, district, or library needs to use systems where the parent or community member submits their e-mail address and subscribes. This will reduce the staff time involved in setting up social media connections and puts the responsibility for keeping e-mail addresses and other account information up to date with the parent or other stakeholder and not on the school staff.

Managing systems in which the school or library staff has to collect and/or enter the addresses or create accounts for users is simply too time consuming and burdensome on educational entities—particularly as there are so many good resources out there that allow for self-management.

THOSE ON THE WRONG SIDE OF THE DIGITAL DIVIDE

Make sure that the organization has some way to provide the same information to those without access to the Internet. Allow parents who don't have Internet access to sign up to receive paper copies of newsletters and other communication. Work with local public libraries or other agencies to ensure those without access to computers at home can access computers somewhere in the community, so that the school doesn't contribute to expanding the digital divide.

GATHERING FEEDBACK FROM THE COMMUNITY

The communication methods mentioned so far in this chapter have generally been focused on one-way communication. One of the potential advantages of social media is the ability to use it for quick and inexpensive two-way communication. At this point, nearly every school and district has a way for people to provide some type of commentary to the website owner, whether by e-mail or by some other form. However, those basic functions don't proactively solicit parent input or input from the wider community.

One of the easiest ways to do this is a short survey, similar to the One Question Survey in *Library Media Connection* each issue. Putting a short survey together is relatively simple. The key often becomes being able to structure questions in such a way as to make sure one is able to get useful data from the answers provided. When creating a survey, take time to craft the questions and make sure multiple pairs of eyes have the chance to review it prior to putting it out for the public. At least some of the online survey engines provide examples for a wide variety of potential surveys that one can modify to create original surveys.

Several of the more popular survey engines include:

- BooRoo: www.booroo.com
- GetSurveyed: http://getsurveyed.com
- Surveys Engine: www.surveys-engine.com
- SurveyMonkey: www.surveymonkey.com
- SurveyShare: www.surveyshare.com
- SurveyTool: www.surveytool.com

Several of the sites, including SurveyMonkey and SurveyShare, allow free limited accounts that will meet the needs of many building-level educators.

These surveys can be given to multiple constituencies, and the information can be disaggregated to show how elementary parents feel as opposed to high school parents or staff as compared to those without children in the district. These survey engines are incredibly flexible and can save an organization both time and money over the cost of traditional paper-and-pencil surveys.

On a less scientific level, one can set up a number of social media to allow people to post comments, but not allow those comments to be seen by anyone but the owner(s) of the blog, etc. This does allow for two-way communication and is more streamlined than requiring an e-mail, but some may be confused when their comment isn't immediately visible.

Surveys can be used by staff to gather input on new curriculum or to communicate the possible options around a building project or a new summer school program. Building leaders will find such surveys an easy way to gather relatively scientific data quickly. Staff, particularly solitary practitioners such as librarians and social workers, can use them to gather information quickly from their colleagues in other buildings or districts as to how they manage process A or B.

The screen shot shows how simple survey questions in SurveyMonkey can allow survey users to disaggregate the responses from survey takers by group. It is part of a survey given to parents, staff, and students to determine the desired characteristics for a new high school principal. It will allow the school to gather information from a variety of stakeholders as to the importance of various characteristics desired by those stakeholders, and then further desegregate that information by the different stakeholder constituencies.

The next example shows a simple survey designed to

Survey monkey principal search

PAGE 1   [Edit Page Options ▼] [Copy]

[+ Add Question ▼]

Q1 [Edit Question ▼] [Move] [Copy] [Delete]

1. How important do you think summer library hours are to you/your child?

	Not important	Somewhat important	Important	Very important	Extremely important
1	○	○	○	○	○

[+ Add Question ▼] [Split Page Here]

Q2 [Edit Question ▼] [Move] [Copy] [Delete]

2. Do you think that reading books from the North Boone school libraries this summer helped you/your child maintain or improve reading skills?

	Not at all	Not much	Somewhat	A lot	Absolutely
1	○	○	○	○	○

[+ Add Question ▼]

Survey monkey summer library hours

solicit parent input as to the effectiveness of summer library hours for elementary students. It allows the library staff to provide the administration with some solid data from parents as to the effectiveness of the library program.

Similar social media communication can be set up directly for students. Most high school students and many middle school students have web-capable digital devices. A school can allow students to sign up for digital copies of daily announcements or even the lunch menu as a text message. Teachers can send reminders of homework and long-term-project due dates or give final-review reminders about quizzes or tests.

FORUM ENGINES

Forum engines are another method of posting information and gathering feedback, but the nature of the forum engine makes them a poor choice for most educational settings, unless the forum is limited to a specific group (like a class or one grade level). The reason for this is twofold. First, spammers love forums and continuously try to post material about such noneducational topics as obtaining your inheritance from Nigeria or Hong Kong or improving one's personal life with this or that pharmaceutical. The second reason is that most public schools could remove such postings only if they rise to the level of obscene, which is a difficult yardstick in many cases. So the most well-intentioned forum may soon be a mix of useless and offensive information with some of the original information mixed in. Forums do work in situations where the users are predetermined, such as class list, but they aren't a great way of generating positive, productive two-way communication with the general public.

COMMUNICATIONS WITH STUDENTS

In the elementary school years, most of a district's communications is directed at the parents and not directly to the children outside of the classroom. However, this changes sometime before students leave the system. Text messages reminding students about upcoming homework due dates, test reminders, or deadlines to purchase prom tickets all have their place.

ELECTRONIC ANNOUNCEMENTS

For decades, teachers or a disembodied voice over the PA system have read the daily announcements to students in schools across the United States who were either indifferent or apathetic to the three- to five-minute recital of information ranging from important to mundane. Sending the school's daily announcements out via social media can assist schools in a number of ways:

- It allows students to read the announcements at their leisure and doesn't take away instructional time
- It allows parents to get the same information at the same time and makes sure they are aware of what is happening at school
- It allows students to go back later to remind themselves about earlier announcements.
- It allows students to obtain the information in a format with which they are generally more comfortable—e.g., via their browser or phone, and not posted on the classroom door
- It is a green approach that can save several trees a year in the average school, as announcements don't have to be posted daily in every classroom
- It allows for personalization of announcements for students in large schools by class, house, or team. So the information important to

9th graders isn't missed due to all of the college visit information posted for 11th graders.

OTHER REMINDERS

For students who wish to sign up, electronic reminders can be generated at any level, from school-wide announcements to classroom-level reminders. Homework due dates, links to textbook resources, and short videos that reinforce the day's lesson can be sent to a blog or, via messaging systems, to e-mail and SMS services.

School-level reminders can help students remember when prom tickets go on sale, when the college recruiter from Loras College is coming to campus, or where tryouts take place for the spring play. Emergency information can also be sent out to students if necessary.

FORMS FOR STUDENTS

Scholarship forms, NHS applications, job applications, and a myriad of other forms can be linked to a school's Facebook page to provide an easy reminder to students about due dates and where to obtain the forms they need to navigate the school year.

COUNSELOR COMMUNICATIONS

Counselors can use social networks to link students and college recruiters together. This is particularly true as colleges and employers are checking out their prospective students and employees on social networks to make sure they are really getting that honor student who plays lacrosse and the clarinet, and not Southeast High's beer pong champion. A separate counseling blog can explain financial aid forms, college applications, and all of the other things the counselors work on from scheduling to graduation requirements. Some exceptional high school counseling blogs are linked at the School Counseling Masters website (www.mastersinschoolcounseling.com/top-50-blogs-by-school-counselors.html). Middle school and elementary counselors might also develop blogs that focus on parenting tips and character education for their student groups.

COACHES

Coaches can use Twitter or Facebook to update scores during the game. This is particularly helpful at the middle school or junior high level, when most games take place immediately after school and many working parents are unable to attend games. It is wonderful to be able to follow a child's game even when you aren't able to attend. Coaches can also use Twitter or Facebook to remind parents about practices, games, and parent meetings along with all of the uses outlined earlier in this section.

COMMUNICATIONS WITH STAFF

All of the methods already articulated above will work as well with staff as with the general public, so it is important to remember to use these resources to communicate with the staff as well. The use of Web 2.0 communication tools and social media can help to more firmly engage employees to the work of the school or district.

EMPLOYEE INFORMATION

As insurance and other benefit information is reviewed and changes occur, most districts send out a great deal of paper to all employees, some of which is actually read. Posting the same information to the district's wiki or such services as SlideShare (www.slideshare.com) can save the district money by not having to print thousands of pages of materials, and it allows staff to obtain the materials whenever one actually needs them without having to search through the bottoms of desk drawers. Similar information about paycheck changes, tax withholdings, etc., can be sent electronically or posted to wikis or other online places for staff to access.

CHANGES IN THE LAW

Particularly in large districts, HR staff or the district's legal team may want to provide a blog or similar media format to update administrative staff on changes in school rules and the law. Whether the issues involve certification or special education, a private blog for administrators could allow principals and other leaders to ask questions and comment in such a way as to make sure the district develops a coherent understanding of how a given change needs to be implemented throughout a district. Special education is another area in which the rules change often and regular updates to a wide range of staff could be beneficial to a school or district.

REQUIRED TRAINING

Many schools and districts are beginning to use video-sharing services to provide required information in a more personalized training-on-demand structure. The types of training required by states, from blood-borne pathogens to ethics training, can be delivered online with much less logistical cost than traditional lecture formats would entail. These types of training tend to take up significant amounts of time, when teachers could otherwise be working on curriculum development or other, more classroom-focused training. The required training videos can be linked into a district's wiki or intranet, and staff can view the videos at their leisure instead of annually during an in-service day that can now be used for more instructional-focused training or staff development.

STAFF INPUT

The survey tools listed earlier in this section can be used to elicit a great deal of feedback and input from staff with minimal work compared with traditional paper-and-pencil surveys. Such surveys can allow teachers to provide their input on everything from what presenters should be brought in for institute days to how the school calendar should be organized for the following year. Survey engines can also be used to allow staff to sign up for various activities or events within the district.

One of the nice features in nearly all of the online survey engines is the ability to sort and disaggregate the survey responses by any number of factors. Employee responses could be sorted by building, grade level taught, level of certification, or how long they have worked in the school.

COMMUNICATING WITH POTENTIAL STAFF

Social media can be an excellent method for recruiting new staff members. However, it is important to know your audience and to make sure that the media one uses is appropriate for the position(s) being searched for. For instance, recent college graduates, the most likely candidates for entry-level teaching positions, use Facebook and Twitter. They are also not shy about posting that they are looking for employment. Posting vacancies on a district's Facebook page or announcing them via Twitter might bring in the needed candidates for entry-level positions. Linking to college and university placement offices with a social network presence can be helpful. Posting short recruiting videos on YouTube or TeacherTube may be helpful. Using a combination of district leaders and young and career teachers allow those staff to explain why the school or district is a good place to work and what new staff can expect during their first year, and to try to answer the basic questions that new candidates might have that would be answered in the three to five minutes they would spend with a recruiter at a job fair. Two examples are DeKalb County, Georgia's teacher recruiting video (available on YouTube at www .youtube.com/watch?v=LX6D-nZ8vTQ) and the Dysart, Arizona, district's video (available at www.youtube.com/watch?v=khiGbrbBmUQ).

However, established teachers and those looking to move into more senior administrative roles may not so readily be posting publicly that they

are looking for a new position. Many of these more "mid-career" professionals are likely to have a presence on LinkedIn, which has a jobs section
and can find people that meet a given set of criteria. It will also present job
opportunities to users based upon their profile. LinkedIn groups provide
another way to announce potential vacancies to those who may be interested
in the position. Start early in the hiring season or before to let people know
about anticipated vacancies as soon as possible. This allows more time for
the information to be passed along via social networks and good-old-
fashioned word of mouth (although much of that might be via electronic
mouth today).

After the recruits have been identified, it isn't a bad idea to search social
media to find out about the potential candidates. One of the potential issues
when searching for information about candidates on social media sites is
that one will probably find out many things about a candidate that you
couldn't ask in the interview process. So, while looking to see if the candidate has posted video of themselves involved in devil worship, one might
also find out:

- Candidate's age (a basic stat on many social networks)
- Marital status (a basic stat on many social networks)
- Number of children (pictures on Facebook, Flickr, etc.)
- Religion (a basic stat on many social networks)
- Race (a basic stat on many social networks, also often evident in
  photos)

Knowing this information early in the hiring process could open a school
or district up to potential discrimination claims. So, the HR department
should have someone who isn't involved in the hiring process search social
networks and simply report whether or not there was anything found of concern. If the district has written administrative procedures for conducting the
hiring process, the review of social media should be clearly identified in
those procedures. Instead of simply having someone search through Facebook and LinkedIn, it makes sense to ensure that the human resources staff
is aware of the people search engines now available which index some of
the more popular social media sites. Wink (http://wink.com) is an example
of such a people search engine. One of the nice features of the site is that it
returns pictures with the search results, which can aid in determining if one
has the right Jane Smith. Pipl (http://pipl.com), another example of a
people search engine, is more exhaustive than Wink but tends to include
results from information that can be nearly a decade out of date, but
still floating in cyberspace. Tweepz (http://tweepz.com) is dedicated
to searching Twitter users. KGBPeople (http://www.kgbpeople.com) is a
pay service, but even in the free introductory screens, it can provide an
amazing amount of information on a person.

Below are some additional resources about recruitment efforts using social media. Many of these are from business, but can easily be translated into the world of educational recruiting.

- Can Your Friend Teach? www.edutopia.org/facebook-social -networking-teacher-recruitment
- 10 Reasons Social Media Should Rock Your World: http:// humanresources.about.com/od/careernetworking/a/social_media .htm
- Relational Recruiting: http://www.scribd.com/doc/53090897/ Relational-Recruiting
- How to Use Social Media for Recruiting: http://mashable.com/2011/ 06/11/social-media-recruiting/
- Recruiting with Social Media: http://www.volt.com/Recruiting _with_Social_Media.aspx
- How to Reach HR and Recruiting with Social Media: www .blogging4jobs.com/business/how-to-reach-hr-recruiting-with -social-media
- Hidden Dangers of Social Media Recruiting: www.intellicorp.net/ marketing/social-media-recruiting/dangers-of-recruiting-with-social -media.aspx

Once a school hires additional staff, take the time to promote the new hires to the community and the staff by announcing those hires on social networking sites. The organization should make sure that people know who the organization is hiring and the common traits that made them good additions to the organization.

Although a more traditional website, Donors' Choose (www.donor schoose.org) is a wonderful way for teachers and librarians to communicate their needs to the wider community. Once a project has been posted on the site, a school would be wise to use Twitter or a blog to update the progress of donations until the donation goal has been reached. Using the school's blog or other media to thank donors is also a simple way to expand the effectiveness of Donor's Choose.

COMMUNICATIONS REMINDERS

One of things that hasn't yet been invented is an "Unsend" key for the keyboard. It is often tempting to respond immediately to a complaint or an anonymous posting on a web forum. However, it isn't really that wise. Dodie Ainslie (2010) has put together some extremely well-done handouts to assist educators in using social networking. One of those articulate the four questions one should ask prior to clicking the Send key:

1. Who will be reading this?
2. Is what I am publishing professional?
3. Am I in a positive state of mind? (this might be the most important of the questions)
4. Am I sharing someone else's private information?

Considering the answers to each of those questions is an excellent way to decide whether or not to post the information on a social media site or even whether or not to send the e-mail. Consider the social media sites an extension of the physical classroom or library. Don't tolerate any behavior or conduct in the virtual realm that wouldn't be tolerated in the actual classroom.

CHAPTER 3

Instructional Uses of Social Media

Some educators might see this book and ask why we are wasting time with social media. Students are much less likely to ask such a question. To most students, particularly by the time they are teenagers, social networks are an integral part of their lives. For schools to embrace these technologies is a way to integrate education more directly in the world as students are viewing it. Social media are real-world applications that can increase student engagement and skill development. Schools are not embracing the Web 2.0 services as quickly as they might. This is in spite of the fact that 48 percent of educators who responded stated students have a higher desire to learn when using Web 2.0 tools and another section of the survey states student engagement was up 39 percent (*Tech & Learning*, 2011).

A May 2011 article in the *Huffington Post* (www.huffingtonpost.com/2011/03/27/social-networking-schools_n_840911.html) outlined increased student engagement as the primary reason for why social media should be integrated into instruction. The article noted that a number of studies show that student participation and engagement increases by more than 50 percent when students are able to incorporate social media into their schoolwork. In one study mentioned in the article, students were found to complete additional assignments and improve their grades by more than 50 percent in comparison to their grades prior to the introduction of social media into a middle school curriculum.

"Progressiveteacher" left the following comment on the *Huffington Post* story:

> I created a teacher facebook page, many of my students are "friends" and I notify them over facebook when I have a new assignment/discussion. Simply put, it's getting the students eyespace and attention and it works.

A University of Minnesota study of social media among 16- to 18-year-old urban high school students found that students who are already engaged in social media can benefit from its incorporation into the instructional program. The study articulated that using social media can increase engagement, increase technological proficiency, and improve collaboration and communication skills. The study was focused on students using MySpace. Ninety-four percent of the students in the study had a social networking site profile. An article about the study quoted Christine Greenhow, a University of Minnesota researcher: "What we found was that students using social networking sites are actually practicing the kinds of 21st-century skills we want them to develop to be successful today" (Feature: Educational benefits of social networking sites, available at www1.umn.edu/news/features/2008f/UR_191308_REGION1.html).

A study published in 2010 by researchers at North Carolina State University showed that social networks provided a number of distinct advantages over a traditional classroom setting when it came to fostering communication and collaboration with classroom peers (Holcomb, Brady, and Smith). The study focused on college students using a Ning as the social networking environment. Among the results presented were that students felt that the Ning environment supported the several improvements in the overall learning process, as shown in Table 3.1.

As the table shows, extremely few of the students in the study felt that the Ning was counterproductive to improving communication, and less than 20 percent felt that it inhibited their abilities to express themselves. Overall, the vast majority of the students found the social networking interactions to be productive and engaging.

A 2009 EdWeb survey found that 61 percent of educators were using social networks. Leading the pack were librarians. Seventy percent of librarians belonged to one or more social networks. At the other end, only 54 percent of principals were engaged in any sort of social networking. (A Survey of K–12 Educators on Social Networking and Content-Sharing Tools, available at www.edweb.net/fimages/op/K12Survey.pdf). The study also found that many educators recognize that they are behind the times in terms of technology and that they need to figure out how to better integrate social networking tools into teaching in order to engage students. One comment provided in the study was fairly direct in the need for educators to embrace social media:

> This kind of tools is not an option in education anymore. As teachers and practitioners preparing 21st century learners we MUST better educate and inform ourselves about how to take the best benefit out of

Table 3.1   **Student Responses to Items by Level of Agreement**

Skill or Function	Strongly Agree or Agree
Communicating with peers and colleagues outside setting of traditional classroom	84%
More time to effectively reflect on others' comments	76%
Collaborating with peers more frequently	72%
Communicating with peers and colleagues who I would not otherwise be able to communicate with	60%
Ning facilitates a more comprehensive understanding of topics	54%
Prefer using Ning to share and discuss ideas due to convenience	54%
Express thoughts more clearly and openly	50%
Comment and discuss ideas with colleagues efficiently	50%
More detailed, in-depth conversation	36%
Comfortable sharing and discussing ideas	32%
Inhibits my ability to express my thoughts and opinions	16%
Does not allow for me to effectively communicate with peers and colleagues	2%

them. The most important reason for this is: THIS IS THE WAY IN WHICH OUR STUDENTS ARE LEARNING TODAY! (p.33)

Emerging EdTech (www.emergingedtech.com) outlined seven reasons to leverage social media tools for instruction in a 2011 posting on its site. Engagement was the first item listed and appears to be universally identified as a top reason for using social media in the classroom. The other reasons include social learning in that since people learn from each other via modeling, etc., it is important for students to have the opportunity to learn appropriate social networking skills and netiquette in a more structured environment, which schools are better suited to offering. This is doubly important, according to the article, as social networks are becoming much more important in business settings, so the impactful and effective use of these networks will be essential for the future success of current students.

Other factors identified in the EdWeb.net report, and actually long articulated as a supportive reason for using the Internet in general, are moving classroom instruction outside the walls and beyond the time constraints of traditional classroom settings. By increasing the amount of time available for collaboration and allowing for less hurried conversations, collaboration and thoughtful communication should increase, as also seen above in the North Carolina State study. All students are able to contribute to blogs, Nings, or other postings, whereas traditional instructional time constraints make it more difficult to allow for everyone to share and comment on ideas presented in class.

Writing is key to most social media. One of the advantages of utilizing social media for writing assignments is that the assignment has a real audience in the case of a social network. Several studies have shown that students produce higher-quality work when they know the writing will be seen by a larger audience than simply their teacher. Students who know their work will be seen by their peers and potentially by a wider audience will generally step up their efforts.

Of course, social media also have their opponents. The majority of those articulating a reason against the inclusion of social media within the instructional program fall into one of two camps: either social media is too prone to danger; or students simply cannot be given the time to work on social media without degrading their face-to-face interpersonal skills. A third group simply finds all social media a waste of time, but that group tends to follow the Luddites of the past and will most likely be as successful at stopping the explosion of social media as the Luddites were at stopping the industrialization of the weaving trade.

The first concern is that of social media being unsafe. Although there is always the possibility of having to deal with online predators and inappropriate materials online, a number of education-focused, kid-friendly social media now exist to allow students and teachers to harness the power of social media without the dangers of playing in the "MySpace street," so to speak. Utilizing Edmodo (www.edmodo.com), Edublogs (http://edublogs .org), or Kidblog (http://kidblog.org), for instance, greatly reduces the concerns that many articulate about using mainstream social media such as Facebook and MySpace. Although anytime one goes into an online environment, no matter how secure, there is always the possibility of someone being contacted by someone with impure intentions. Chapter 5 contains more on how to address this.

The need to educate students about how to use social media properly to ensure that they understand privacy concerns and what can happen with the information they put online is more a reason to embrace social networking in schools than it is a reason to avoid or ban it. Some of the other concerns that people articulate that social media should be banned from schools include:

- The sites are a proven haven for malicious content and hackers
- Social networking sites don't verify personal information, so people may not be who they say they are
- The sites foster cyberbullying

- The use of social media can lead to personality and brain disorders such as ADHD, according to some

The other common concern is the reduction of face-to-face contact by those utilizing social networks. This is probably the most realistic concern, but unfortunately, to some extent it is the way of the future. Many in business work through e-mail, LinkedIn, and Google Apps in ways that they never connect face to face. Graduate students routinely complete degrees online and may rarely, if ever, meet all of their professors face to face. People use Skype to attend family reunions, and webinars are replacing seminars in many areas of business and industry.

Use of social networking is up, and nearly 75 percent of teens and young adults use social media as of 2012. So, if schools are to prepare them for a post–high school world in which they are using social media, it is best that schools do that by educating students on how to use social media effectively and ethically. A Pew Internet Project survey showed that although teens are heavy users of social media, they are not heavy users of blogs or Twitter. Currently, use of those particular tools peaks among the 18- to 29-year-olds, college-age students, and often the age group of primary school–aged children. Only 14 percent of teens were found to blog in the Pew study, and another 8 percent used Twitter. However, 52 percent of teens stated they commented on the blogs of their friends. Most teen use of social media is focused around the larger social networking sites such as Facebook and Google+. In comparison, about 1 in 10 adult Americans maintains a personal blog of some sort (Pew Internet, Social media and young adults, available at www.pewinternet.org/Reports/2010/Social-Media-and-Young-Adults.aspx).

However, the Future of Children, a joint venture between the Brookings Institution and Princeton University, released a study more than a decade ago showing that children using computers show the same social interactions and development that children show in other forms of group play. The quote below comes from the Future of Children's Fall–Winter 2000 journal article, by Ellen Watella and Nancy Jennings, "Children and computers: New technology—old concerns."

Similarly, the research being conducted today indicates that computer use can contribute to a child's self-perception and affect a child's socialization in a variety of ways in school and at home. In the school environment, shared computers often have been found to lead to group interaction and cooperation rather than social isolation. Young children's social interactions in a computer center were found to resemble their interactions in other play areas, and various studies have shown that computers can facilitate social interaction and cooperation,

friendship formation, and constructive group play. (http://www
.princeton.edu/futureofchildren/publications/journals/article/index.xml
?journalid=45&articleid=201&sectionid=1311)

The same study also supported the engagement argument in favor of integrating all forms of technology into the curriculum, as students are more
likely to be engaged when technology is integrated into the instructional program. Of course, simply using technology isn't enough. Handing a child a
laptop or a tablet is no different from dropping a textbook in his or her
lap. Good instruction and real, engaged learning can occur only when the
teachers, librarians, and other instructional staff work to develop a strong
instructional plan.

Dan Tapscott (2008) summed up the issue well with the following quote:

> [W]hen kids are online, they're reading, thinking, analyzing, criticizing
> and authenticating—composing their thoughts. Kids use computers for
> activities that go hand-in-hand with our understanding of what consti-
> tutes a traditional childhood. They use the technology to play, learn,
> communicate and form relationships as children always have. Devel-
> opment is enhanced in an interactive world. We need the rationale
> but we need the how also—maybe a little less rationale here and more
> how.

DEVELOPING A STRONG INSTRUCTIONAL PLAN
USING SOCIAL MEDIA

Determine the Core Learning Objectives/Goals
to Be Taught

Always start with the development of the core curricular objectives or
goals. Make sure the learning objectives are clear to both students and any
other staff involved in the lesson. Social media and other technology tools
are to good educators what hammers are to carpenters. They are simply
tools to complete a larger objective and shouldn't be an end it itself.

Ensure that the Assignments or Activities Are Enhanced
by the Use of Social Media and that the Social Media
Tools Are Not Simply a Replacement for a Traditional
Assignment

Every school librarian has nightmares about the Internet version of the
almanac worksheet that reared its head in schools across the county when
the Internet first ventured into classrooms. It was simply the old almanac
assignment in which students had to look up random facts about one or

more countries. Now however, they were to do so using the Internet. Of course, at the time of its initial development, the web was slow. Students weren't used to using it for information, and Google didn't exist. So it usually took students much longer to complete the same assignment using the computer than had they simply picked up an almanac.

The same has been true of PowerPoint presentations that simply buzzed, flashed, or danced across the screen without providing any additional learning opportunities for the children completing them. Make sure that the social media tools enhance and expand the learning objects and not simply replace an older technology with a newer one. As an example, the blog is an exceptional means to further deepen and extend conversations about a book chapter. If the teacher begins the conversation in class, as traditionally has been done, it would end with the ringing of the bell. All students wouldn't generally be able to participate, and a few might not even have completed the reading assignment. (Please, Mr. Brimmeyer, that wouldn't have been me.) However, by posting the leading questions on a blog, the teacher can even require the students to have responded prior to class. Setting the comments to not be made public until after class meets would ensure that students couldn't simply parrot the answers of others; but after the class discussion, the blog comments could be made public and the students could further comment on each other's thoughts regarding the text, etc. This use of social media helps to expand the time students are engaged in the piece of literature and requires a higher level of participation. Therefore, it is a strong use of social media.

For a more complete perspective on this issue, see the Technology Position Statement and Guidelines from the National Council for the Social Studies, available at http://www.socialstudies.org/positions/technology.

Make Sure the Social Media Tools Are Appropriate and Safe for the Students Involved

Where possible, limit the tools for students to those that are developed purposefully for education, such as Kidblogs, as opposed to using a more general tool like WordPress for student work. Through the middle school level, serious consideration should be given only to tools that allow the teacher to fully moderate the conversations among students.

A corollary to the above is to *collaborate with other instructional staff so that the students are using a finite set of tools.* Students shouldn't have to learn four different versions of blogging software because each teacher uses something different. District and school technology leaders and librarians need to take a leadership role in ensuring that students don't spend too much time learning a lot of different tools that basically do the same thing. At a school or district level, work to choose a suite of tools that will work for most applications and stick to them. That will allow the students to spend more time learning about the content of the curriculum and less time focused on the technology "how to."

Be Clear about What Tasks the Students Are to Complete Using Social Media Tools and Ensure They Know How to Use Those Tools

Teachers shouldn't make the assumption that students will all know how to use whatever technology tool simply because they are from a "digital generation." When planning the lesson, determine whether or not students will have a range of tools they can use to complete a given assignment, or if they will all be asked to follow a standard format. Obviously, the more flexibility students have, the greater level of engagement they will often have. Flexibility and variation also often allow students of differing learning styles to complete activities in a way that is more meaningful to them.

It is important that teachers can complete the assignment themselves before asking a student to do so. Particularly for librarians and technology facilitator types, it is essential to make sure the classroom teacher understands how to complete the assignment being asked of the students. Sadly, it is still possible to see teachers giving assignments that require technology skills the teacher is unable to complete himself. This almost always causes frustration among the students and a loss of real learning time. It also often gives instructional technology in general a bad name, as students get frustrated with difficult or even unreasonable expectations. Practice ahead of time, if necessary, and make sure students have clear directions on how to complete the assignment(s).

Coordinate with the IT Staff Ahead of Time to Ensure that the Social Media Tools Being Used Will Work through the District's Firewall(s) and Filters

Unfortunately, firewalls, filters, and various network restrictions are a fact of life. By themselves, they are neither benign nor evil. However, many teachers view them as evil when they waste instructional time by not checking out the filtering issues ahead of time. However, to not do so endangers learning time and is a responsibility for those planning any lesson using technology, as otherwise students will have to wait while the IT staff makes whatever changes are necessary to allow the lesson to proceed. It will also ingratiate one to the IT staff if they get some lead time to address the issue instead of a help desk emergency. Never make the assumption that what works under a teacher login will automatically work from a student account. Always check ahead of time.

Consider if It Is Necessary to Make Accommodations for Students Who May Not Have Adequate Technology Access at Home

A significant concern in using technology-based assignments is whether or not it is equitable for students who don't have ready access to computers or the Internet at home. Make sure that students who might not have such access have alternative access either via extended hours in the school library or through a public library or local college.

Create a Rubric or Other Assessment Instruments for the Students

This will help students use their time effectively and create a clear set of expectations. The development of such rubrics can also be helpful to teachers to ensure that the focus of the assignment is on a content-based end product rather than on the technology tools. The social media tools, in a perfect world, should be like a light switch. They should be barely noticed. The subject matter content should always be the focus—unless, of course, it is a technology course!

There are a number of exceptional rubric sites for teachers. There is no need to start from scratch. A great number of teachers, librarians, and other educators share their materials on the web. A couple of example sites to find teacher rubrics include:

Kathy Schrock's Guide for Educators (http://school.discoveryeducation
.com/schrockguide/assess.html): This site includes a number of Web
2.0–specific rubrics.
Laurie Fowler's Rubric Sites for Teachers (www.lauriefowler.com/
rubrics.html): This site links to about 10 rubric development sites.
Rubrics 4 Teachers (www.rubrics4teachers.com): Select multimedia
rubrics for a number of rubrics that can be modified for social
media.
Rubistar (http://rubistar.4teachers.org/): Requires free registration to
make and save online rubrics. This would be a good tool for a team
of collaborative educators to use to share amongst themselves.
TeacherVision Rubrics Library for Teachers (www.teachervision.fen
.com/rubrics/assessment/26773.html): Provides both general and
customizable rubrics for a variety of areas.
Teachnology Rubric Maker (www.teach-nology.com/web_tools/
rubrics/): This site has a tool to create rubrics in addition to many
pre-made rubrics.

WHILE CONDUCTING THE LESSON

Make Sure to Reinforce Proper Conduct and Netiquette among the Students

When a teacher gives assignments requiring social media, those media tools effectively become an extension of the classroom. Teachers need to enforce the same conduct rules that they would in a classroom. Make sure to enforce copyright and fair use as well. Educators must realize that what happens in these settings might require school authorities to act. Recent laws in several states require school authorities to investigate and discipline students for some types of online conduct.

Report Inappropriate Contact from Outsiders, Cyberbullying, or Any Other Inappropriate Conduct to the Administration and/or Law Enforcement Authorities

Don't take any chances by ignoring what seems like odd or inappropriate conduct. If it seems like it might be a concern, report it to the appropriate authorities.

Continually Monitor the Functionalities of Social Media Tools

One of the frustrating things about social media is that they are particularly fluid forms of technology. So from time to time, something that worked a week ago may no longer be a supported feature of a given tool. This can cause great levels of frustration and a loss of learning time for students, so teachers or librarians must monitor the tools being used to make sure they still work as required. This is particularly true when reusing lessons developed with social media tools in the next semester or even the next year.

Developing a well-understood code of online conduct or netiquette is as important in a technology-rich school as it is to development conduct guidelines for the cafeteria. Below is a short basic set of netiquette expectations for social media tools like Edmodo, blogs, etc., along with traditional e-mail.

Sample Netiquette Guidelines[1]

- Stay on topic and be concise when possible.
- Be careful what you write about others. Assume that anyone about whom you are writing will read your comments or receive them in a way other than intended.

- Online messages can be quite informal, but try, nevertheless, to express yourself using proper spelling, capitalization, grammar, usage, and punctuation.
- Be truthful. Do not pretend to be someone or do something that you are not.
- Use titles that accurately and concisely describe the contents of e-mail and other postings.
- Do not use offensive language or any comments that might be construed as discriminatory.
- Remember that the law still applies in cyberspace. Do not commit illegal acts online, such as libeling or slandering others, and do not joke about committing illegal acts.
- Avoid putting words into full capitals. Online, all-caps is considered SHOUTING. Be careful with humor and sarcasm; it doesn't transfer well online. One person's humorous comment may push another person's buttons or may even be seen as offensive.
- Avoid chastising others for their online typos. Misspellings and typos occur. Do not retype the message or correct unless the message cannot be understood. In discussions please be sure to use proper spelling, capitalization, grammar, usage, and punctuation.
- Read existing follow-up postings and don't repeat what has already been said.
- Respect other people's intellectual property. Don't post, display, or otherwise provide access to materials belonging to others, and cite references as appropriate.
- Online expressions of hostility will not be tolerated.
- Do not send e-mail to people who might have no interest in it. In particular, avoid automatically copying e-mail to large numbers of people. Never send online chain letters.
- If you run across inappropriate material that makes you feel uncomfortable, tell your teacher.

Additional Netiquette Guidelines for Students

Boston Public Library Netiquette for Kids: www.bpl.org/kids/netiquette .htm

Education.com Netiquette: www.education.com/reference/article/ netiquette-rules-behavior-internet

Internet Suite 101 Top 10 Netiquette Guidelines: http://www.suite101 .com/content/netiquette-guidelines-a26615

Kids and Media Netiquette: www.kidsandmedia.co.uk/netiquette

Cyber Safety Lesson Grades 7–8

Overview

Provide students with a basic understanding of the security concerns when using social media and other Web 2.0 tools.

Instructional Standards Being Addressed (Based on ISTE NET-S)

2. Communication and Collaboration
   a. Interact, collaborate, and publish with peers, experts, or others employing a variety of digital environments and media.
5. Digital Citizenship
   a. Advocate and practice safe, legal, and responsible use of information and technology.

Introduction

Find out which students are familiar with social media sites, like Facebook, Google+, etc. Ask them to explain how they are using the sites through the following or similar questions:

- How many friends do you have on Facebook? Do you actually know all of your "friends"?
- Do you set your privacy settings so only friends can see your information? Do you know how to do that? Why should you restrict who can see your information online?
- How many of you have ever been surprised to click a link that took you somewhere you didn't want or shouldn't have gone?

Instruction

Then explain the following points about cyber safety with regard to social media accounts:

- Only friend people you actually know.
- Limit your privacy settings only to your friends.
- Don't share your physical address or phone number with strangers online.
- Realize that once something has been posted to your page/site, others can take that information, and it may never disappear or be entirely deleted.
- Don't accept friend requests unless you are sure who the person really is. Not everyone on the Internet is always honest about who they really are.
- Never agree to meet someone you met online without getting your parent's permission.
- Don't chat with people you don't know. Never open links from people you don't know.

- Often people posing as a friend will send viruses or other malware to your account. Never open documents or attachments from people unless you are expecting them.
- Sometimes even your friends' accounts can get hacked and malicious e-mail can be sent from real friends' e-mail accounts.
- Offers for "free stuff" or other "too good to be true" offers probably are not legitimate.
- If you get unsolicited requests to friend people you don't know, share that information with a trusted adult.

Guided Practice

Ask the students to work in small groups to determine how to respond to the following types of situations:

- Ralph received an e-mail from a friend's account saying that he needs him to send Ralph's mom's credit card number, so he can afford to take a taxi home from downtown, since his mom lost her wallet and they are stuck.
- Sari gets an online message says "Want to party with us? Click here." She doesn't recognize the account that sent the message.
- Jose is online and a girl named Catherine sends him a message asking for him to join her in a private chat room by clicking a link. He looks her profile up and it says she is a 14-year-old girl living in another state.
- A message that appears to be from iTunes is in Shelia's inbox. It asks her to update her iTunes account information.

As a group, discuss the appropriate responses that the small groups report out on and also discuss what to do if they do accidentally make a poor choice in responding.

Independent Practice

Ask students to create a short comic strip, electronic presentation, or poster that illustrates how to properly handle one of the situations discussed in class.

Web 2.0 Assignment Option

Have students use StumbleUpon or another social bookmarking site to identify additional resources for their classmates or their parents on how to be "Safe Surfers."

AFTER THE LESSON

Gather Feedback from Students on the Usefulness of the Tools and the Effectiveness of the Assignment

Many social media tools allow students to provide feedback and give the instructor the ability to easily sort and review that feedback. If possible, teachers should use the functions of those tools to gather feedback on how the students felt the assignment worked—what they learned, and how the assignment could be enhanced in the future. Using such feedback will almost certainly improve the learning of future students.

Share What Worked and What Didn't with Colleagues

As social media tools are constantly emerging and fairly fluid, sharing what one learned at the end of the lesson with colleagues will help everyone and improve the experience for students in the future. It also helps to make sure no one has to reinvent the wheel; more about that in Chapter 4.

EXAMPLES

The Micro Blogs

As we are always being told to start small, it makes sense to begin again with the microblogs. Since Twitter and its ilk are limited to 140 characters or so, it seems like an easy place to start as well. There are many "100 Ways to Teach with Twitter" web pages. If you don't believe it, do a quick search and you will be surprised.

A couple of truly simple ideas stand out. The library word of the day is one. It could also be the class word of the day; the sixth-grade team word of the day, etc. Working with something like Marzano's Academic Vocabulary List or similarly well-developed list, tweet a word a day or week. Ask parents to support the word as well, so they can try to work on the word at home as well. Students who use the word properly during a visit to the library would be rewarded with some small token or a chance to enter a weekly or monthly drawing, for instance. Strong vocabulary is a cornerstone to success, according to Marzano's research.

Principals or deans could tweet the behavior or conduct rule of the week to students. Parents would be encouraged to follow along and reinforce the development of good-behavior standards at home. If the school sets up a private TweetGroup, students "caught being good" could be recognized via a tweet to other students, staff, and parents (who would have to log in) to see such tweets.

Tweeting book reviews or book talks is another. Links to book talks could be tweeted to students or teachers. If the librarians in an area all got together to each create a few short book-talk videos of the state contest books, for instance, it would be easy to share those throughout the area and tweet a book or two a week. Of course, a wide range of commercially available book reviews and trailers are available at Amazon and elsewhere.

Tweet what one is currently reading. Hopefully that will not only raise interest in reading that title, but will spur on the conversation among students and staff about what else is being read throughout the building or district.

Tweet course updates and homework reminders. Students can never be reminded often enough that the solar system project is due on Friday. Parents, counselors, and special education case managers would be able to follow the reminders as well.

Send tweets out to language students in the language being studied. Ask them to either tweet back a translation or an appropriate response in the target language.

Steve Wheeler (http://steve-wheeler.blogspot.com) suggests "Twitter Stalking." This has the class follow a famous person and document their progress. Particularly during election time, as candidates are using more and more social media, this could be an interesting project for students at a variety of levels. Some analysis of the activity could make for an exceptional assignment.

Twitter can also be used as a makeshift student response system. English teachers and others assigning writing prompts can tweet writing prompts to students. Students can be allowed to tweet questions during class that they may not be willing to ask in front of everyone. Students could also be asked to use Twitter to provide constructive feedback for oral presentations in class.

Twitter also offers a Public Timeline (http://www.twitter.com/public_timeline) that can be useful for current events courses or history courses during events with a national or global impact. Classes can also follow specific political leaders or candidates to watch and analyze what they say and how they use Twitter and other social media.

Assign a class to write a twittory. Twittories are stories written collectively, but 140 characters at a time using the rules of Twitter. Many such twittories are stored at http://twittories.wikispaces.com.

George Mayo, a Maryland eighth-grade teacher, set up a creative writing project called "@manyvoices" using this approach. The result was a story in which over 100 students from six countries contributed. It is available as a published book through Lulu (www.lulu.com/product/paperback/%40manyvoices/2579032). It may be downloaded for free as a PDF document.

Many of the suggestions for Twitter, which will be covered in Chapter 4, can be modified for use with older students as well.

More Resources for Twitter as an Instructional Tool

30 Ways to Use Twitter to Accelerate Learning: http://taitcoles.word press.com/2011/01/12/30-ways-to-use-twitter-to-accelerate-learning

Can We Use Twitter for Educational Activities? http://www.scribd.com/doc/2286799/Can-we-use-Twitter-for-educational-activities

Instructional Design with Twitter: http://jenny.wakefield.net/instruction/instructional-design/web2/twitter.html

Tips for Using Chat as an Instructional Tool: http://campustechnology.com/articles/2007/10/tips-for-using-chat-as-an-instructional-tool.aspx

Facebook

One of the advantages mentioned by students over using other learning management systems (LMS) such as Blackboard or Moodle is that students are generally already comfortable with the Facebook interface and don't have to learn another system for class. The Facebook wall allows for a threaded discussion forum similar to those found in other LMS. By setting up course or other student groups, it isn't necessary to "friend" other students or groups and personal information that you wouldn't necessarily want the rest of the class to have can remain private.

Facebook Polls

Polls are an easy way to gather information about a class or to receive feedback about how an assignment worked. For a teacher or librarian just stating with social media, this is a good place to start. Public and school library Facebook pages can use polls to track all types of reading interests, etc.

Facebook Election

A Canadian ninth-grade history teacher, Richard Cossette, developed a Facebook assignment in which students had to research a former world leader, create a Facebook profile for the leader and then use Facebook to electioneer to become the world leader. This assignment has been featured in a number of blogs and other social media. The student assignment sheet is available at http://emergingedtech.com/pdfs/FacebookAssignment TriFold.pdf. This assignment could easily be modified to discuss authors, determine the finest Civil War general or the most impactful scientist of the millennium, etc.

The Flat Stanley Project (www.flatstanley.com) has a presence in a multitude of venues including Twitter, Facebook, and the web. Flat Stanley blogs are available from the main website. Students can view other FS blogs as well. In addition to teacher resources, there are also sections for Girl Scouts, Boy Scouts, and some specific special education resources.

Other Facebook-related resources include:

To Create a Poll in Facebook

1. Select a poll app or type "poll" in the search box (Figure 1A).
2. Select Allow (Figure 1B).
3. Facebook will then ask for permission to share your information with the Poll App (Figure 2). Click Allow.

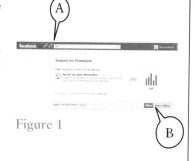

Figure 1

Figure 2

4. Select *Click here to get started* (Figure 3).
5. Figure 4 Dialog box will appear:
   a. You can select where you want the poll to post (Figure 4A).
   b. Enter the question to be polled (Figure 4B).
   c. Enter the possible answers (Figure 4C).
   d. Select Create Poll (Figure 4D).

Figure 3

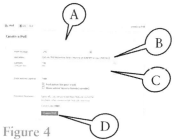

Figure 4

6. Then select Post in the next dialog box
7. Another dialog box will allow for more ways to share the poll (Figure 5).
8. Figure 6 shows the poll on the creator's Facebook wall.

Figure 5

Figure 6

Cyber Polling Lesson Grades 9–12

Overview

Provide students with a basic understanding of how to use Web 2.0 polling tools. (This could easily be combined into a lesson on probability or statistics in math or science or a social science lesson on political polling or electioneering. It could be used to support a journalism lesson or a lesson on spreadsheet graphs and charts.)

Instructional Standards Being Addressed (Based on ISTE NET-S)

1. Creativity and Innovation
    d. Identify trends and forecast possibilities
3. Research and Information Fluency
    d. Process data and report results

Introduction

Bring into the class an example of a poll or remind the students about a recent poll conducted by the school.

- Ask students what recent polls they are familiar with.
- Why do people conduct polls? What do they do with the results?
- Do you ever wonder if the results would be the same if you conducted the poll here in school?

Share results from some recent web-based polls. Some example sites would include:

Fox News Polls: www.foxnews.com/topics/fox-news-polls.htm
Gallup Polls: www.gallup.com
Teen Ink: www.teenink.com
Wall Street Journal/NBC Polls: http://topics.wsj.com/subject/W/wall-street-journal/nbc-news-polls/6052

Review some polls together in class and ask the students to interpret what the results mean to them. The two samples shown here are from Teen Ink.

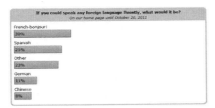

Discuss how these results show what the students would have expected.

Instruction

Then explain how polls are used by the media, politicians, and other organizations to determine and then shape public opinion.

Guided Practice

Provide instruction on how to use the Web 2.0 polling engine of the school's choice. (Some choices include Edmodo, Facebook Polls, and SurveyMonkey.)

Walk the students through setting up a poll and then opening it for input. As an example, use the polling question:

Will knowing the results of a poll potentially influence your opinion on a topic?

1. Yes, I would want to know what other people think.
2. Maybe, if it is a topic I am not familiar with.
3. No, I don't care what the crowd thinks; I will make up my own opinion.

Then have the class take the poll, and export the results. Then review the results and ask the students to put the results into a graph or chart and write a paragraph or two which interprets the results.

Independent Practice

Ask students to break into teams of between two and three and select a national poll from the web to reproduce in the school. After the students gather the results, ask them to write a short explanation of why they think the results of the local school based poll either did or didn't replicate the results of the national poll.

Facebook as a Learning Platform: http://elearningtech.blogspot.com/2007/10/facebook-as-learning-platform.html

One Hundred Ways You Should Be Using Facebook in Your Classroom: www.onlinecollege.org/2009/10/20/100-ways-you-should-be-using-facebook-in-your-classroom

Using Formspring (www.formspring.me), a social media service similar to Facebook, one Illinois teen set up an anonymous compliment website for her high school. This allows for students to leave anonymous compliments for each other through the service. The creator stated that she did this in order to combat all of the negativity on the Internet. The creator feels that the positive compliments have helped set a different tone in the school and has helped make the school climate a little more positive. The site is moderated, so no negative postings will show up even if they are received (Zwang, 2011 September).

Skype (Voice, Chat, and Video Services)

Skype (www.skype.net) is a two-way voice, chat, and video service. It is the most popular of the video /chat services. Skype has a specific Twitter account for classroom ideas at @Skype Classroom. Information on how to use Skype is at How to Skype (http://howtoskype.net). Eduwikius .wikispaces.com/SKYPE is dedicated to using Skype in the classroom as well. There are a number of commercial products available as well that provide similar functionality to Skype.

One of the easiest ways to use Skype is for modern language or ESL learning. Allowing students to Skype with a native speaker is a great way to improve language fluency. Whether it is done as a required assignment for all students in a lab setting, in an enrichment activity, or for students needing additional support or practice, it is an incredibly easy way to bring native speakers into the classroom.

Librarians can use Skype to allow authors to visit virtually without the travel expenses associated with traditional author visits. Authors can interact via Skype or other video services with students to answer questions or explain their works in a much less costly venue than on-site author visits once a year or so. A list of experts willing to Skype into a classroom is available at www.skypeforeducators.com/educators.htm. There is also a Skype in Schools wiki at http://skypeinschools.pbworks.com.

Virtual field trips to museums or historic sites are another possible way to use Skype to instructional advantage. Classrooms can arrange virtual exchanges with students from other countries. Former foreign exchange students can keep in touch with their former teachers and classmates.

Home- or hospital-bound students can be Skyped into the regular classroom in order to not miss material as can other students with special needs. Skype can be used to allow military parents who have been deployed to participate in parent-teacher conferences or watch the school play they would otherwise have to miss.

Other similar chat/video services include:

FaceFlow: www.faceflow.com
Fring: www.fring.com
ooVoo: www.oovoo.com
SnapYap: www.SnapYap.com
TokBox: www.TokBox.com

Wikis in the Classroom

Wikis can be an excellent learning tool for many classroom environments. Wikis are excellent for coordinating information, documents, and other materials in a collaborative format. Wikipedia is probably the most famous wiki, and though many shudder at its use as a definitive resource (which it isn't), its popularity ensures that most students will be familiar with the basic concepts of how to navigate through a wiki environment.

Nearly any class or subject could use a wiki for developing student-produced study guides. Allowing students to develop their own study guide in a wiki environment is an easy way to start using wikis in the classroom. Assign small teams of students to each research a topic and create one or more entries in a class wiki is an easy way to introduce students to wikis.

Here are some additional ideas for using wikis in instructional settings, from TeachersFirst (www.teachersfirst.com/content/wiki/wikiideas1.cfm):

1. Be clear about your purpose for using the wiki
2. Link it closely with the objectives
3. Ensure adequate rewards for learning the basics
4. Build in milestones on editing skills where possible
5. Reward both product (pages produced) and process (edits, messages, and other features where available)
6. Be prepared to be overwhelmed by some students
7. Be clear about the assessment criteria and that it may shift as some classes evolve more quickly than others.
8. Trust the wiki to keep the information available to you.

Some great ideas for wiki projects include collaborative writing projects for students. The web is full of wikis devoted to discussing classic literature, ranging from Shakespeare to *1984*. Wikis allow users to post and discuss articles, links to blogs and other resources, etc. Check out the following examples:

AP English Literature Circle: http://apenglishliteraturecircles. wikispaces.com
British Literature Wiki: http://britlitwiki.wikispaces.com
Children's Literature collaborative: http://childrensliterature. wetpaint.com
Literawiki: http://literature.wikia.com/wiki/Literawiki

Some good school library wiki examples include:

Central Middle Library Wiki: http://centralmiddle.wikispaces.com
JES Library Wiki: http://jamestownreads.wikispaces.com/home

Creating a Wiki with Wikispaces

1. Sign in to www.wikispaces.com. Creating an account will create your first wiki.

2. Enter the following:

a. A username

b. A password

c. A valid e-mail address

d. Select Yes for making a wiki.

e. Select if you want a Public or Private wiki.

f. If for K–12 use, select K–12 to obtain the Wiki free without advertisements.

g. Click on the Join button.

3. To add a page to the wiki, select New Page from the left-hand menu

4. Then add a page name and descriptive tags. Click on the Create button.

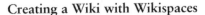

5. The newly created page will appear in edit mode, as in the example below. Add content and then click on Save. The new page will appear in the left-hand menu of the wiki.

6. Selecting Manage Wiki will bring up a list of control panel options.

7. Selecting People will show the options for how to manage members of your wiki and to invite potential members.

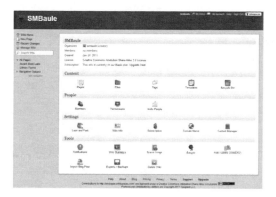

8. Selecting Invite People will open a dialog box to allow you to invite up to 100 people to the wiki.

9. To be notified of any changes to the wiki, set notification settings by selecting the NOTIFY ME tab at the top of the wiki.

Select the type of e-mail or RSS feed notification that you desire.

Media in the Middle Wiki: http://media-in-the-middle.wikispaces.com/home

Mt. Harmony's Library Media Center Wiki: http://mhesmedia.wikispaces.com

Produce a study guide page for the school linked from the library web page. Allow students and teachers to develop study guides for common assessments, etc. Work with teachers to get them to support the project by providing support for students who create the best study guides for a given topic or project.

A school-wide vocabulary resource wiki could provide definitions and examples for difficult words that students encounter in their reading. Particularly where students are involved in differentiated reading programs, it would expose students to a wider range of vocabulary than otherwise possible. Student participation could be easily measured.

Wiki Development Lesson Grades 7–10

Overview

Provide students with a basic understanding of how to create a Wiki and populate it with useful information about an Asian County as part of a geography course. (This could easily be combined into a lesson on local history or many other social studies courses.)

Instructional Standards Being Addressed (Based on ISTE NET-S)

1. Creativity and Innovation
    b. Create original works as a means of personal or group expression
3. Critical Thinking, Problem Solving, and Decision Making
    b. Plan and manage activities to develop a solution or complete a project.

Introduction

Ask students how they might gather and organize information about their upcoming project to research a country in Asia. Review some of the ways country information is organized, using examples like CIA World Factbook, CultureGrams, almanacs, traditional encyclopedias, and other print and on-line materials. After discussing the advantages and disadvantages of each, ask the students to consider the ways in which wikis display and organize information. Ask the student how many have used Wikipedia or similar wiki tools. Discuss with the students how they like or dislike the wiki approach to organizing information.

Instruction

Ask the students to determine what essential and optional pieces of information should be included in the wiki for each country. After cooperatively agreeing on what those items are, have the students divide into groups of three to four students to develop a wiki entry on an assigned country.

As a minimal example:

Required Information	Optional Information
Name	Famous people from the country
Population	Travel destinations
Area	How the current borders came to be
Flag	Ethnic breakdown of the nation
Type of government	
Ruler/head of state	
History timeline	

Provide instruction on how to add pages to the wiki created for the project. (Some choices include Edmodo, Wet Paint, Wikia, or Wikipedia.)

Walk the students through setting up a page for their country. Include how to add images, videos, timelines, etc.

Then have the class review and rate each of the country pages. For extra credit, ask the students to individually add one or more additional facts into the page(s) of one or more other countries not covered by their group to help reinforce the collaborative nature of wikis.

Assessment

Assess the wiki entries based upon a rubric developed based upon the Wiki rubric included in this text.

A collaborative pathfinder page could be developed using both student and staff contributions throughout a school, district, or even a wider region. This could be particularly helpful for those portions of the curriculum that are regionally or even locally important, but on which textbook writers do not regularly focus.

Local history wikis may be a great way to collaborate with a local museum or historical society. Students can post presentations or projects they did on local history topics. It is also a great way to make students aware of local primary source materials, photographs, and other materials that can help bring historical periods to life.

A related project would be to develop a wiki to further inform the community about the names on a monument in a community. Almost every community has some sort of monument raised either to soldiers who fought in a given war or to the community leaders who helped support the development of some community project. Ask students to research those people at the local library or historical society and then develop a short biographical entry for each in a wiki format. Schools with long histories or their own archives may wish to have students start to build a school history wiki that can be shared with the public and that can highlight some of the more interesting historical resources of the school.

Some wikis are developed simply to create a virtual base for an individual course and all of the resources related to the course can be linked from the wiki. In many ways, the Learning Management Systems (LMS) create this functionality whether it is Blackboard, Moodle, etc. Teachers can easily post their notes, presentations, and assignment rubrics into a wiki for easy student reference.

Special education case managers can also create a wiki for posting assignments and accommodative type materials that students and their parents can access from home as well as in class. One major problem with special education students with organizational problems or ADHD is that they misplace materials. By putting them into a wiki, the students will always be able to find their assignment sheets, worksheets, and rubrics.

Most of the examples above include the teacher creating the structure of the wiki and asking the students to use and/or contribute to the resources available. However, there is no reason why students or groups of students can't be asked to create their own wikis for a variety of assignments. Some of the easiest places to use to build a wiki are listed below.

Sources to start a wiki include:

Edmodo: http://www.edmodo.com
Wet Paint: http://www.wetpaint.com
Wikia: http://schools.wikia.com
Wikispaces: http://www.wikispaces.com

Students can be asked to develop a wiki for a specific assignment or to create an online portfolio of their work across the curriculum. Wikis may be the best tool for students and schools who wish to develop strong online portfolios. Some online portfolio resources are listed below:

MERLOT: http://eportfolio.merlot.org
Nuventive: http://www.nuventive.com
Pupil Pages: http://www.pupilpages.com

Wikis make an exceptional place to gather open educational resource (OER) content for students to either supplement or supplant traditional textbooks. OER Commons (www.oercommons.org) is a site that organizes and shares OER content. A growing number of open textbooks are available through the OER Commons. Particularly as more schools and districts look to moving towards 1:1 instructional computing models, there is an increased desire to provide electronic resources aligned to state standards and the Common Core.

Virtual Bookshelves

Goodreads (www.goodreads.com) is a social media site to share reading lists. It is sort of a virtual book club. It has some of the characteristics of both a blog and a wiki. The purpose of the site is to allow users to share what they are reading and their recommendations with others. It allows users to designate what they are currently reading, as shown in the Goodreads screen shot. One's friends are able to share and recommend titles to each other.

Students could use this to easily keep track of their reading during the school year as well as over the summer. This would allow teachers and librarians to see what both their students and their colleagues are reading and make recommendations to students based upon what they have read and liked. This is some ways is a simple to use virtual readers' advisory site. The reviews added in Goodreads are easily moved into a blog. It also allows for interactive comments on the reviews. Particularly at the secondary level, this resource has a great deal of potential for helping guide students along a path of good literature. More on similar sites is found in Chapter 4.

Blogs (or Web Logs)

Blogs are another relatively easy Web 2.0 technology to bring into the classroom. For many years, students have been asked to journal or write other thought pieces about their responses to a given assignment, piece of art, etc. Blogs allow for the same type of journaling, but with the added capability of collaboration available in a Web 2.0 environment.

Goodreads screen shot

Instructional blogging can take place in three basic ways:

- Teacher-directed blog with students asked to comment on teacher postings
- Student blogs in which the teacher can comment on the student responses to a given prompt
- Student blogs in which students comment on each other's postings with some moderation and prompting from the teacher, but the goal is student collaboration and discussion

These follow what can happen in a traditional classroom setting, where often the best teachers simply set up the discussion and may put out a prompt or two to begin the discussion. The biggest difference is that a blog-based discussion doesn't need to end at the bell, and all of the students in a class will have the opportunity (if not the expectation) to contribute to the conversion. This ability to extend the learning beyond the school day is clearly one of the strong points of a blog. The Escapbooking site (http://escrapbooking.com) gives the following reasons why teachers like blogs:

- Easy for the teacher to provide written feedback
- Much easier for students and teachers to maintain than web pages
- Time stamps show when students made entries
- Multiple blogs for many purposes
- Students have ownership and access beyond the school setting
- Students enjoy the writing experience
- Students don't get lost in the "glitz" of the technology
- Teachers can add password protection and membership restrictions as needed
- Communication with the community and parents is essential; blogs are the tool
- Extends learning beyond the period or school day (i.e., guest e-speakers, questions, and answers)

Blogs are in fact one of the easiest to use Web 2.0 technologies. As mentioned above, the blog can be secured, so only the students in a given class or section can see the blog or post to the blog. Most blogs can also accept video clips, images, and even presentations as entries, so a blog doesn't have to be limited to text.

One of the easiest ways to jump into the Web 2.0 world is to take the traditional classroom, library, or school newsletter and transform it into a blog. It is extremely simple to make this transformation and is a good way to begin to move parents toward looking to the web for class information. Allowing parents to comment is a good way to get feedback, but one probably wants to view the comments, but not let them be visible to others on the blog. Posting student assignment dates and other information also provides a good resource for students. Linking to specific resources to remind students about exam prep or review sheets, for example, is an easy step into the interactive web.

Many schools work to encourage summer reading, but a blog is a great way for students to stay connected to each other and to library or classroom staff over the summer. Set up a blog to allow students to comment and respond about their summer reading lists. To help motivate students, look to provide top contributors with some small reward at the end of the summer similar to the traditional rewards given in summer reading programs.

Students in a health course could be asked to develop and post public service announcements on a blog tied to the week's instruction in class. Foods students could post original or favorite recipes to a blog. Language students could be asked to blog in the target language only. Linking with a classroom in a country where the target language is spoken would allow students to directly communicate with native speakers.

Students can also be asked to interact with existing blogs. Looking to newsblogs from various parts of the country or the world can be an easy way to start to discuss the concepts of perspective with young writers. Why do the blogs of the BBC, for instance, differ in their viewpoint from those of NBC or Fox News?

Instructional Blog Resources

David Warlick's Class Blogmeister: http://classblogmeister.com
Mr. B-G's Blogging with Students: http://bgexemplar.blogspot.com
Robert Runte's Assigning and Assessing Student Blogs: http://www
   .slideshare.net/Runte/assigning-and-assessing-blog-assignments
Student Blogging Challenge: http://studentchallenge.edublogs.org

Some Sample School Library Blogs

AIBS Library Blog, Budapest: http://www.trycuriosity.com
Monarch's Library Blog: http://monarchlibrarian.blogspot.com
New Trier Library Blog: http://newtrierlibrary.blogspot.com
Nicholas Senn High School Library Blog: http://sennlibrary.blogspot.com
Pollard Middle School Library Blog: http://yourschoollibrary
   .wordpress.com

Some Sample Principal and Counselor Blogs

From Palmer's Pen (Middle school principal): http://tpsmiddlestaff
   .blogspot.com
Mr. Ackerman's Blog (Principal): http://rackerman.wordpress
   .bedford.k12.ma.us
Smart Futures (Counselor): http://blog.smartfutures.org
Westmont High School Guidance News Blog: http://www.cusd201
   .org/srhigh/student_services/guidance/news

Creating a Blog with Blogger

1. Sign in to www.blogger.com. If necessary, you may have to create a Google account first.

2. Once signed in, click on Create a Blog.

3. Complete the Name page

   a. Enter a title for your blog.

   b. Enter the address you want for the blog.

   c. Enter the verification code and click Continue.

4. Select a template from the options presented and click Continue.

5. Select Start Blogging.

6. Complete a first post.

   a. Enter a title.

   b. Enter the text of your initial message.

   c. Select Preview to review the post before publishing it.

   d. Enter subject label(s) for the post (optional).

   e. Once the posting is complete, click PUBLISH POST.

YouTube, Slide Share, and Flickr

Most students and educators are at least familiar with YouTube and similar video-sharing sites. Many educators and students use these sites as a resource, but contributing to them is an effective way to contribute to the interactive web. Uploading videos to YouTube or TeacherTube is an easy way to share one's classroom successes with the wider world. Besides simply taping class presentations and posting them to the web, students can also interview local celebrities about issues in the community and create school-based news broadcasts, commercials, and even game shows to review course materials. These opportunities can help increase student motivation to produce their best work. Some of these videos could then be embedded into a blog to allow others to comment on the content and or quality of the work produced.

Librarians could record student or teacher book talks and develop a small library for students to view if they need some ideas on book selection. Physical education teachers could make short videos on basic sports fundamentals or rules that students could use to either practice or review.

Teachers with interactive whiteboards may be able to capture their presentations and post those notes and presentations directly to the web in order to share with students who were absent or who may want to review the materials at a later date. Posting videos prior to a course session allows the students to gather the "lecture" information ahead of time and leaves more time in class for discussion or other group work.

Uploading one's classroom presentations to SlideShare or a similar resource makes it easy for students to retrieve them. It would also allow special education teachers, parents, or tutors to review the content when they are helping a student with homework.

Documenting a field trip using either of these resources can both serve as a student assignment and as a way to share the field trip with students who were unable to participate.

Uploading student presentations to SlideShare is a great way to reward student effort and allow their work to be viewed by a wider audience. Students could also reduce their presentations to movie forms and post them to Flickr or YouTube as well. See the image of a sample presentation using SlideShare.

Students and teachers can also build and share presentations directly through the web using sites like Prezi (http://prezi.com), which provides some exceptional instructional videos. Making a Prezi video is fairly simple. However, the presentation engine is robust and allows for embedded video from YouTube or other sources. Some educational examples of Prezi presentations include:

A Brief Overview of World War II: http://prezi.com/qiknryuwyzjt/ipt
-prezi-history-class

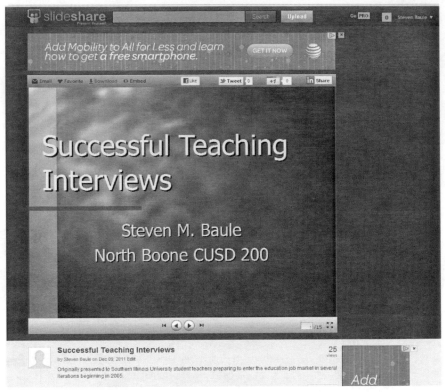

A sample presentation viewed in Slideshare

Ancient Rome: http://prezi.com/npkt318odke0/chapter-9-section-3
-ancient-rome

AP Bio: http://prezi.com/boa21ytdaoxy/ap-bio-evolution-6-brief
-history-of-life

Chemistry Semester Review: http://prezi.com/2ykmsj4rymuq/
chemistry-review

Important Dates in American History: http://prezi.com/w9dl_psc7a3t/
important-dates-in-american-history

The image of a Prezi page shows a list of prezis prepared by a school librarian.

Tagging Sites

The basic reasons for utilizing tagging or social bookmarking sites for instruction are to allow collaboration among students and to ease the organizing and managing of the sites or other bookmark lists. StumbleUpon (www.stumbleupon.com) and Delicious (http://delicious.com), among

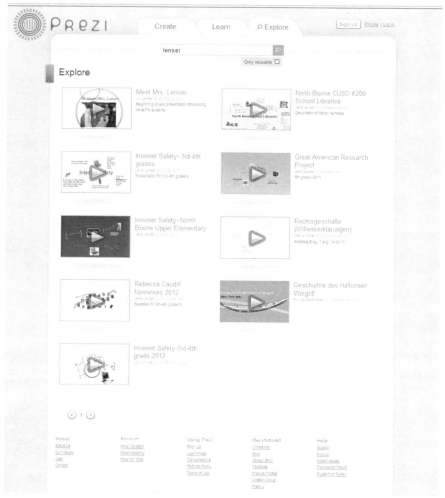

A School Librarians prezis

others, allow a user to keep a record of sites very much like favorites or bookmarks in a web browser. However, these collections of sites can be shared with other users. Teachers and librarians can use these social media sites to preview and gather resources for students in the same way that librarians and teachers once developed reserve book collections in the library.

A teacher or librarian can wade through all of the immense information on the Internet and then bookmark only the best resources for students to use. This allows for a librarian to go out and search for the most exceptional sites regarding Ernest Hemingway, Eva Peron, Pope Julian II, etc., and then make all of those links available to anyone with access to that librarian's StumbleUpon account. It also allows any registered user to comment on the links. In the case of an ancient history project, the librarian could search out the 40–50 best sites to support the project on Carthage and then each of the teachers involved could comment on the specific strengths of the various sites based on the needs of the project options.

Students could also be asked to identify a particular subject or subjects as being of interest to them. This will generate a weekly random set of suggestions from StumbleUpon based upon their interest inventory, an example of which appears in the StumbleUpon image. So, U.S. history teachers could asked students to "Stumble" through various U.S. history sites and report on those from which they learned something new or something related to the current period of study in class.

Diigo (www.diigo.com) gives an interesting twist to tagging. Users not only collect sites, but they are allowed to annotate those sites and share that information. It is as close to highlighting and posting sticky notes to websites as you can get without messing up your monitor. One of the disadvantages of this site is that it limits a user to 1,000 highlights per year unless they upgrade to a fee-based plan. However, the fee is modest, at approximately $20 per year.

StumbleUpon

Hi Steve!

We've gathered a personalized selection of sites we think you'll like, enjoy!

Stumble >

Want even better recommendations? Choose more interests or find people you know on StumbleUpon.

Weekly StumbleUpon website recommendations based upon an individually defined

Google Bookmarks also allows a user to share their bookmarks with others. This is a relatively new feature in Google. This feature would serve the same purpose as one of the other tagging services above, so a teacher in a Google Apps environment may wish to use this bookmarking feature instead. The disadvantage is that Google Bookmarks doesn't suggest additional sites based upon your preferences or previously visited sites.

News Ranking Websites

Digg (www.digg.com) and similar news ranking services allow users to comment on the importance of given news stories. Digg will allow a user to search by topic, such as presidential election, Middle East conflict, etc. One can also view the news stories as they are captured and vote on whether the item is newsworthy and should be at the top of the Digg Top News, or buried. Students could easily use the service to both gather current news on a range of topics or watch what people around the world think is important. These sites have value as a potential educational tool at the high school level, but the vocabulary associated with many of the comments don't make them child friendly. Digg does allow accounts to filter out what they consider adult content, making it one of the better options among these services.

Survey Sites

SurveyMonkey (www.surveymonkey.com) and similar sites can be used to gather student responses, to elicit parent or student feedback, or even to create quizzes or other assessments. Survey sites were also discussed in the last section on communications tools. SurveyMonkey includes a bank of potential survey questions for a variety of types of surveys. The current education bank includes teacher and parent feedback surveys, a bullying survey template, and a high school sports survey template. However, these tools are incredibly malleable and can be used for a wide range of classroom applications.

Teachers could use these engines to develop pretests for gauging student knowledge at the beginning of a unit or course. For example, teachers could ask about student learning styles in order to better differentiate or to add a couple of feedback questions to the end of a quiz and get some additional feedback about how the students feel the course is being paced or how the class work is being presented.

Students can be taught how to create surveys and can gather input for their own polls or other data-gathering assignments. Most of these sites are free for users who are only surveying small groups of people, and even the largest class loads for high school teachers will generally allow them to use a free account.

Similar to full survey sites, Yahoo Groups, Facebook, and Google Apps also allow for survey development and polling on a smaller scale. Yahoo Groups polls are easy to set up and administer to anyone who is already a member of the group. Teachers could easily create a group for their students and then use the internal polling structure of Yahoo Groups to elicit feedback or gather other information from students.

Multiplayer Games

It is only a matter of time before the software engines used to drive massively multiplayer online games (MMOs) or massively multiplayer online role playing games (MMORPGs), are harnessed to provide direct educational instruction. In fact, a few such examples already exist. These games allow users to create a user account and then develop or create one or more avatars (toons, characters, etc.) that will allow them to make their way through the virtual environment. Fantasy games such as World of Warcraft (WOW) and Dungeons and Dragons Online (DDO) are just two examples of such programs available on the web. Many now allow free registration and then require users to purchase upgrades to allow one to travel to different areas or purchase upgraded equipment or powers.

One such educational "game" is Zon (http://enterzon.com), which has been developed to help users learn Chinese. According to the website: "Zon is a virtual environment where the community of Chinese language learners can connect, practice their language skills and learn about the Chinese culture. Participate in tutor sessions, live classes and practice one on one with other players. Every item in Zon has information attached, allowing you to explore culture and language at your own pace." Zon is a product of the Confucius Institute at Michigan State University. It is the first of its kind in education, but it is doubtful that it will be the last.

McLarin's Adventures (http://k20center.publishpath.com/mclarin) is a similarly developed MMORPG created by the University of Oklahoma. According to the University of Oklahoma's K20 Center, McLarin's Adventure "is set in a survivor story mode where gamers explore an uninhabited, uncharted island to test their skills at finding necessary resources. Through a series of tasks, student teams must work together to apply math, bioscience, geography and geology to maneuver through the game. McLarin will send the winning team into outer space to explore colonization of other planets."

According to the K20 Center, only six research centers throughout the United States are currently working on harnessing MMORPG engines for education. However, it seems straightforward that these engines, which create significant motivation and interest, will eventually be harnessed to an educational cart. Whyville (www.whyville.net) is a similar game system on a less intense scale focused on primary-aged children. Its games focus on

How to Create a Yahoo Group

1. Sign into groups.yahoo.com

   (see the sample moderated group to the right; it includes a notice of messages needing to be approved).

2. Select Start a Group.

3. This will open up a dialog box like that shown below.

4. If you select Schools & Education/K–12 as the subject of the group, you can further refine the group's subject category.

5. Complete the next dialog box.

a. Give the group a name.

b. Create an address for
   the group.

c. Write a description
   of the group.

6. You will then be asked which profile you want to manage the group,
   etc. Then click Continue to finish creating the group.

7. If everything is completed correctly, you should see a dialog box
   congratulating you on the creation of the group and asking if you
   want to customize the group or invite people to join.

8. Select Customize the Group.

  a. Determine if you want the group to be in the Yahoo directory.

  b. Determine if it should be moderated or if anyone can join.

  c. Determine who can e-mail the group.

9. Again, select the choices that are appropriate for your group.

10. Select the choices as to whether or not nonmembers can access group resources.

11. Click Finish.

STEM-related curriculum and topics. One of the key components of its being school friendly is that the chat system automatically filters out curse words and similar speech. This allows it to be used in school settings with less trepidation than some other similar systems.

For more information on the future of gaming in education, check out the following resources:

EduRealms (a blog about using WOW and other games for education):
   http://edurealms.com
The Minecraft Teacher: http://minecraftteacher.net/
Second Life: http://secondlife.com
WOWinSchool: www.scribd.com/doc/58293619/WoWinSchool-A
   -Hero-s-Journey

RUBRICS TO SUPPORT THE INSTRUCTIONAL USE OF SOCIAL MEDIA

Rubrics provide students with a clear set of expectations about what students are being asked to create, do, or present. Rubric development is often an ongoing process in which teachers will want to further refine the rubric after each iteration of student projects to make sure that the rubric is providing the best guidance possible for students. Some general information and guidelines about rubrics for Web 2.0 projects are available at the sites below:

Educational Origami: http://edorigami.wikispaces.com/
LCI Quality Rubrics Wiki: http://qualityrubrics.pbworks.com/w/page/
   992395/Home
TeachersFirst: www.teachersfirst.com/istecre8/rubrics.cfm

Sample Blog Rubric

The sample blog rubric outlined in Table 3.2 can be used for evaluating single blog posts or long-term blog assignments. The additional sections can be added to the rubric based upon the focus of the assignment. For instance, if the blog is to discuss world events in a high school geography course, the Understanding Global Perspectives section could be added.

Additional blog rubrics are available at:

A+ Rubric, University of Wisconsin–Stout, A Rubric for Evaluating
   Student Blogs: http://www2.uwstout.edu/content/profdev/rubrics/
   blogrubric.html
Blog Grading Rubric: www.frenchteachers.org/technology/Grading
   .Rubric.pdf

Table 3.2 Sample Blog Rubric

	1 Beginner	2 Developing	3 Proficient	4 Expert
Quality of writing	• Post has little or no style • Doesn't add any information to the strand • Poorly organized	• Post has little style • Adds little new information • Poorly organized	• Post has an interesting style • New information or reflections are evident • Well organized	• Post has an interesting style • Information or reflections are compelling/significant • Well organized
Presentation	• Many grammar or spelling errors • Formatting makes post difficult to follow	• Several grammar or spelling errors • Formatting makes it difficult to follow	• Minor mechanical errors • Formatting makes the post easier to read	• No mechanical errors • Formatting makes the post more interesting and/or easier to read
Multimedia	• No media included in post	• Media isn't truly on point of the topic or doesn't function properly	• Media is on point and adds to the reader's understanding	• Media is on point and adds to the reader's understanding without overwhelming the post itself
Community	• No appropriate links • Post is not tagged or otherwise categorized	• One or more appropriate links • Post is tagged	• Several appropriate links • Post is tagged	• Several links to places that significantly add to the reader's understanding • Post is completely tagged
References	• Sources lack documentation	• Most sources are documents	• All sources are accurately documented.	• All sources are accurately documented in the desired format.

(continued)

Table 3.2 (continued)

	1 Beginner	2 Developing	3 Proficient	4 Expert
Optional Sections				
Connecting and Networking	• Displays inappropriate behavior online • No thought given to creating or sustaining a network	• Usually uses proper netiquette • Usually connects with others safely • Regularly reviews self-chosen RSS feeds • Network changes only with support	• Uses proper netiquette • Connects with others safely • Regularly reviews self-chosen RSS feeds • Network sometimes changes, growing or shrinking slowly	• Supportive of others online • Connects with others safely • Regularly reviews RSS feeds subscribed to • Deletes and adds feeds as needed • Network is flexible, changing to meet needs
Commenting	• Never comments on others work • Few comments approved in own space	• Occasionally comments on others work • Comments in own space approved late	• Regularly comments on others work • Comments are approved in a timely manner	• Often comments on the work of others • Comments ask questions and drive forward thinking
Understanding Global Perspectives	• Accesses information only from the United States • Little to no understanding of global perspectives	• Accesses information from at least two countries • Vague understanding of global perspectives	• Accesses information from at least two continents • Some understanding of global perspectives	• Accesses information from at least three continents • Shows clear understanding of global perspectives

Blog Reflection Rubric: http://edweb.sdsu.edu/courses/edtec296/ assignments/blog_rubric.html

Educational Origami, Bloom's Digital Taxonomy: http://edorigami. wikispaces.com/file/view/blogging+rubric.pdf

Sample Wiki Rubric

The sample wiki rubric shown in Table 3.3 can be used for evaluating student wikis. When groups of students are involved in the development, adding the collaboration element would make sense to be included.

Additional Wiki rubrics are available at:

Rubric Assessment: http://flatclassroomproject.wikispaces.com/ Rubrics

Rubrics/Wiki Rubric Development: http://wikieducator.org/Rubrics/ Wiki_Rubric_Development

Wiki Grading Rubric: http://k12online.wm.edu/WikiGradingRubric .pdf

Twitter Rubric

The Twitter rubric outlined in Table 3.4 could be used for assessments in which the students are using Twitter over a unit or longer period, not tied to a specific or short-term assignment.

Additional Twitter rubrics are available at:

A+ Rubric, University of Wisconsin–Stout, Twitter Rubric: http:// www2.uwstout.edu/content/profdcv/rubrics/Twitter_Rubric.html

Education with Technology, Harry G. Tuttle, Twitter Rubric: http:// eduwithtechn.wordpress.com/2009/06/23/assessing-learning-with -web-2-0-twitter-in-the-classroom/

SOCIAL NETWORKS AND CHEATING

Unfortunately, there are students who have figured out many ways to use social networks to cheat on academic assignments, quizzes, and tests. According to a NewsOne report in 2011, 8 out of 10 high schoolers cheat. The report states that not only do low-performing students cheat, but many upper-level students cheat, trying to deal with the pressures of trying to produce in order to get into good schools and meet family expectations.

Technology and social media are not making cheating more difficult. According to NewsOne, 82 percent of students plagiarized from Wikipedia,

Table 3.3 Sample Wiki Rubric

	Needs Improvement	Emerging	Proficient	Excellent
Content	Coverage is not complete; sections are lacking or nonexistent	Provides significant coverage of the topic, but coverage lacks completeness	Provides complete coverage of the topic	Covers topic in depth with details and examples; content knowledge is exceptional
Organization	Site is not coherently organized	Classification of content is not complete or not user friendly	Content is well organized	Content is well organized and properly grouped under subheadings/divisions
Attractiveness	Design elements distract from the message/usability of the site	Design elements are neutral to the message/usability of the site	Design elements support the use and understanding of the site	Excellent use of design to enhance the wiki
Mechanics (Grammar)	Mechanical errors impact the message/usability of the site	Some mechanical errors are present	Only minor mechanical errors that don't impact the message/usability of the site	No mechanical errors
Technology	Technology errors, bad links, etc., impact the usability of the site	Some technology errors are present; images are slow loading, etc.	Only minor technology errors are present	No technology errors; links work; images optimized for the web, etc.
Collaboration	Is not a positive contributor to the team, is disruptive, etc.	Contributes less than proportionally to the wiki	Proportionally contributes to the development of the wiki	Contributes greatly to the development of the wiki

Table 3.4 Sample Twitter Rubric

	Needs Improvement	Emerging	Proficient	Excellent
Content	The tweets were unclear and not easy to understand	The content of the supplemental material was adequately summarized	The tweets were somewhat clear and easy to understand	The tweets were clear and easy to understand
Mechanics	Significant mechanical errors	Mechanical errors that don't interfere with the message	Minor mechanical errors that don't interfere with the message	No mechanical errors
Hashtags	The appropriate hashtag was rarely or not used	The appropriate hashtag was used for some of the tweets	The appropriate hashtag was used for most of the tweets	The appropriate hashtag was used for all of the tweets
Hyperlinks	Hyperlinks are either absent or not appropriate or broken	Hyperlinks are occasionally included	Hyperlinks are appropriately included	Hyperlinks are appropriate and recent
Responses and Retweets	Responses are not present; retweets are not present or not appropriate	Responses to tweets not always appropriate or present; retweets are not always present or not appropriate	Responses to tweets are appropriate; retweets are generally timely and appropriate	Responses to tweets are appropriate and positive; retweets are timely and appropriate

one of the most famous Web 2.0 tools. Only 5 percent are caught, according to the article. Thirty-eight percent of students have copied directly from another website. Similarly, a full one-third of high school students have used their cell phone to cheat, and a full one-half of students ignore their school's rules about cell phone use. Almost two-thirds of college students admit to some type of cyber cheating.[2]

Some of the most common ways to address those issues are the same methods used to fight crib notes and other less technologically spectacular forms of cheating. One of the easiest ways to combat cheating is to provide for assessments and exams which require responses that tap the higher levels of Bloom's Taxonomy, as such responses are more likely to need to be individualized and provided in a context. In comparison, a multiple-choice exam is much easier to cheat on than an essay exam, which asks for synthesis of ideas.

Rotating exam questions for multiple-section courses and giving randomly generated sections of exams will also help to both discourage and deter cheating within a classroom. The ease of developing such random-item quizzes and exams is remarkable given the ubiquitous nature of test generation software.

Of course, others will argue that using social media and engaging students in more authentic ways will reduce cheating, since cheating is generally a response to boredom and practiced by the unengaged learner. If one asks their students to comment on a piece of literature on a Facebook page or a wiki, it will be fairly evident if three or four students post the same exact responses.

Caroline Knorr (2011) suggests proactively discussing cheating with children to make sure they understand what collaboration is and what is cheating. She states that children don't always understand the concept of "cheat" based on the video and online gaming industries, which build in "cheats" as special codes or Easter egg type surprises as a bonus for users to uncover. However, homework doesn't work that way, and children need to be encouraged to use only the types of collaboration and technologies that the teacher or school intended.

As technology allows collaboration among students at all times of the day and night, it is important for parents to be involved in monitoring cyber cheating, and engaging parents to assist in watching for cheating is an excellent way of helping inform parents about the capabilities of the technology in their children's hands. The school library may choose to hold a parent night to explain some of the emerging technologies and work with the school administration in order to share with parents how they might check up on their own children to make sure they are working properly and aren't cheating on homework or other assignments.

NOTES

1. Based upon the Netiquette Guidelines of Inver Hills (Minnesota) Community College.

2. News One (2011), Shocking Stats on Cheating from Kindergarten through College, available at http://newsone.com/the-education-zone/newsonestaff2/cheating-kids-school-college (accessed September 21, 2011).

CHAPTER 4

Professional Development

Social media applications are also a wonderful set of tools to enhance professional development for educators. Social media is the cutting edge of professional development in many ways. New ideas and instructional uses for technology are evolving through social media conversations every day. If one searches the Internet for information about how to use social media to support their professional development, they will be nearly overwhelmed by the amount of information retrieved. Of course, with the exponential expansion of digital information sources, the same could be said about searching for information about how to make ice cream or how to read hieroglyphics.

With regard to professional development, social media resources are particularly important, as fewer resources are available for the more traditional professional development methods. Conference attendance is down significantly across most strata of educational programming. It is a confluence of many factors, including fewer resources available for travel, fewer people doing what more people used to do, and the ability to utilize virtual meeting environments for some tasks. More staff members are being asked to work in multiple buildings, which also lead to a feeling of separation from the rest of the staff and a loss of camaraderie.

For some career educators, who don't often get out of their individual districts, social media has the ability to provide new perspectives from districts across the state and around the world. Due to economic issues, child care issues, etc., some staff are not able or willing to travel to conferences away from the district. Those staff members often have a rather limited outlook with regard to professional development due to not being exposed to a wide variety of other staff, perspectives, and opinions. Social media can help impact those issues and provide all staff with a wider perspective.

Online professional development can assist in combating some of those feelings of loss and isolation by providing virtual colleagues and opportunities for learning. Virtual staff development can also assist in reducing travel and lodging costs to schools by significantly reducing the time away from school for travel. This is particularly true for rural districts, where travel even to in-state conferences can drive up costs in additional travel expenses.

Many of the reasons and rationales for using social media for professional development are the same reasons that have been articulated earlier for integrating social media into the instructional and communications processes of a school or district. Some of the reasons for embracing social media for professional development are discussed below.

Brian Croxall (www.briancroxall.net) articulated three reasons why college faculty should embrace social media for professional development: It's faster, cheaper, and more open. As mentioned above, the time and money needed to travel to a conference or meeting aren't required for most conferences using social media engines. Due to the speed and lack of travel time needed, the cost is almost always lower. Additional cost savings include the lack of needing meeting halls or other spaces to meet.

Social media professional development is more open in part because more people can participate. Whereas even in the best-heeled schools, the principal couldn't afford to send the entire staff to a conference, all of the staff could participate in a virtual conference or collaborate via a wiki. All of the staff can view presentations available via YouTube, SlideShare, or other social media and aren't limited to those able to fit in the room at the same time or to those whose schedule accommodated traveling to a given workshop or conference.

Social media allow for more interaction between participants and the presenters or facilitators. In virtual presentation settings, the participants are able to share with each other and interact in ways that aren't limited in terms of time or location, as opposed to traditional workshops. The virtual presentations allow for a much wider scope of participation than traditional conference settings and are more likely to draw a much more diverse audience. When participants are able to comment and interact, the flow of ideas can become much richer than in traditional settings. Many conferences are now investing in the resources to ensure the availability of virtual participation opportunities for those unable to attend the physical conference site.

Beyond offering hybrid conference opportunities, social media can also enrich traditional conferences through the use of backchannel communications or backchanneling, during sessions. Backchanneling can be an effective way to engage the audience and solicit feedback without taking significant time out of the presentation.

According to TodaysMeet, the backchannel is "everything going on in the room that isn't coming from the presenter. The backchannel is where people ask each other questions, pass notes, get distracted, and give you the most immediate feedback you'll ever get."

The backchannel can be impromptu via Twitter, instant messaging, or a range of other social media. However, for particular presentations or workshops in which a presenter wants to be able to gather and utilize the feedback available from the backchannel, a number of specific tools are available for backchannel communications, including:

Chatzy: www.chatzy.com
Edmodo: www.edmodo.com
TodaysMeet: http://todaysmeet.com/

Basically, the backchannel allows participants to share their ideas, queries, and feedback with the presenters in real time without disrupting the flow of the presentation itself. Some presenters may even take some brief "Twitter breaks" to review the backchannel commentary and make sure that the participants are getting what they want from the session. Backchannel communications can also be harnessed for student instruction in 1:1 classrooms. Particularly where students are watching longer movie clips, etc., the backchannel would allow students to ask questions or comment without needing to stop the video to address individual questions. Special education students or ESL learners could even be assigned their own backchannels to allow them to get additional help from their resource teachers without needing to pose their questions before the entire class.

Some additional resources on how to harness the power of the backchannel include:

Tony Karrer's Presentation Backchannel Multitasking: http://elearning tech.blogspot.com/2009/10/presentation-backchannel-multitasking .html

Kyle Mackie's Thinking, Learning, Teaching on the Backchannel: www.slideshare.net/kylemackie/thinking-learning-teaching-on-the -backchannel

Christopher Machielse's How Technology Empowers the Shy Student to Participate in Class: http://info.lecturetools.com/blog/bid/39488/ How-Technology-Empowers-the-Shy-Student-to-Participate-in -Class

When presenting as part of a group, it is simple to assign one of the presenters to monitor backchannel feedback. Some solo presenters will take a short break to address those issues. Other presenters might ask one of the participants to monitor the backchannels and bring forward any important questions or comments they notice. The authors, when they present together, bring an extra table or laptop to monitor the backchannel. The authors often use Wallwisher (www.wallwisher.com) as a simple backchannel medium for participants to post questions and comments in the way that the "parking lot" was often previously used with butcher paper to put questions or ideas that the presenter wanted to speak to later. Wallwisher is discussed in greater detail later in this chapter.

Examples of how social media can enhance professional development follow.

BLOGS

Blogs are a powerful tool for professional development. They may also be the easiest plan for educators new to social media to begin their forays into Web 2.0. They allow the exploration of new ideas and interaction with other educators, and they facilitate professional discussions among educators. Reading blogs, responding to other blog posts, and starting one's own blog are excellent first steps toward becoming familiar with many aspects of social media.

Unlike Twitter and some of the other forms of social media, blogs are relatively easy to explain and understand. As the easiest way to begin, reading educational blogs isn't much different from reading professional journals, except that one is often able to respond directly to the author via the comment features available on most blogs.

Blogs can be used as simply a way to enrich and supplement traditional professional reading. Many of the mainstream educational journals and newspapers now include mentions of blogs that have raised questions or provided deeper review of the issues covered in the print issue. This is an excellent place to start for those new to social media.

The following are some lists and blog search engines to help one find educational blogs of note:

Blogarama: www.blogarama.com
Edublogs at SupportBlogging.com: http://supportblogging.com
EatonWeb: http://portal.eatonweb.com
Technorati Blog Directory: http://technorati.com
25 EduBlogs You Simply Don't Want to Miss: www.slideshare.net/
    zaid/25-edublogs-you-simply-dont-want-to-miss-presentation

Some education blogs worth reviewing include:

Jeff Cobb, Mission to Learn: http://blog.missiontolearn.com
Dan Colman, Open Culture: www.openculture.com
Will Richardson, Weblogg-ed: http://willrichardson.com
Kathy Schrock, Kaffeeklatsch: http://blog.kathyschrock.net/
David Warlick, 2¢ Worth: http://davidwarlick.com/2cents/

Some (mostly school) library blogs worth reviewing include:

Bib 2.0 (Jeri Hurd): http://bib20.blogspot.com
The Blue Skunk Blog (Doug Johnson): http://doug-johnson.squarespace
.com
Disruptive Library Technology Jester (Peter Murray): http://dltj.org
Eliterate Librarian (Anonymous): http://e-literatelibrarian.blogspot
.com
Gargoyles Loose in the Library (Frances Jacobson): www.uni.illinois
.edu/libraryblog
Info-fetishist (Anne-Marie Deitering): http://info-fetishist.org
Judging the Books (by Beth, high school librarian): http://judgingthe
books.blogspot.com
100 Scope Notes (Travis Jonker): http://100scopenotes.com
Musings of a School Librarian (Caroline Roche): http://uulibrarian
.wordpress.com
Shelf Consumed (Leigh Ann Jones): www.shelfconsumed.com
The Unquiet Librarian (Buffy Hamilton): http://theunquietlibrarian
.wordpress.com

Also worth reviewing is the blog comic Unshelved, by Gene Ambaum and Bill Barnes (www.unshelved.com).

An easy way to keep current with blogs is to use an RSS reader like Good Noows or Google Reader to check one's blogs and website for updates and new posts. Setting up most readers is fairly simple. For instance, when one creates a Good Noows account, the next screen will provide a listing of types of newsfeeds and allow one to simply select the sources one wants to receive. Then one only has to add any blogs or other URLs that one wants to stay up on and any updates will show up in the reader. Some of the reader tools even allow the information to be displayed in newspaper format, so one's customized morning paper really can show up on the computer desktop.

Some feed-organizing options:

BlogBridge: www.blogbridge.com
Good Noows: http://goodnoows.com
Google Reader: www.google.com/reader
Netvibes Wasabi: www.netvibes.com/en
Readefine Desktop: http://readefine.anirudhsasikumar.net

After becoming comfortable with reading blogs and comments, a teacher or librarian may want to begin his or her own blog to share thoughts with the world or just find out if others agree or disagree with what they are trying instructionally, etc.

The first thing to do is set up a blog using one of the services mentioned in the first section of the book. Then gather ideas about what to write about. Some of the things one might write about include:

- An introductory post articulating how one got involved in wanting to blog or share in a Web 2.0 environment
- What one did last week, yesterday, or today in the classroom, with a solicitation for commentary about what could be done better or simply one's own reflections on the process.
- What one learned on the last professional development day and how it is being used
- Comments or reflections about changes in state or federal legislation
- Reflections about the use of a new instructional method, intervention, or technology in the classroom
- A post about a lesson plan or unit plan that really worked well

There are a great many articles and help pages on how to start writing a blog. For more information and ideas to stimulate the launching on a blog, search for "how to start a blog" or "how to write a blog"; you will find a great many useful hits.

TWITTER

Twitter has the potential to be an excellent professional development tool. Part of the ability to use Twitter effectively is learning how to strip away the constant inane posts from some users that post such "important" information as the fact they are going to the grocery store, that they just got their haircut, or that they just ordered a Red Stripe. Such information might be stimulating and engaging for some, but many educators are looking for good professional development information and not a laundry list of one's Saturday errands.

One of the first questions people have concerns how to find people to follow. There is no simple answer to determine who to follow, but Todd Zeigler (www.bivingsreport.com/2008/the-twitter-disconnect) gave the following advice on his blog:

1. Identify a few people you know in real life and follow them by searching for their name on Twitter. Then go through the list of the people they follow and add some of the people that you know and/or that look interesting.
2. Check out a list of the most popular Twitter users and follow the interesting ones.
3. Once you are following around 20 or so Twitter feeds, just sit back and listen. You'll see lots of little conversations break out through

the use of the @ sign. Check out the accounts of the people your friends are talking to and add them if they make a good impression.
4. At this point, new users will start following you. Follow the ones that you find that seem cool.
5. Don't be afraid to stop following people you find uninteresting.

For most educators, it is easy to start with finding educators in similar positions who are already tweeting. Find out who they follow and determine if some of the people they follow are suitable to follow.

Hashtags use the # character at the beginning of the tag to identify the tweet as dealing with that item—such as #echat for education, or #library for library. If you search Twitter using the hashtag, it will return only tweets identified with the hashtag. This will bring in more accurate results than simply searching "library," for instance. There are more than 400 hashtags specific to education. For a specific event, like an in-service day, a workshop, or a conference, a specific hashtag can be developed for the conference participants to share information during the conference. Some popular educational hashtags to follow include:

#echat	Education	#ntchat	New Teachers
#edtech	Educational technology	#TUalg1	Algebra 1
#educhat	Education	#mathchat	Math
#ukedchat	UK Education	#engchat	English
#gtchat	Gifted and Talented	#edapp	Educational Apps
#vitalcpd	Effective use of EdTech	#spedchat	Special Education

Here are some additional hashtag resources:

A–Z Dictionary of Educational Twitter Hashtags: http://edudemic
  .com/2011/10/twitter-hashtag-dictionary/
Advice from the Twitter Hashtag Queen: http://theinnovativeeducator
  .blogspot.com/2011/05/advice-from-twitter-hashtag-queen-steve
  .html
Creative Education Blog, Top Twitter Hashtags for Teachers: www
  .creativeeducation.co.uk/blog/index.php/2010/12/top-twitter-hashtags
  -for-uk-teachers/

Cybrary Man's Educational Web Sites, Some Educational Hashtags:
    www.cybraryman.com/edhashtags.html
Hashtag.org: http://hashtags.org/
TwitterU's Listing of Hashtags: http://twitteru.wikispaces.com

Twitter chats can also be developed to focus on a specific topic, ranging from general professional development to what one had for lunch. Currently there are over 550 scheduled Twitter chats. #libchat is currently scheduled weekly "for librarians and information students, booksellers, vendors, book critics and everyone who loves libraries and books." #schoolschat is devoted to a biweekly conversation on the latest education news and studies. It would be easy for a librarian to set up a Twitter chat like #rtilibrary to discuss the role of the librarian in implementing response to intervention (RtI) throughout a district or a region.

Twitter lists allow users to follow a group of Twitter users on a single list. These lists can be either public or private. Creating a private list for workshop attendees, peers, or all of the librarians within a district is an easy task. A couple of sample public Twitter lists include:

Joe Jacquot's EdTech List: http://twitter.com/#!/WackJacq/edtech
Laura Spangler's Library Land: http://twitter.com/#!/laurajspangler/
    library-land
Michelle's Librarianship: http://twitter.com/#!/michellefromtx/
    librarianship
PublicAgenda's In the Principals Office: http://twitter.com/#!/
    PublicAgenda/in-the-principals-office

In the end, the best thing to do with Twitter is set up an account and start to explore and experiment. Look for things that are interesting and follow up those leads.

Additional Twitter Resources

Boss, S. (2011). Twittering, Not Frittering: Professional Development
    in 140 Characters. www.edutopia.org/twitter-professional-develop
    ment-technology-microblogging
Childs C. (2011). Twitter: Use It Productively. www.lifehack.org/
    articles/lifehack/twitter-use-it-productively.html
Flowing Data (2008). 17 Ways to Visualize the Twitter Universe.
    http://flowingdata.com/2008/03/12/17-ways-to-visualize-the-twitter
    -universe/
Twittaholic (listing the most popular Twitter users). http://twitaholic
    .com/

FACEBOOK, GOOGLE+, LINKEDIN, AND MYSPACE

Although Facebook, Google+, and MySpace have a wide variety of tools and services that can be harnessed for professional development, they have their drawbacks for professional educators. The authors would recommend keeping a Facebook or other profile for friends and family and not using it for professional networking. LinkedIn is a much better professional resource and using a divergent source and not Facebook, etc. will help separate an educator's professional life from his or her personal life.

Once in LinkedIn, users can connect with colleagues, former teachers and professors, and even students (but in a more professional tone than Facebook, etc.). Groups in LinkedIn allow users to connect with like-minded individuals, post questions, and begin conversations. Many professional organizations have a group presence on LinkedIn, and it is an easy way for members of a professional organization to become more active in their professional organization(s).

One of the additional features of LinkedIn is the ability to search for people by skills and expertise. More than 50 categories of skills and expertise are directly tied to school and library work in LinkedIn. This could be used to help find a speaker for an in-service day or just to do one's own homework prior to attending a conference or a workshop.

LISTSERVS AND GROUPS IN GOOGLE AND YAHOO

There are a tremendous number of groups and listservs devoted to an astounding array of topics tied to education and libraries. Although some of these more traditional listservs and other services are being supplanted by newer social media, many of these groups and listservs continue to have

---

Commentary from a Teacher Using Facebook: Anonymous Teacher posted 16 Nov 2009

I have been debating all weekend about whether or not to take down my FaceBook page. My mother insists that I should do so, just in case, but I don't feel there is anything inappropriate included on my page. I try to be careful of how I am photographed in any situation because many of my friends have pages where they post photos. So even if I remove my page, there are still photos of me on the internet. I use FaceBook to keep in touch with relatives and friends who live all over the country, and it bothers me that, as a teacher, I can't enjoy the same format of communication enjoyed by so many others. What concerns me most, however, is that one anonymous email can derail a career in so short a time. I have been teaching for seven years now, and it seems each year the cons list grows while the pros list diminishes . . . sigh!

active and vibrant followings. A good list of educational listservs can be found at www.shambles.net/pages/staff/ListMail. LM_NET, the library media listserv, was one of the earliest listservs in education and is still listed at the top of the Shambles' list. An LM_NET wiki has been set up at http://lmnet.wikispaces.com to support the listserv.

Listings of Groups and Listservs

Classroom 2.0 Groups: www.classroom20.com/groups
Google Groups: https://groups.google.com
Yahoo Groups: http://groups.yahoo.com
L-Soft Listserv Catalog: www.lsoft.com/catalist.html

For districts using Google Apps as a district-wide solution, it is easy to create groups for specific clusters of teachers, librarians, and other education professionals that will provide the same functionality of outside groups, but will be limited to members of the district's staff. This is an excellent resource for those schools that wish to develop a collaborative culture without the need to train school staff in new technology, as most if not all of the staff should be familiar with e-mail at this point. Professional learning communities (PLCs) can use such groups to share information. The functionality of both the Google and Yahoo groups really resemble more the scope of a wiki than a traditional listserv, as they allow for posting files and other data along with providing for surveys and polls among the members.

SKYPE

Many of the things discussed earlier in the instructional section covering Skype can be used for professional development as well. Assuming one finds a contact for an author or an outside expert, it is relatively easy and inexpensive to bring them into a workshop via Skype. Skype can also be used for individual coaching or professional development sessions with experts from across the district or around the world. If the web is to be believed, Skype is being used in many districts to allow teachers to collaborate for grade-level and departmental- or subject-area meetings without requiring travel throughout the district. Teachers or librarians looking for others to collaborate via Skype can check out the Skype in the Classroom directory at http://education.skype.com.

WIKIS

Wikis and similar collaborative workplaces are an easy way for educators to share materials. Some of these can be managed through the traditional free sites such as Wikispaces and others mentioned earlier. See the KIDS Wiki screen shot example. However, education-specific tools, such as Edmodo and Elgg, offer more closed environments for users within a school. In either case, professional-development wikis make an exceptional place for educators to share lesson plans, faculty meeting minutes, common assessments, rubrics, and all of the other "tools of the trade." With the current increases in expectations that are impacting teachers and other educators, there isn't time to continually recreate the wheel.

Educators need to do a better job of sharing resources and collaborating across the hallway as well as across the country. Wikis make that extremely easy.

A few of the exceptional wiki-type professional resource sites include the following:

Multimedia Education Resource for Learning and Online Teaching (MERLOT): www.merlot.org/merlot/index.htm
Read, Write, Think: www.readwritethink.org
Thinkfinity: www.thinkfinity.org
WetPaint's Wikis in Education: http://wikisineducation.wetpaint.com
WikiSpaces, Educational Wiki Examples: http://educationalwikis .wikispaces.com/Examples+of+educational+wikis

If one is just getting started with building a professional wiki, create a simple school-level wiki for teachers to share lesson plans and other materials. Requiring departments, teams, and/or grade-level teacher groups to post their minutes to the wiki is a great way to get people started with using wikis. Librarians can post book lists, new materials lists, and other information to the wiki. Principals can post faculty meeting agendas, schedules, and other important items to the wiki as another way to get users used to obtaining and sharing materials via a wiki.

VIRTUAL BOOK LISTS

Goodreads (www.goodreads.com), which was mentioned in Chapter 3, is another tool that can be harnessed for staff development. If a librarian creates a Goodreads account for his or her students, it is easy to separate materials into various "shelves." Creating a professional shelf allows a librarian or principal to recommend books to the rest of the staff. If the school's staff all use Goodreads with their students, it is easy for them to all create, recommend, and review professional reading materials to each other. Some similar resources include:

LibraryThing: www.librarything.com
Revish: www.revish.com
Shelfari: www.shelfari.com

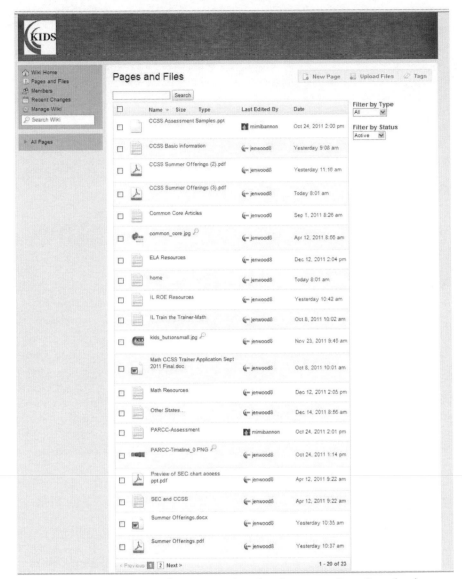

KIDS (IL) Regional Wiki for Supporting the Common Core Standards

It seems like almost every school library should be using one of these sites for students, parents, and staff. Reading, as a core of lifelong learning and modeling for students, is going to remain an essential skill for the twenty-first century just as it was for the nineteenth century.

VIDEO AND PRESENTATION SHARING

Sharing presentations and videos is easy with today's social media tools. While videos from YouTube are good instructional resources, they are also exceptional opportunities for professional development available in the video-sharing sites. For teachers and librarians early in their careers, watching videos of master teachers can be an excellent way to become aware of strong instructional techniques. TeacherTube has a specific section (called "channels") about how to make educational videos and other tutorials for teachers. The Teaching Channel (www.teachingchannel.org), a product of PBS, provides a range of professional-development videos for teachers. It has a specific section for new teachers.

Other channels are specifically devoted to RTI and professional development.

My Learning Tube: http://mylearningtube.com
PBS Teachers: www.pbs.org/teachers
TeacherTube: www.teachertube.com

SlideShare provides a method for sharing presentations in PowerPoint and other formats. Teachers involved in professional development can share in-service presentations, find other professional development materials, and find "how to" presentations on a variety of topics. Video and audio clips can also be included in SlideShare as "SlideCasts." Scribd is a similar site to SlideShare and allows for similar document types. Both have 100 MB limits for files, but SlideShare allows up to 500 MB for video.

Presentation Sharing Resources

authorSTREAM: www.authorstream.com
SlideShare: http://slideshare.net
SlideBoom: http://slideboom.com
SlideServe: www.slideserve.com
Scribd: www.scribd.com

SOCIAL BOOKMARKING OR TAGGING SITES

These sites allow one to gather bookmarks or "tag" their favorite sites that they can then share with other users, friends, or the public in general. Most of the systems organize these site links into folders, or "stacks" in the case of Delicious (www.delicious.com). StumbleUpon (www.stumbleupon.com) is similar but adds the facet of making recommendations for a user based upon what they tell the service they like. StumbleUpon allows users both to enter a great deal of information about themselves and to manage their interests. These interest categories will generally recommend websites to visit on a weekly basis. Categories range from ancient history to Internet tools. Users are also able to review sites, which makes it easy for teachers or librarians to identify exactly how colleagues may wish to utilize the sites they identify as favorites.

Diigo allows educators a more advanced free account that includes being able to share with student or staff groups.

Social Bookmarking Resources

BlogBookMark: www.blogbookmark.com
BuddyMarks: www.buddymarks.com
Diigo: http://diigo.com
Gather: www.gather.com
MyBookmarks: www.mybookmarks.com
Whitelinks: www.whitelinks.com

SURVEY SITES

Survey sites can be used to determine staff concerns or needs for staff development in the same ways they can be used to communicate with parents and be used instructionally with students. Professional learning communities are able to use sites like SurveyMonkey to gather input and feedback from their groups or teams. Individual teachers may want to use these services to elicit feedback from parents or students to help them refine their practices.

SCHEDULING AND ORGANIZING

There are a number of sites that can help organize meetings for professional groups. These sites allow members to poll users as to the dates and times that a meeting can be scheduled or when people can meet for a committee meeting. These sites can be used by teachers getting together to work on common assessments, graduate school research groups, etc. One of these, Doodle, is probably the simplest of the schedulers to use, but it lacks some of the more advanced features. Several of the others also have iPhone apps, allow each person to suggest the best times for them, and more.

Doodle: http://doodle.me
ScheduleOnce: www.scheduleonce.com
TimeBridge: www.timebridge.com
Tungle: www.tungle.me/Home

Sample Professional Development Survey

This survey was designed to support the district's technology plan and allowed the library and IT staff to differentiate between the needs of the various buildings and type of employees.

First Section

Asked for demographic information to be able to stratify the responses by building (Question #1) and then by job category (Question #2).

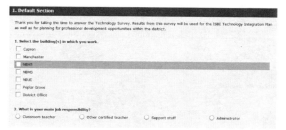

Second Section

This section asks questions as to what people need/want to learn about.

3. I would benefit from technology professional development on...	Strongly Agree	Agree	Neither Agree or Disagree	Disagree	Strongly Disagree	Do Not Know
Research based practices I can use in my teaching.	○	○	○	○	○	○
Identification and evaluation of technology resources, e.g., websites that I can use with my students.	○	○	○	○	○	○
Performance based assessment of my students.	○	○	○	○	○	○
Use of technology to collect and analyze student assessment data.	○	○	○	○	○	○
Learner-centered teaching strategies that incorporate technology, e.g., project-based or cooperative learning.	○	○	○	○	○	○
Online security and safety.	○	○	○	○	○	○
Use of technology in differentiating instruction for students with special learning needs e.g., gifted, autistic, etc.	○	○	○	○	○	○
Ways to use technology to communicate and collaborate with families about school programs and student learning.	○	○	○	○	○	○
Ways to use technology to communicate and collaborate with other educators outside of the district.	○	○	○	○	○	○

Third Section

This section allows the staff to provide input in another format than Section 2. This allows for some verification of the Section 2 answers as well as some open-ended opportunities for feedback.

4. I am interested in learning more about the following areas of technology: (Check all that apply.)

- ☐ Microsoft Word
- ☐ Excel
- ☐ Options for presentation software e.g., PowerPoint
- ☐ Educational social networking sites
- ☐ Multi-media presentation software e.g, MovieMaker
- ☐ Basic troubleshooting
- ☐ SmartBoard classroom usage
- ☐ StarBoard classroom usage
- ☐ Developing teacher websites
- ☐ Using other equipment currently owned e.g., Student Response System, ELMO, etc.

5. Please list any other professional development technology needs.

6. How would you rate your overall comfort level and proficiency with technology?

- ○ Other people come to me as a technology resource
- ○ I am a strong user
- ○ I know enough to get by
- ○ I am technologically challenged

7. Is there any technology equipment or software that you would like to see added to your classroom that could impact student learning?

8. How often do you use instructional technology in your job assignment and for what purposes? (Check all that apply.)

- ☐ I use an interactive whiteboard throughout the day.
- ☐ I use an interactive whiteboard occasionally.
- ☐ I take my students to the computer lab once a week.
- ☐ I take my students to the computer lab more than once a week.
- ☐ I require my students to use technology tools for their assignments.
- ☐ I regularly introduce new technology to my students.
- ☐ I read my email daily.
- ☐ I use email to communicate with parents.
- ☐ I keep records/lessons electronically.
- ☐ I do not normally feel comfortable using technology with students.

VIRTUAL WORLDS

As mentioned in Chapter 3, there is a small but growing segment dealing with instructional gaming. There are other virtual worlds as well, and these virtual worlds are being used to provide significant professional development opportunities. Second Life (http://secondlife.com) is probably one of the most well known and has been used for a great deal of graduate instruction.

Some graduate courses are available via Second Life or other virtual-world settings. OpenSimulator, or OpenSim, is a free version similar to Second Life with some of the less desirable aspects of Second Life minimized. Drury University and North Carolina State are two institutions that are using Second Life to offer for-credit courses.

A number of virtual worlds exist, ready to be explored. Some are fairly open and allow significant flexibility, while others are more stable.

Active Worlds: www.activeworlds.com
Kaneva: www.kaneva.com
Moove Online: www.moove.com
OpenSimulator: http://opensimulator.org
There: www.there.com

VIRTUAL BULLETIN BOARDS/BRAINSTORMING TOOLS

Being exactly what they sound like, these services create virtual bulletin boards on which people may post virtual notes. For instance, a professional learning team could use one for the "parking lot" questions raised during a work session. Then no one would have to transcribe the real post it notes on a piece of flip chart paper; that work would already be completed. Some like Wallwisher (www.wallwisher.com) are limited to Post-It notes and linking URLs. These can be used by groups, but they are also any easy way for individuals who work between multiple computers during the day or week to organize their personal task or to-do lists. These boards can also be used collaboratively to develop digital "data walls" for classes or intervention groups. In conjunction with an interactive whiteboard, these programs can be used to show student progress, interventions, and other information with amazing ease.

Some virtual bulletin board sites are below:

Corkboard: http://corkboard.me
Edistorm: http://edistorm.com
Linoit: http://en.linoit.com
PrimaryWall: http://primarywall.com
Skrbl: www.skrbl.com
Wallwisher: www.wallwisher.com

Goal-setting sites are another way for teachers or librarians to use the web for professional and personal development. There are a range of goal-setting sites that allow one to keep track of goals and the progress toward completing them.

Some online goal-setting and management sites include:

Forty-three Things: www.43things.com
Goal-Buddy: www.goal-buddy.com
Goals on Track: www.goalsontrack.com

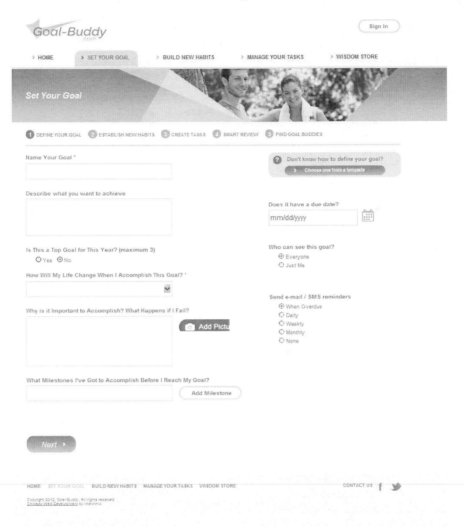

Goal Buddy screenshot

    LifeTango: www.lifetango.com
    Solid Goals: www.solidgoals.net

    Goal-Buddy requires that the goals be in SMART Goal form; see the image from the Goal-Buddy site. The SMART Goal format, which is required by so many schools for PLC team goals, school improvement plans, and individual goal-setting, is a nice requirement for this goal site. It could easily be modified for use by a PLC team, a department or even a school as a way to collaboratively track goals.

How to Use the 43 Things Website to Track Your Goals

1. Register at http://43things.com.

2. Enter your first goal and then click ADD.

3. Continue to add goals until you have all of them enumerated.

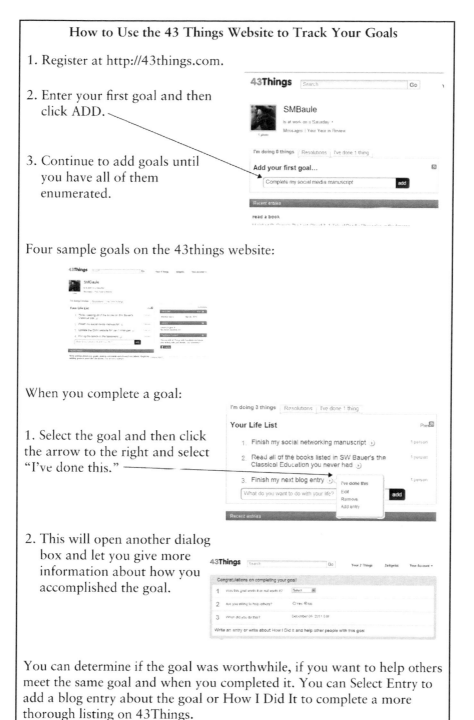

Four sample goals on the 43things website:

When you complete a goal:

1. Select the goal and then click the arrow to the right and select "I've done this."

2. This will open another dialog box and let you give more information about how you accomplished the goal.

You can determine if the goal was worthwhile, if you want to help others meet the same goal and when you completed it. You can Select Entry to add a blog entry about the goal or How I Did It to complete a more thorough listing on 43Things.

3. If you selected Entry, the dialog box to the right appears and allows you to enter information for a blog entry and then post it to the blog of your choice. The entry will remain on the 43 Things website as well, even if you don't post to a blog.

You can attach an image as well

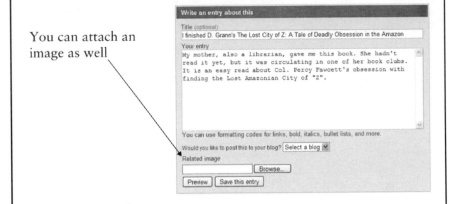

If someone isn't certain about the goal they want to add, 43 Things provides some options that one can click on to see what others are doing.

The How I Did It Entry Option allows for more complete, but formalized input.

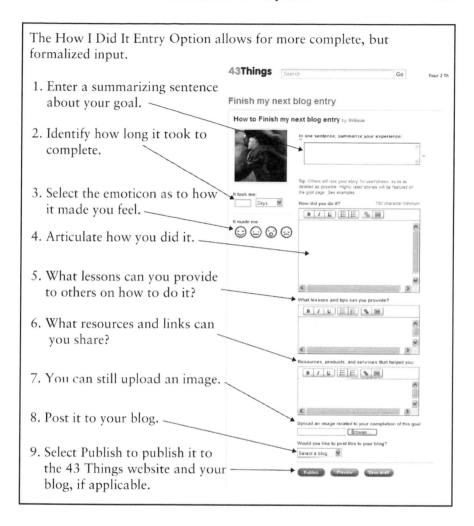

1. Enter a summarizing sentence about your goal.

2. Identify how long it took to complete.

3. Select the emoticon as to how it made you feel.

4. Articulate how you did it.

5. What lessons can you provide to others on how to do it?

6. What resources and links can you share?

7. You can still upload an image.

8. Post it to your blog.

9. Select Publish to publish it to the 43 Things website and your blog, if applicable.

NEWS SERVICES

As the educational environment is changing rapidly, it is important for educators at all levels to remain up to date with the changes and issues that are in the news. Keeping up to date can be difficult these days with all of the various news sources, but Newsvine and other news aggregators can help manage the news. Newsvine allows users to choose which news sources and topics they wish to focus on. Digg offers a similar service to users, and both services allow users to rank news stories. Google News (illustrated in the screen shot) allows users to completely personalize a news

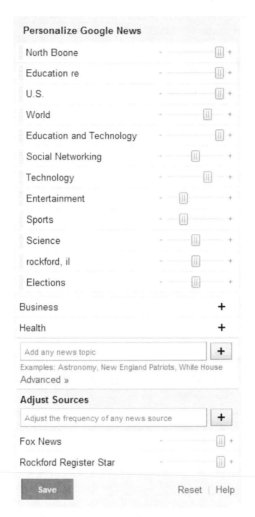

Personalize Google News

North Boone   –   ⊞ +

Education re   –   ⊞ +

U.S.   –   ⊞ +

World   –   ⊞   +

Education and Technology   –   ⊞ +

Social Networking   –   ⊞   +

Technology   –   ⊞   +

Entertainment   –   ⊞   +

Sports   –   ⊞   +

Science   –   ⊞   +

rockford, il   –   ⊞   +

Elections   –   ⊞   +

Business   **+**

Health   **+**

| Add any news topic | **+** |

Examples: Astronomy, New England Patriots, White House
Advanced »

Adjust Sources

| Adjust the frequency of any news source | **+** |

Fox News   –   ⊞ +

Rockford Register Star   –   ⊞ +

Save   Reset | Help

Google News Personalization

stream by topic and news source. Google Reader allows for similar personalization, plus it allows for blog content to be included along with the more traditional news services. Some news feeds can be bundled and shared with others.

Some news services available on the Internet:

Digg: http://digg.com
myYahoo: http://my.yahoo .com
NewsGator: www.news gator.com
Newsvine: www.news vine.com
PageFlakes: www.page flakes.com
Sofomo: www.sofomo .com

One can create a personalized newspaper using PaperLi (http://paper.li). This is a great resource to share with students working on a specific topic to gather and edit news. It could be an excellent way to start off an in-service day or a workshop by providing all of the participants with a newspaper specifically designed to provide the necessary background knowledge to prepare for the coursework or content. Librarians could use the site to develop theme-based issues to supplement book talk subjects, book awards, or other particular themes. The main page allows one to search by keyword to find pre-generated newspapers of interest as well as creating one's own paper.

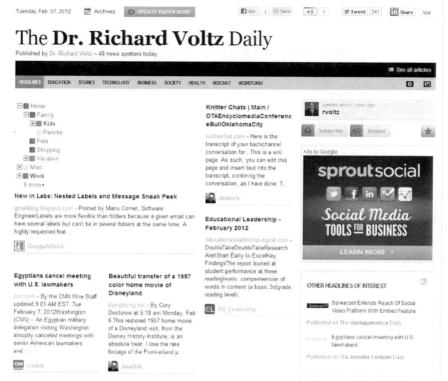

A sample Paper. Li publication: Dr. Voltz is the IASA professional development director and publishes this "daily" for superintendents

A sample Paper. Li issue from a middle school library

CHAPTER 5

Legal and Policy Issues

The U.S. Department of Education ("USED") and the American Library Association have publicly supported the use of social media in schools. A 2010 USED report calls on school districts to apply "the advanced technologies used in our daily personal and professional lives to our entire education system to improve student learning" (U.S. Department of Education, Office of Educational Technology, 2010).

DEVELOPING A BALANCED SOCIAL MEDIA POLICY

This is the question that gets asked most often: How does a school district or other governmental entity create a social media policy that enables its students, employees, or constituents to take advantage of social media in an appropriate way to further the educational mission of the school (or mission of the governmental unit), but also takes into account that social media can be used in inappropriate ways, while not infringing upon the users' constitutional rights? There are ways to accomplish this. For example, this can be achieved by allowing anyone to comment on the page but by hiding or not posting/publishing the comments. In doing this, everyone and anyone can provide feedback or voice their opinion on important issues, but those opinions are not posted for everyone to see. Those individuals who would post potentially inappropriate comments, or comments that would not be protected by the First Amendment—such as defamatory, lewd, vulgar, or offensive comments—will not be able to see their comments online. This often takes the "fun" out of doing so. This method allows those monitoring the website to view the comments and ensure that the feedback gets to the

Suggested blogger comment settings

appropriate individuals within the entity, while not enabling those who would detract from the mission or conversation to do so. For an example of how one school district did this by changing the comments settings in Blogger from the defaults, see the screen shot of the North Boone District Blog.

This allows for comments to be sent to the district but doesn't post them directly for the world to see. This allows the district to maintain two-way communication with the public without creating a public forum that would be difficult for the district to productively maintain.

WHERE DOES THE SOCIAL MEDIA POLICY FIT IN AMONG OTHER POLICIES?

The school district's policy on social media will not stand alone. It will be one of several technology, personnel, and student policies in the school board policy manual, and together they should appropriately address and communicate the district's stance regarding technology and social media—how and when to use it, and how and when *not* to use it. For example, the social media policy could be included within the acceptable use policy (applicable to both employees and students), the bullying and harassment policy, the ethics policy, and student publication policies, or it could be a separate policy that supports and refers to the other policies. Either approach is acceptable, but both need to be regularly reviewed and potentially revised given the fluid nature of social media. (Some sample policies are included as an appendix to this chapter.)

According to the law firm of Schwartz, Janes & Reed (2008), an acceptable use policy should include the following:

- Scope of use—for educational purposes only
- Prohibited uses
- Rules of use, including full disciplinary options
- Liability—the district is not liable for the accuracy of information on the web, etc.
- Privacy statement—that the e-mail and other technology used on the district's computers are district property, and that users should have no expectation of privacy
- Password responsibility
- Cyberbullying and sexting should be addressed here as well as in your bullying and harassment policies

Notification of Acceptable Use Policy Standards

It is considered a best practice to annually notify employees and students of the district's acceptable use policy, and to require them to sign a statement that they have read and received a copy of it. Courts will find that the employee/student did not have a reasonable expectation of privacy in the information stored in the work/school computer such that the school district has violated the employee's/student's Fourth Amendment rights where a school district engages in this type of routine annual notification, and where the district requires acknowledgment of the district's acceptable use policy each time an employee/student accesses a district computer (see, e.g., *U.S. v. Bailey*, 272 F.Supp.2d 822 (D.Neb. 2003)). Courts have also found that the existence of a clear policy banning personal e-mails can diminish the reasonableness of an employee's claim to privacy in e-mail messages (see, e.g., *Scott v. Beth Israel Medical Center*, 847 N.Y.S.2d 436, 441 (N.Y.Sup. 2007)) (The court determined that e-mails sent to the attorney by the employee were not privileged and noted that company's e-mail policy prohibiting personal use was "critical to the outcome."). Courts generally consider four factors when measuring an employee's expectation of privacy in his computer files and e-mail: (1) whether his employer maintains policy banning personal or other objectionable use; (2) whether the employer monitors use of employee's computer or e-mail; (3) whether third parties have right of access to the employee's computer or e-mail; and (4) whether the employer notified the employee, or whether the employee was aware of any use and monitoring policies (see *In re Asia Global Crossing, Ltd.*, 322 B.R. 247, 257 (S.D.N.Y. 2005)). Accordingly, if a district wants to minimize the potential for a successful Fourth Amendment challenge to a search of an employee's work computer or school-district-issued student computer, the district's acceptable use policy that is given to all employees and students each year, and for which they sign a notification statement, should: (1) include language that bans personal or other specifically delineated objectionable use (do not merely state that the district bans "objectionable use" or the policy will be stricken down as overbroad and vague by a court of law); (2) create an internal policy for your director of technology to randomly and periodically monitor computers and e-mails; (3) require your director of technology to keep a log of third-party access to employee computers and e-mail (e.g., other agencies, documents produced pursuant to Freedom of Information Act requests); and (4) maintain the annual notification forms on which employees indicate they have read and received the acceptable use policy.

Basic Tenets of a Social Networking Policy

1. Purpose of social networking for the organization
2. Be responsible for what you write
3. Be authentic
4. Consider your audience
5. Exercise good judgment
6. Respect copyright laws
7. Protect confidential information
8. Bring value to the organization

When developing social media policies or integrating them into existing policies, it may be helpful to develop a purpose statement as to why social media is being used by the school or district. An excellent example of a social media purpose statement is provided by the Federal Emergency Management Agency (FEMA):

> FEMA has been engaging in Web 2.0 tools and on social media sites nationwide as part of its mission to prepare the nation for disasters. FEMA's goals with social media are: to provide timely and accurate information related to disaster preparedness response and recovery; provide the public with another avenue for insight into the agency's operations; and engage in what has already become a critical medium in today's world of communications. FEMA's social media ventures function as supplemental outreach, and as appropriate channels for unofficial input.

Reviewing the statement, the important purposes identified in the purpose statement are:

- Provide timely and accurate information related to the organization/entity

- Provide the public with another avenue for insight
- Engage in what has already become a critical medium in today's world of communications
- As a supplemental method for informal outreach and input

Any school or district could modify that statement to its own ends and create something similar to the example below:

School District 133 engages Web 2.0 tools and social media sites as part of its mission to educate children and communicate with the wider community of stakeholders. SD 133's goals with social media are: to provide timely and accurate information related to school district operations and events; provide the public with another avenue for insight into the district's operations; and engage in what has already become a critical medium in today's world of communications. SD 133's social media ventures function as important educational and professional development tools, an avenue of community outreach, and as appropriate channels for community input.

Below is a sample acceptable use policy that includes social media within its scope.

(SAMPLE POLICY) ACCEPTABLE USE OF ELECTRONIC RESOURCES

Electronic resources, including but not limited to, hardware, software, network access, data files, virtual files, Internet-resources, social networks, other Web 2.0 resources and personal technology devices, are a part of the District's instructional program in order to promote educational excellence by facilitating resource sharing, innovation, and communication. The Superintendent or designee shall develop an implementation plan for this policy and appoint a system administrator/(s). The School District is not responsible for any information that may be lost, damaged, or unavailable when using the resources, or for any information that is retrieved or transmitted via the Internet. Furthermore, the District will not be responsible for any unauthorized charges or fees resulting from access to the Internet.

Curriculum

The use of the District's electronic resources shall: (1) be consistent with the curriculum adopted by the District as well as the varied instructional needs, learning styles, abilities, and developmental levels of the students, and (2) comply with the selection criteria for instructional materials and library resource center materials. Staff members may, consistent with the Superintendent's implementation plan, use electronic resources throughout the curriculum.

The District's electronic resources, including social networks, are part of the curriculum and are not a public forum for general use.

Acceptable Use

All of the District's electronic resources must be: (1) in support of education and/or research, and be in furtherance of the Board of Education's stated goals; or (2) for a legitimate school business purpose. Use is a privilege not a right. Students and staff have no expectation of privacy in any materials that are stored, transmitted or received via the District's electronic network or District computers. General rules for behavior and communications apply when using electronic resources. The District's Authorization for Electronic Resource Access contains the appropriate uses, ethics and protocol. Electronic communications and downloaded material, including files deleted from a user's account, may be monitored or read by school officials.

Internet Safety

Each District computer with Internet Access shall have a filtering device that blocks entry to visual depictions that are: (1) obscene; (2) pornographic; and/or (3) harmful or inappropriate for students, as defined by applicable federal law(s), and as determined by the Superintendent or designee. The Superintendent or designee shall enforce the use of such filtering devices. An administrator, supervisor, or other authorized person may disable the filtering device for bona fide research or other lawful purpose, provided the person receives prior permission from the Superintendent or system administrator. The Superintendent or designee shall include measures in this policy's implementation plan to address the following:

1. Ensure staff supervision of student access to electronic resources including social networking and other Web 2.0 resources;
2. Restrict access to inappropriate matter as well as restricting access to harmful materials;
3. Ensure student and staff privacy, safety, and security when using electronic resources;
4. Restrict unauthorized access, including "hacking" and other unlawful activities; and
5. Restrict unauthorized disclosure, use, and dissemination of personal identification information, such as names and addresses.

Social Networks, other Web 2.0 Resources and Personal Technologies

Definitions:

Includes–means "includes without limitation" or "includes but is not limited to."

Social Network–media for social interaction, using highly accessible communication techniques through the use of web-based and mobile technologies to turn communication into interactive dialogue. Examples include Facebook, LinkedIn, MySpace, Twitter, and YouTube.

Personal Technology–any device that is not owned or leased by the District or otherwise authorized for District use and: (1) transmits sounds, images, text, messages, videos or electronic information; (2) electronically records, plays, or stores information; or (3) accesses the Internet, or private communication or information networks. This includes smartphones, tablet computers and other personal electronic devices.

Usage and Conduct

All District employees and students who use personal technology and social media shall:

1. Adhere to the high standards for appropriate school relationships in policy, Ethics and Conduct at all times, regardless of the ever-changing social media and personal technology platforms available. This includes District employees posting images or private information about themselves or others in a manner readily accessible to students and other employees that is inappropriate as defined by Workplace Harassment Prohibited; Ethics and Conduct; and Harassment of Students Prohibited; Use only District-provided or approved methods to communicate with students and their parents/guardians.
2. Not interfere with or disrupt the educational or working environment, or the delivery of education or educational support services.
3. Comply with the Responsibilities Concerning Internal Information policy. This means that personal technology and social media may not be used to share, publish, or transmit information about or images of students and/or District employees without proper approval.
4. Refrain from using the District's logos without permission and follow Board Copyright policy, and all District copyright compliance procedures.

5. Use personal technology and social media for personal purposes only during non-work times or hours. Any duty-free use must occur during times and places that the use will not interfere with job duties or otherwise be disruptive to the school environment or its operation.

6. Assume all risks associated with the use of personal technology and social media at school or school-sponsored activities, including students' viewing of inappropriate Internet materials through the District employee's personal technology or social media. The Board expressly disclaims any responsibility for imposing content filters, blocking lists, or monitoring of its employees' personal technology.

7. Be subject to remedial and any other appropriate disciplinary action for violations of this policy.

Authorization for Electronic Resource Access

Each staff member must sign the District's *Authorization for Electronic Resource Access* as a condition for using the District's electronic resources. Each student and his or her parent(s)/guardian(s) must sign the *Authorization* before being granted use.

All users of the District's computers shall maintain the confidentiality of student records. Reasonable measures to protect against unreasonable access shall be taken before confidential student information is loaded onto the network.

The failure of any student or staff member to follow the terms of the *Authorization for Electronic Resource Access*, or this policy, will result in the loss of privileges, disciplinary action, and/or appropriate legal action.

FREEDOM OF INFORMATION ACT

Each state, as well as the federal government, has enacted a freedom of information act that applies to school boards and all of their committees and subcommittees. Often, the definition of the term "public records" is very broad. In Illinois, the definition is as follows:

[A]ll records, reports, forms, writings, letters, memoranda, books, papers, maps, photographs, microfilms, cards, tapes, recordings, electronic data processing records, electronic communications, recorded information and all other documentary materials pertaining to the transaction of public business, regardless of physical form or characteristics, having been prepared by or for, or having been or being used by, received by, in the possession of, or under the control of any public body.

According to Illinois state statute, e-mail communications that have been prepared, or have been or are being used, received, possessed, or under the control of a public body, are treated as public records under the Illinois Freedom of Information Act. E-mail messages produced on one's personal computer in all likelihood will not constitute public records under the act. However, if a school board member regularly uses his or her personal e-mail account to respond to board inquiries and conduct board business, those messages would most likely constitute public records under the Act. Also, "personal" or "private" e-mails sent or received by school employees on a school's computers should not be considered public records under the Act because they were not made or received pursuant to any law or ordinance or in connection with the official business of the school and, therefore, do not come under the control of the school. It is important for affected public officials to be conversant with the types of records that must be provided upon request and those that are exempt.

Educators need to ensure that both students and staff understand what types of digital communications are potentially disclosable under FOIA or the Family Educational Rights and Privacy Act (FEPPA). As a general guideline, any e-mail, tweet, or text that would have been reduced to a memo or letter in the past is probably disclosable if it is under the possession of and maintained by the school. Mentioning a student by name in a writing may create a student record that would be disclosable to the parents or the child. It is essential to refer to your state's specific statute in this area and/or consult with your school attorney for guidance as to what constitutes a "record."

SUNSHINE LAWS AND OPEN MEETINGS ACTS

It is important to check your state's open meetings act and ascertain how a meeting is defined under that act. For example, in Illinois, a meeting is defined as "any gathering, whether in person or by video or audio conference, telephone call, electronic means (such as, without limitation, electronic mail, electronic chat, and instant messaging), or other means of contemporaneous interactive communication, of a quorum of the members of a public body held for the purpose of discussing public business or, for a 5-member public body, a quorum of the members of a public body held for the purpose of discussing public business." These laws are intended to ensure that the public is able to view the workings of the government at all levels and avoid decision making in "smoke-filled back rooms."

Under this definition, interactive communication by a quorum of the members of the school board on the school's social networking site could be considered a gathering by electronic means, and thus be considered a meeting under the open meetings act. In checking your state's statute, be aware of the specific provisions as to: (1) whether a public body can meet electronically, and if a public body can do so; and (2) be certain not to violate the statutory provision by communicating with a quorum of the members of the public body about public business that must be addressed before the public in a properly noticed meeting. In Illinois, there must be an *intent* to discuss public business before the "gathering" will be held to be a meeting covered by the Open Meetings Act. Moreover, the Illinois Open Meetings Act allows certain units of local government to attend meetings subject to the act electronically, but requires them to adopt procedural rules to conform to the requirements and restrictions of the Act.

Best Practice: Elected officials should refrain from posting, commenting, or discussing public business via social networking platforms, especially if a quorum of the members of the public body is commenting on or discussing the same topic.

FIRST AMENDMENT PUBLIC FORUM ANALYSIS AND SOCIAL MEDIA

The First Amendment to the U.S. Constitution prohibits the making of any law abridging the freedom of speech. The U.S. Supreme Court has held that the due process clause of the Fourteenth Amendment applies the First Amendment to each state, including any unit of local government.

The U.S. Supreme Court has identified three types of fora for purposes of identifying the level of First Amendment scrutiny applicable to content-based restrictions on speech on government property: (1) a traditional or open public forum, (2) a limited or designated public forum, and (3) a closed or nonpublic forum. Traditional or open public fora include sidewalks, squares, and public parks:

> [S]treets and parks . . . have immemorially been held in trust for the use of the public and, time out of mind, have been used for purposes of assembly, communicating thoughts between citizens, and discussing public questions. Such use of the streets and public places has, from ancient times, been a part of the privileges, immunities, rights, and liberties of citizens. (*Hague v. CIO*, 307 U.S. 496, 515 (1939))

Typically, the government can impose only content-neutral time, place, and manner restrictions on speech in a public forum and any restrictions that are based on the content of the speech will be struck down, unless the government can show that the restriction is necessary to further a compelling governmental interest. As stated by the U.S. Supreme Court, "[i]n these quintessential public forums, . . . [f]or the State to enforce a content-based exclusion it must show that its regulation is necessary to serve a compelling state interest and that it is narrowly drawn to achieve that end." (see *Perry Education Association v. Perry Local Educators' Association*, 460 U.S. 37, 45 (1983); see also *International Society for Krishna Consciousness*, 505 U.S. 672, 678 (1992)

("[R]egulation of speech on government property that has traditionally been available for public expression is subject to the highest scrutiny"); *Frisby v. Schultz*, 487 U.S. 474, 480 (1988) ("[W]e have repeatedly referred to public streets as the archetype of a traditional public forum").

A limited or designated public forum "consists of public property which the State has opened for use by the public as a place for expressive activity" (*Perry*, 460 U.S. at 46). Whereas any content-based restriction on the use of a traditional public forum is subject to strict scrutiny, the state is generally permitted to limit a designated public forum to certain speakers or the discussion of certain subjects, as long as it does not discriminate on the basis of viewpoint. See *Perry*, 460 U.S. at 45 n.7. Once it has defined the limits of a designated public forum, however, "[r]egulation of such property is subject to the same limitations as that governing a traditional public forum" (*Int'l Soc'y for Krishna Consciousness*, 505 U.S. at 678). Examples of designated fora include university meeting facilities (see *Widmar v. Vincent*, 454 U.S. 263 (1981)), school board meetings (see *City of Madison Joint School Dist. v. Wisconsin Employment Relations Comm'n*, 429 U.S. 167 (1976)), and municipal theaters (see *Southeastern Promotions, Ltd. v. Conrad*, 420 U.S. 546 (1975)).

The third category—the closed or nonpublic forum—includes places that have not been open to public expression, such as jails or military bases. "Limitations on expressive activity conducted on this last category of property must survive only a much more limited review. The challenged regulation need only be reasonable, as long as the regulation is not an effort to suppress the speaker's activity due to disagreement with the speaker's view" (*Int'l Soc'y for Krishna Consciousness*, 505 U.S. at 679).

This analysis is important because if your school district decides to use social media—or if it is already using social media—it should consider whether it has created or will create an open or limited public forum such that any attempt to regulate speech on the site based on content would be a violation of that individual's First Amendment rights. A school district must uphold free speech rights on school property and at school-sponsored events, and this includes any social media site established by and/or sponsored by the school district. It is important to note, however, that blogs or other sites created solely for curricular purposes would be considered a closed or nonpublic forum, such that the teacher in charge of the blog or site could limit the expressive activity on the site.

LESSONS LEARNED FROM U.S. SUPREME COURT PRECEDENT: WHAT YOUR POLICY SHOULD SAY IN REGARD TO AN EMPLOYEE'S EXPECTATION OF PRIVACY IN GOVERNMENT-ISSUED TECHNOLOGY

Does your district currently make clear whether employees have an expectation of privacy in district-issued technology? In *City of Ontario v.*

Quon, 529 F.3d 892 (2010), the U.S. Supreme Court held that the City of Ontario Police Department's search of an officer/employee's text messages on a city-issued pager was reasonable and that the City did not violate the employee's Fourth Amendment rights. In that case, the City of Ontario had a no-privacy policy regarding computers and e-mails, but it did not explicitly include text messages. Nonetheless, the U.S. Supreme Court held that the employer's search was reasonable because the search: (1) had a non-investigatory, work-related purpose, (2) was justified at its inception, and (3) was not excessive in scope. The court determined that the search had a non-investigatory purpose because the purpose behind the search arose when the police department's chief sought to determine whether the existing limit on text messages was too low or whether the overages were for personal messages when police officers exceeded the number of text messages allowed to be sent based on the department's contract with its wireless carrier for several months. Once the wireless provider sent transcripts of the text messages, it was discovered that many of Quon's messages were not work related, and some were sexually explicit. At that time, the chief referred the matter to the internal affairs division. Quon and fellow officers sued the City, alleging that it had violated their Fourth Amendment rights and the federal Stored Communications Act by obtaining and reviewing the transcript of Quon's pager messages. They also sued the wireless provider, alleging that it violated the Stored Communications Act. Ultimately, the Ninth Circuit Court of Appeals determined that the wireless provider had violated the Stored Communications Act by providing transcripts of the employee's text messages to the City. While the U.S. Supreme Court granted the petition for writ of certiorari filed by the City, the police department and the chief on the issue of whether the employees' Fourth Amendment rights had been violated, the court did not grant certiorari on the issue of whether the wireless provider had violated the Stored Communications Act. Thus, the Ninth Circuit Court of Appeals decision on that issue stands.

The lesson to be learned for public employers, such as school districts, from the *Quon* case is that they must:

- Have a clear policy that all employer-owned communication facilities/devices are subject to search at any time and that no employee should have any expectation of privacy
- Only conduct a search if it is based on a legitimate, work-related purpose
- Make sure that the search is reasonable in scope—don't be more intrusive than necessary

The Stored Communications Act, 18 U.S.C. § 2701, *et seq.*, presents another reason to tread carefully when conducting a search of employees' social media use.

For example, if an employer searches an employee's work computer, discovers the employee's username and password for electronic accounts unrelated to the employer's system (e.g., Facebook, Twitter, Gmail, or Hotmail), and then examines the employee's communications in the private account, this could be a violation of the Stored Communications Act. The Act prohibits unauthorized access to an electronic "facility" to examine stored communications. It is a criminal offense with civil fines of $1,000 per violation in statutory damages, without need for proof of actual damages. It is unclear whether the act of access is a single violation or whether each communication retrieved and reviewed is a separate violation. The financial implications of this question are enormous. School personnel should not search a student's or staff member's personal accounts under any circumstances. If such a need arises, staff should contact local law enforcement and have them conduct the search. If local law enforcement refuses but there is a critical need to obtain records contained in a personal account, contact your school attorney and work with that individual to obtain a subpoena.

EMPLOYMENT OR STUDENT DISCIPLINE DECISIONS BASED ON SOCIAL MEDIA ACTIVITY

What if an employer or school district attempts to discipline an employee or student based on social media posts? This area of the law is growing day by day, and attempting to discipline employees and students for this type of behavior could:

1. Violate their First Amendment rights
2. Result in the punishment being held to be excessive
3. Violate their Fourteenth Amendment rights; the punishment could be determined to be unconstitutional because the policy under which the employee or student was disciplined was vague or overbroad, did not put the employee/student on notice that they would be punished if they engaged in that type of behavior, did not adequately define terms and could be applied arbitrarily, and/or because policy could be interpreted to prohibit protected speech

Important Considerations in Developing Policy

- Does a school policy specifically define the offense such that it puts employees and students on notice that if they do it, they will be punished—and indicate how they will be punished? If not, the policy is vague, overbroad, and arbitrary.
- A school policy is constitutionally invalid on its face if it allows school administrators to punish employees or students for any

action judged to be "inappropriate" because it is too vague; too much discretion is in the hands of the administrators. It must include a clear definition of what behavior is included within the scope of transgression.

- A school policy constitutes a prior restraint on speech, and a violation of the First Amendment, if it is overbroad and vague and can be interpreted to limit all speech, including speech that is protected under the First Amendment (for example, speech has to result in a material and substantial disruption—or the likelihood of a material and substantial disruption—under *Tinker v. Des Moines Indep. Community Sch. Dist.*, 393 U.S. 503 (1969), must constitute a true threat or must be sexually explicit, lewd, or vulgar in accordance with *Bethel Sch. Dist. No. 403 v. Fraser*, 478 U.S. 675 (1986)).

EMPLOYEES

In *Pickering v. Board of Education*, 391 U.S. 563 (1968), a teacher was dismissed after writing a letter to the local newspaper, which criticized how the school board and the superintendent handled funds. Ultimately, the U.S. Supreme Court held that this violated the teacher's First Amendment rights. *Pickering* established that public employees have First Amendment rights when they are speaking as a citizen (not as a part of their duties as an employee), and when they are speaking on issues of public concern. This has resulted in a balancing act for public employers, because even if an employee speaks as a private citizen on a matter of public concern, he or she may still be disciplined:

- Where speech infringes on the employer's operations or on its ability to provide effective and efficient services.

On the other hand, speech is not protected by the First Amendment when a public employee makes statements pursuant to his or her public duties. This was the holding of the U.S. Supreme Court in *Garcetti v. Ceballos*, 547 U.S. 410 (2006). In *Garcetti*, a deputy district attorney filed a complaint against the county and his supervisors, alleging that he was subject to adverse employment actions in retaliation for engaging in protected speech—that is, for writing a disposition memorandum in which he recommended dismissal of a case on the basis of purported governmental misconduct. The U.S. Supreme Court held that: (1) when public employees make statements pursuant to their official duties, they are not speaking as citizens for First Amendment purposes, and the Constitution does not insulate their communications from employer discipline; and (2) the district attorney did not speak as a citizen when he wrote his memorandum and, thus, his speech was not protected by the First Amendment.

A policy on employee social networking should include:

- All employer-owned electronic resources are subject to search—no expectation of privacy.
- Any social networking activities done pursuant to the employee's job duties or that occur during working time or while at work are not private and are subject to employer monitoring.
- Schools should suggest that employees make clear that they are not representing their employer when engaging in personal social networking.

Employees should be encouraged to be cautious when engaging in social networking on their own time, to make clear that their opinions do not represent those of their employer, and to not post anything that undermines the ability of the employer to operate effectively.

STUDENTS, SOCIAL MEDIA, AND SOCIAL NETWORKING

How can schools regulate the behavior of students that takes place on social media or through electronic resources? Can schools search cell phones and other electronic communication devices? When can schools regulate off-campus conduct?

The standard most often used as to whether and how schools can regulate student behavior was established by the U.S. Supreme Court in *Tinker v. Des Moines*, 393 U.S. 503 (1969). In that case, the court held that schools may limit students' First Amendment or other constitutional rights only when the students' conduct causes a material or substantial disruption in the orderly operation of the school. However, this standard is not always easy to apply. For example, just recently, the Third Circuit Court of Appeals struggled mightily with this issue in the following two cases: (1) *Layshock v. Hermitage School Dist.*, 593 F.3d 249 (3rd Cir. 2010), *vacated for rehearing en banc* (3rd Cir. 2010) and (2) *J.S. ex rel. Snyder v. Blue Mountain School Dist.*, 593 F.3d 286 (3rd Cir. 2010), *vacated for rehearing en banc.*

These two opinions were issued by panels of the Third Circuit Court of Appeals on the same day and dealt with almost factually identical issues in which students created parody profiles of their principals on MySpace. However, since that time, the full Third Circuit, sitting *en banc*, heard arguments on these two cases in June 2010. On June 13, 2011, the court ruled that the students could not be suspended for creating the parody profiles on MySpace of their principals on home computers because there was not a sufficient nexus between their behavior and school.

After the two three-judge panels of the U.S. Third Circuit Court of Appeals issued the contradictory rulings in June 2010, the full Third Circuit determined that their creation of the profiles did not cause a material and substantial disruption—nor was it likely to create such a disruption—at school. In the *J.S. v. Blue Mountain School District* case, in which the majority opinion included 8 of the 14 justices, the court found that the student's First Amendment free speech rights were violated because "J.S. was suspended from school for speech that indisputably caused no substantial disruption in school and that could not reasonably have led school officials to forecast substantial disruption in school." However, Judge D. Michael Fisher, who was joined by five other justices, wrote the following about the majority opinion in the dissent: "It allows a student to target a school official and his family with malicious and unfounded accusations about their character in vulgar, obscene, and personal language." The dissenting justices were of the opinion that the school district had the right to discipline J.S. because substantial disruption was reasonably foreseeable. In that case, an eighth-grade student who had been disciplined previously for dress code violations created a MySpace page using an actual photo of the principal with a fake name. In the profile, she casted the principal as a pedophile and sex addict, and the Internet address for the profile was www.myspace.com/kidsrockmybed.

In the second case, *Layshock v. Hermitage School District*, a high school student created a fake Internet profile of his principal at his grandmother's house using a photograph of the principal from the school district's website. In the profile, the student indicated that his principal smoked marijuana, used steroids, and was a "big fag." The student was suspended for creating the fake Internet profile, and the parents sued the school district. The district court overturned the suspension, that decision was upheld by an appeals panel, and the full Third Circuit upheld that decision. The student voluntarily apologized to Principal Eric W. Trosch, an apology the principal found "respectful and sincere." In that opinion, the unanimous Third Circuit said, "We do not think that the First Amendment can tolerate the School District stretching its authority into Justin's grandmother's home and reaching Justin while he is sitting at her computer after school."

On January 17, 2012, the U.S. Supreme Court denied the Blue Mountain School District's petition for writ of certiorari, thus declining to review that case as well as the *Hermitage School District v. Layshock* case that had been combined with the *Blue Mountain School District v. J.S.* case. As such, the decisions of the U.S. Court of Appeals for the Third Circuit will now stand as to both cases.

If your school district encounters an issue involving student speech that takes place off campus, be certain to document specifically how it impacts your school and how a nexus with the school campus was created by the speech. Provide specific and detailed information as to how that off-campus conduct or speech substantially and materially disrupts the normal school day; did staff have to alter their routines? Did school administrators have to conduct an investigation? If so, how many people were involved, and how much time was taken? Which specific school policies or provisions of the school code were violated? Did parents and students notify school officials of the speech? Did students and/or staff view the speech on campus? Documentation is key. In addition, be certain to check whether or not your state has a specific statute that addresses this type of conduct. If it does, your school district should implement a policy reflective of that statute. Illinois recently passed Public Act 97-340, which amends the School Code (105 ILCS 5/10-22.6) and enables school boards to expel pupils guilty of gross disobedience or misconduct, including gross disobedience or misconduct perpetuated by electronic means.

Every case dealing with issues of online speech and the First Amendment is extremely fact specific. A review of the cases is instructive as your district prepares its policies and learns to address these situations. In *Beussink v. Woodland R-IV School District*, 30 F.Supp.2d 1175 (E.D.Mo. 1998), the court determined that the school district could not punish the student for his online speech. Brandon Beussink made a home page on his computer, which contained a hyperlink to the school's website, criticizing the school and its administrators. He invited students to contact the principal about their opinions of the high school. A friend who was angry at Brandon showed the web page to a teacher, who showed it to the principal. Brandon was suspended for 10 days. The suspension caused Brandon to fail all of his classes. The court determined that Brandon's home page did not create a substantial disruption or material interference with school activities, and was therefore entitled to First Amendment protection.

Similarly, in *Emmett v. Kent School District*, 92 F.Supp.2d 1088 (W.D.Wash. 2000), the court held that the student was entitled to a preliminary injunction because he was able to show that he had a substantial likelihood of success on the merits of his claim. In that case, Nick Emmett created a web page from his home, which he entitled the "Unofficial Kentlake High Home Page," but he included disclaimers warning a visitor that the site was not sponsored by the school and was for entertainment purposes only. The site contained some commentary on the school administration and faculty, and also included mock "obituaries" of at least two of his friends. The obituaries were inspired by a creative writing class in which students had to write their own obituary, and these were done in a tongue-in-cheek manner. Nick allowed visitors to the site to vote on who should "die" next, thus becoming the subject of the next mock obituary. The mock obituaries became a topic of discussion at the high school among students, faculty, and administrators. Three days after Nick posted the website, an evening television news story characterized his website as featuring a "hit list" of people to be killed. That same night, Nick removed the site from the Internet. The next day, he was summoned to the school principal's office, and eventually told that he was placed on emergency expulsion for intimidation, harassment, disruption to the educational process, and violation of Kent School District copyright. The emergency expulsion was subsequently modified to a five-day short-term suspension, beginning that Friday. The court noted that the school district failed to present any evidence that any student actually felt threatened by the website, although it stated at oral argument that it believes that some students did feel intimidated. The court also indicated that the school district failed to present any evidence that Nick intended to intimidate or threaten anyone. The court determined that Nick would suffer irreparable harm if the suspension occurred and enjoined the school district from suspending him.

In *Killion v. Franklin Regional School District*, 136 F.Supp.2d 446 (W.D.Pa. 2001), Zachariah Paul served 3 days of a 10-day suspension before the court determined that the school had violated his First Amendment rights because it failed to show that his actions had caused a material and substantial disruption at school. The court also determined that the discipline policy applied by the school district was vague and overbroad because it could be interpreted to prohibit speech protected by the First Amendment, as it failed to specifically define the infraction, failed to limit its geographical reach, failed to refer to a substantial disruption, and could be applied arbitrarily. In this case, the student made a derogatory top 10 list about the athletic director and e-mailed it to his friends after he was denied a parking permit on campus and because of regulations placed on members of the track team. The list read as follows:

1. The school store does not sell twinkies.
2. He is constantly tripping over his own chins.
3. The girls at the 900 #'s keep hanging up on him.
4. For him, becoming Franklin's "Athletic Director" was considered "moving up in the world."
5. He has to use a pencil to type and make phone calls because his fingers are unable to hit only one key at a time.
6. As stated in the previous list, he's just not getting any.
7. He is no longer allowed in any "All You Can Eat" restaurants.
8. He has constant flashbacks of when he was in high school and the athletes used to pick on him, instead of him picking on the athletes.
9. Because of his extensive gut factor, the "man" hasn't seen his own penis in over a decade.
10. Even if it wasn't for his gut, it would still take a magnifying glass and extensive searching to find it. (*Killion*, 136 F.Supp.2d at 448)

Another case that illustrates the importance of carefully spelling out the types of behavior that will violate the school district's discipline code is *Coy v. Board of Education of North Canton City Schools*, 205 F.Supp.2d 791 (N.D.Ohio 2002). In that case, Jon Coy created a website at home that he accessed on a school computer that labeled pictures of three of his fellow classmates as "losers" and made other derogatory comments about them and then accessed it at school. Among other sections of the school district's student code of conduct, school administrators charged Jon with violating Section 21, which stated: "Inappropriate Action or Behavior: Any action or behavior judged by school officials to be inappropriate and not specifically mentioned in other sections shall be in violation of the Student Conduct Code." While the school district claimed that it disciplined Jon for accessing the unauthorized website and not for the content of the postings on the website, the court determined that Section 21 of the school district's student code of conduct was constitutionally invalid on its face because it was vague and allowed administrators to punish students arbitrarily.

The next case, *Flaherty v. Keystone Oaks School District*, 247 F.Supp.2d 698 (W.D.Pa. 2003), shows that carefully defining the terms used in board policies and not overreaching in drafting policies are two very important steps to take in limiting the number of successful suits by students and their parents for disciplining students. In *Flaherty*, the parents of Jack Flaherty brought an action on his behalf against the Keystone Oaks School District, the superintendent, the principal, the assistant principal, the athletic director, and a coach. In the case, Jack engaged in a message board conversation regarding an upcoming volleyball game in which he posted three messages from his parents' home and one from school. He was punished for violating the district's discipline, student responsibility, and technology policies. Jack's parents sought a declaration from the court that certain policies in the student handbook were overbroad and vague because particular portions allowed for punishment of speech that school officials deem to be "inappropriate, harassing, offensive or abusive" without defining those terms or limiting them in relation to geographic boundaries at school or school sponsored events or to speech that causes a material and substantial disruption to the school day. "An overbroad statute is one that is designed to punish activities that are not constitutionally protected, but which prohibits protected activities as well" (*Killion v. Franklin Regional Sch. Dist.*, 136 F.Supp.2d 446, 458 (W.D.Pa. 2001)). Under the " 'void for vagueness doctrine,' a governmental regulation may be declared void if it fails to give a person adequate warning that his conduct is prohibited or if it fails to set out adequate standards to prevent arbitrary and discriminatory enforcement" (*Killion*, 136 F.Supp.2d at 459, *citing Chicago v. Morales*, 527 U.S. 41, 56, 144 L.Ed.2d 67 (1999); *Kolender v. Lawson*, 461 U.S. 352, 357, 75 L.Ed.2d 903 (1983)).

The court determined that the breadth of the handbook policies relating to discipline, student responsibility, and technology were overreaching and violated the students' free speech rights, and that even if the handbook policies were not overbroad, they were unconstitutionally vague in the definitions that they used and as applied. Finally the student handbook policies that did not geographically limit the school officials' authority to discipline expressions that occurred on school premises or at school-related activities were overbroad and vague and in violation of students' First Amendment free speech rights.

In a case that is analogous to *J.C. v. Beverly Hills Unified School District* (see below), two high school–aged girls were suspended from participating in extracurricular activities for posting provocative photographs to MySpace, Facebook, and/or Photo Bucket (*T.V. v. Smith-Green Community School Corporation*, 807 F.Supp.2d 767 (N.D.Ind. 2011)). The two students at Churubusco High School sued the school district, alleging that their First Amendment rights were violated. The two girls, 16-year-old T.V. and 15-year-old M.K., posed for the racy photographs during a summer sleepover and then later posted the photographs online. When school officials discovered the online display, they suspended the girls from extracurricular activities—which included volleyball, cheerleading, and choir—for a portion of the upcoming school year. School officials were made aware of the photographs when a parent (whose child did not play volleyball that year) brought printouts of them to the superintendent and stated that the photos were causing "divisiveness" among the girls on the volleyball team.

The Churubusco High School Student Handbook for 2008–2009 contained an "Extracurricular/Co–Curricular Code of Conduct and Athletic Code of Conduct," which provided as follows:

> The purpose of the "Extra-Curricular Code of Conduct" is to demonstrate to students at Churubusco High School who participate in organized extra-curricular activities that they not only represent themselves, but also represent Churubusco High School, as well. Therefore, those students who choose to participate in extra-curricular activities are expected to demonstrate good conduct at school and outside of school. . . . This code will be in force for the entire year including out of season and during the summer.

Separately, under the heading "Extra-Curricular/Co–Curricular Activities," the Student Handbook read as follows:

> If you act in a manner in school or out of school that brings discredit or dishonor upon yourself or your school, you may be removed from extra-curricular activities for all or part of the year.

The principal suspended the girls from extracurricular activities after he determined that the photographs had the potential for causing disruption of school activities and brought discredit upon the school. The court held that the students' conduct was speech protected by the First Amendment, that the photographs did not substantially interfere with requirements of appropriate discipline in operation of school, that the principal was entitled to qualified immunity, and that the student handbook provision was impermissibly overbroad and vague.

In *Mahaffey v. Aldrich*, 236 F.Supp.2d 779 (E.D.Mich. 2002), the parents of Joshua Mahaffey sued the board of education and the school director after Joshua was suspended for contributing objectionable material, including a list of people he wished would die, to an Internet website. According to Joshua, the website—called "Satan's web page"—was created by another student "for laughs," because they were bored and "wanted something to do." The website stated as follows:

This site has no purpose. It is here to say what is cool, and what sucks. For example, Music is cool. School sucks. If you are reading this you probably know me and Think Im evil, sick and twisted. Well, Some might call it evil. I like to call it ___ well evil I guess. so what? If you don't know me you will see. I hope you enjoy the page.

The website then listed "people I wish would die," "people that are cool," "movies that rock," "music I hate," and "music that is cool." Near the bottom, the web page stated:

SATAN'S MISSION FOR YOU THIS WEEK: Stab someone for no reason then set them on fire throw them off of a cliff, watch them suffer and with their last breath, just before everything goes black, spit on their face. Killing people is wrong don't do It. unless Im there to watch. ___ Or just go to Detroit. Hell is right in the middle. Drop by and say hi. PS: NOW THAT YOU'VE READ MY WEB PAGE PLEASE DON'T GO KILL-ING PEOPLE AND STUFF THEN BLAMING IT ON ME. OK? (*Mahaffey v. Aldrich*, 236 F.Supp.2d at 781–82)

A parent of a student in the school district notified the police about the website, who in turn notified the school district. Joshua admitted that he contributed to the website and that school computers may have been used to create the website. The principal recommended Joshua for expulsion "based upon the admitted and alleged violation of Categories 5-Behavior Dangerous to Self and Others, 23-Internet Violations and 24-Intimidation and Threats of the Waterford School District Code of Conduct" (*Id.* at 782). Joshua eventually graduated from another school district one year early. The court found that the student's suspension violated his First Amendment rights, absent proof of disruption to the school by the website or that the website was created on school property. The court also determined that the student's statements on the website did not constitute threats, and that his speech was therefore protected by the First Amendment. The court also held that the student's due process rights under the Fourteenth Amendment were violated when he was suspended for a semester without being afforded the specific due process rights provided for in the district's code of conduct.

" 'True threats' encompass those statements where the speaker means to communicate a serious expression of an intent to commit an act of unlawful violence to a particular individual or group of individuals" (*Virginia v. Black*, 538 U.S. 343, 359 (2003)). In *Latour v. Riverside Beaver School District*, No. 05-1076, 2005 WL 2106562 (W.D.Pa. Aug. 24, 2005), the court considered the above, as well as the speaker's intent, how the intended victim reacted to the alleged threat, whether it was communicated directly to its victim, whether the threat was conditional, and whether the victim had reason to believe that the maker of the threat had a propensity to engage in violence (*Latour v. Riverside Beaver School District*, 2005 WL 2106562 at *1).

In *Latour v. Riverside Beaver School District*, Anthony Latour was expelled for two years due to four rap songs that he wrote and recorded in his home over a two-year period. Anthony never brought any of the songs to school. Anthony and his parents filed a motion for a preliminary injunction seeking an order from the court enjoining the Riverside Beaver School District in Pennsylvania from expelling Anthony and from banning Anthony from attending school-sponsored events and from being present on school grounds after hours, and enjoining the school district from imposing any other sanctions against Anthony for expressions, or as retaliation for his expressions. The court found that "[t]he evidence at the hearing shows that Anthony's songs were written in the rap genre and that rap songs are 'just rhymes' and are metaphors. Thus, while some rap songs contain violent language, it is violent imagery and no actual violence is intended" (*Latour*, at *2, citing testimony of individuals at preliminary injunction hearing). The court also noted that there was no evidence that: (1) Anthony communicated his songs directly to the students mentioned in the songs, (2) the student mentioned in one of the songs felt threatened, or (3) Anthony had a history of violence. The court also determined that the school district failed to demonstrate that the songs caused a material and substantial disruption. As such, the district was enjoined from expelling Anthony and from banning Anthony from attending school-sponsored events.

In *Wisniewski v. Board of Education of the Weedsport Central School District*, 494 F.3d 34 (2nd Cir. 2007), cert. denied, 552 U.S. 1296 (2008), Aaron Wisniewski, an eighth-grade student at Weedsport Middle School in the Weesport Central School District in upstate New York, was using AOL Instant Messaging on his parents' home computer. Aaron's IM icon was a small drawing of a pistol firing a bullet at a person's head, above which were dots representing splattered blood. Beneath the drawing appeared the words "Kill Mr. VanderMolen." Philip VanderMolen was Aaron's English teacher at the time. Aaron created the icon after his class had been instructed that threats would not be tolerated by the school and would be treated as acts of violence. He sent instant messages to approximately 15 members of his buddy list, on which the icon appeared and could be viewed for a total of three weeks. Eventually, one of Aaron's classmates informed Mr. VanderMolen and supplied him with a copy of the icon. The Court of Appeals for the Second Circuit ultimately held that the student's actions posed a reasonably foreseeable risk that the drawing/icon would come to the attention of school authorities and would materially and substantially disrupt the school.

The next two cases are similar to the Blue Mountain and Hermitage School District cases mentioned earlier, in which students created fake MySpace profiles of their principals; however, the outcomes are different. In *Barnett v. Tipton County Board of Education*, 601 F.Supp.2d 980 (W.D.Tenn. 2009), Christopher Barnett and Kevin Black created fake MySpace profiles in October 2006 of Earl LeFlore, the assistant principal at Brighton High School in Brighton, Tennessee, and of Charles Nute, a coach at the school. The profile contained LeFlore's photograph and biography from the Tipton County Board of Education's website as well as sexually suggestive comments about female students in the district. The district first heard about the websites when it received a phone call from a concerned parent and a local reporter who believed that LeFlore was the author of the website and that he was engaging in inappropriate conversations with students. School officials conducted an investigation and discovered that plaintiff Gary Moses contributed to the profiles, and Moses identified Barnett and Black as the creators of the profiles. School officials discovered that Barnett had accessed LeFlore's fake profile during his classes in the school's computer lab. Ultimately, Barnett was suspended for two days and received an 8-day in-school suspension. Black received an 11-day in-school suspension, and Moses received a 2-day in-school suspension. Following his suspension, Barnett created a website with a "Wanted" poster containing a photograph of the student whom Barnett believed told school officials that he created the profiles. After the board conducted a disciplinary hearing for Barnett, it concluded that he should be sent to an alternative school for the remainder of the school year. The plaintiffs sued, contending that the district violated their free speech rights and deprived them of their right to a public education without due process of law. The plaintiffs argued that the MySpace profiles were "parodies" and that parodies are not "reasonably believable" and are clearly exaggerated to enhance the humor of the parody (*Barnett*, 601 F.Supp.2d at 984, *citing Hustler Magazine, Inc. v. Falwell*, 485 U.S. 46,

57, 99 L.Ed.2d 41 (1988)). However, the court found that visitors to the profile believed it was authentic, that LeFlore had created it himself, and that he had engaged in the inappropriate behavior and communication. The court also determined that the disciplinary hearing satisfied due process.

In *Kowalski v. Berkeley County Schools*, 652 F.3d 565 (4th Cir. 2011), Kara Kowalski, a senior at Musselman High School, was suspended for creating and posting to MySpace a discussion group web page entitled " S.A.S.H." that ridiculed a fellow student and included pictures of her. Kara testified in her deposition that S.A.S.H. stood for "Students Against Sluts Herpes," but another student stated that it was an acronym for "Students Against Shay's Herpes," referring to another classmate, Shay N., who was the main subject of the discussion web page. After creating the group, Kara invited approximately 100 people on her friends list to join the group. Several students joined and posted comments and pictures. The next day, Shay N.'s parents, along with Shay, went to the high school to file a harassment complaint with the vice principal. At that time, they provided her with a printout of the S.A.S.H. web page.

School administrators ultimately determined that Kara had created a "hate website" in violation of school policy against "harassment, bullying, and intimidation." As a result, they suspended Kara from school for 10 days and issued her a 90-day "social suspension," which prevented her from attending school events in which she was not a direct participant. Kara was also prevented from crowning the next "Queen of Charm" in that year's Charm Review, having been elected "Queen" herself the previous year. In addition, she was not allowed to participate on the cheerleading squad for the remainder of the year. After Kara's father asked school administrators to reduce or revoke the suspension, the assistant superintendent reduced Kara's out-of-school suspension to 5 days, but retained the 90-day social suspension. Kara sued the school district and school officials alleging that the suspension violated her free speech rights under the First Amendment and her due process rights under the Fourteenth Amendment. The Fourth Circuit Court of Appeals held that the school district did not violate Kara's free speech rights or her due process rights.

The Court noted that "[t]here is surely a limit to the scope of a high school's interest in the order, safety, and well-being of its students when the speech at issue originates outside the schoolhouse gate," but determined that they were "satisfied that the nexus of Kowalski's speech to Musselman High School's pedagogical interests was sufficiently strong to justify the action taken by school officials in carrying out their role as the trustees of the student body's well-being" (*Kowalski*, 652 F.3d at 573). Kara Kowalski petitioned the U.S. Supreme Court to review the decision of the U.S. Circuit Court of Appeals for the Third Circuit, and her petition was denied.

Evans v. Bayer, 684 F.Supp.2d 1365 (S.D.Fla. 2010), is an important case because it resulted in the possibility of a principal having to pay attorneys' fees and damages as a result of suspending a student who created a group on Facebook to express dislike for a teacher. The student sued the principal in his individual capacity, alleging that her suspension violated her First and Fourteenth Amendment rights. The student, Katherine Evans, was a senior at Pembroke Pines Charter High School in November 2007, when she created a group on Facebook called "Ms. Sarah Phelps is the worst teacher I've ever met." The Facebook page included a picture of Ms. Phelps. The group's purpose was to allow students to voice their dislike of Ms. Phelps, and Katherine posted the following on the website:

> Ms. Sarah Phelps is the worst teacher I've ever met! To those select students who have had the displeasure of having Ms. Sarah Phelps, or simply knowing her and her insane antics: Here is the place to express your feelings of hatred.

The posting did not contain any threats, was made after school hours from Katherine's home computer, and did not disrupt school activities. Katherine removed it after two days. After the removal, Peter Bayer, the school's principal, suspended Katherine from school for three days and forced her to move from her advanced placement classes into lesser-weighted honors classes. Katherine's notice of suspension said that she was suspended for "bullying/cyberbullying/harassment towards a staff member" and "disruptive behavior." The court found that there was no evidence of a well-founded expectation of disruption and that school officials could not restrict Katherine's speech based upon a concern for the potential of defamation, as the principal claimed because her speech fell under the "wide umbrella of protected speech . . . as an opinion about a teacher, that was published off-campus, did not cause any disruption on-campus, and was not lewd, vulgar, threatening, or advocating illegal or dangerous behavior" (*Evans*, 684 F.Supp.2d at 1374). The court next determined that the principal did not have qualified immunity and was subject to the possibility of paying attorneys' fees.

The next case is important because students routinely use their cell phones and other equipment to videotape and record students and teachers both at school and outside of the school setting. Now, students can post these videos to Facebook, YouTube, and other social media sites. In *J.C. v. Beverly Hills Unified School District*, 711 F.Supp.2d 1094 (C.D.Cal. 2010), J.C., a student at Beverly Vista High School, sued the school district after she received a two-day suspension for posting a video clip on YouTube. In May 2008, J.C. was at a local restaurant with some friends after school and recorded a four-minute video of her friends talking about a classmate, C.C. They called her a "slut," said she was "spoiled," and used profanity during the recording. J.C. went home and posted the video on YouTube, then contacted 5–10 students and told them to look at the video. J.C. also contacted C.C.

and told her to look at the video. C.C. told J.C. that she thought the video was mean. J.C. asked C.C. whether she would like her to take the video off the website, but C.C. told her to keep the video up, as her mother told her to do so such that they could present it to the school the next day. The next day, C.C.'s mother told the school about the video and C.C. spoke with the school counselor about her hurt feelings and humiliation as a result of the video.

J.C. sued the school district and several others, alleging that they violated her First Amendment rights by punishing her for making the YouTube video and posting it on the Internet because she posted it from home. The court determined that J.C.'s geography-based argument—that the school could not regulate her behavior because it originated off campus—failed. The Court went on to say that even if it applied the approach utilized by some courts wherein some threshold consideration be given to the location of the speech, the YouTube video clearly made its way to the school campus, thereby creating a sufficient connection when C.C.'s mother made the school aware of the video and when the video was viewed at school by the school counselor and a participating student and her father in the administrative offices. The court also noted that it was reasonably foreseeable that the video would make its way to campus. However, the court found that there was no material and substantial disruption and that "the word 'substantial' must equate to something more than the ordinary personality conflicts among middle school students that may leave one student feeling hurt or insecure" (*J.C.*, 711 F.Supp.2d at 1119). Accordingly, the two-day suspension violated J.C.'s First Amendment rights.

The student in the next case also petitioned the U.S. Supreme Court to review the Second Circuit Court of Appeals decision upholding the district court's decision that the school district's punishment did not violate her rights. However, on October 31, 2011, the U.S. Supreme Court declined to accept the case, which means that the decision of the U.S. Circuit Court of Appeals for the Second Circuit will stand. Interestingly, that Court included now U.S. Supreme Court justice Sonia Sotomayor at the time the decision was issued. In *Doninger v. Niehoff*, 642 F.3d 334 (2nd Cir. 2011), Avery Doninger was punished for sending an e-mail to students and parents affiliated with the school and for posting a message on her personal blog criticizing the school for cancelling a school event. Avery's e-mail and blog encouraged people to contact school officials and complain about the cancellation of "Jamfest," an annual battle-of-the-bands concert that Avery and other Student Council members helped to plan. Avery called school officials "douchebags" on her blog, and her e-mail stated that she wanted people to contact the superintendent to "piss her off even more." Avery had accessed an e-mail account of the father of one of the students from the school's computer lab to send the mass e-mail in spite of a school policy that specifically restricted "[a]ccess of the internet or e-mail using accounts other than those provided by the district for school purposes" (*Doninger*, 642 F.3d at 340). The next day, students gathered outside the administration office to protest the cancellation. The court concluded that the substantial disruption test established by *Tinker* was met and that school officials could prohibit Avery from running for class secretary. The school district had a policy in place regarding eligibility to represent its schools in elected offices that read as follows:

> All students elected to student offices, or who represent their schools in extracurricular activities, shall have and maintain good citizenship records. Any student who does not maintain a good citizenship record shall not be allowed to represent fellow students nor the schools for a period of time recommended by the student's principal, but in no case, except when approved by the board of education, shall the time exceed twelve calendar months.

Avery had signed the policy, attesting that she had reviewed it with her family.

GOING TOO FAR? THE STATE OF MISSOURI

The state of Missouri passed a law, Senate Bill 54,[1] forcing all school districts to implement no-social-media policies. The bill is also known as the Amy Hestir Davis Student Protection Act, named after a student—now 40 years old—who was allegedly sexually abused by her 30-year-old art teacher when she was 13 years old and in the seventh grade. She did not report him at the time, out of fear that she would disappoint and hurt her family and her art teacher. The bill, among other things, required annual background checks for teachers, got rid of the nondisclosure clauses between districts, and added a number of offenses to the list of conduct for which a teacher can lose their teaching certification. The Bill also removed or extended the statute of limitations law for specific sex crimes.

The Missouri State Teachers' Association (MSTA) filed a lawsuit in Cole County Circuit Court on August 19, 2011, challenging the state's new law, which was enacted to protect students from sexual misconduct, and seeking a preliminary and permanent injunction to prevent the state from implementing and enforcing the law.[2] In their lawsuit, MSTA asserted that the language in Senate Bill 54 would prevent an educator from communicating with current and former students by way of texts and social media, and therefore infringe upon a teacher's right to free speech. The complaint stated that "[t]he Act is so vague and overbroad that the Plaintiffs cannot know with confidence what conduct is permitted and what is prohibited and thereby 'chills' the exercise of first amendment rights of speech, association, religion, collective bargaining and other constitutional rights by school teachers" (MSTA Complaint, p. 3, para. 14). The complaint argued that the bill was a prior restraint on a teacher's right to free speech under both the state constitution and the U.S. Constitution (Complaint, p. 4, para. 19a).

The American Civil Liberties Union (ACLU) also filed a class action lawsuit in the U.S. District Court for the Eastern District of Missouri, challenging the constitutionality of Senate Bill 54 and seeking a preliminary and permanent injunction.[3] The ACLU's named plaintiff, Christina Thomas, was a teacher and a parent, and the complaint asserted that the offending provision in Senate Bill 54 was so overbroad that it prevented her from communicating with her own child (ACLU Complaint, p. 1, para. 1).

Cole County Circuit Court judge Jon Beetem granted MSTA's request for a preliminary injunction on August 26, 2011, which took effect immediately for a period of 180 days.[4] The injunction, which expired on February 20, 2012, allowed for a trial to take place before implementation of the statute. In a press release, Judge Beetem indicated that based upon the evidence presented by the parties, teachers in Missouri use social media as one of their primary forms of communication and that the law "clearly prohibits communication between family members and their teacher parents using these types of sites. The Court finds that the statute would have a chilling effect on speech." In his press release, Missouri governor Jay Nixon announced:

> In a digital world, we must recognize that social media can be an important tool for teaching and learning. At the same time, we must be vigilant about threats posed to students through the Internet and other means. Because of confusion and concern among educators, students and families over this specific provision of Senate Bill 54, I will ask the General Assembly to repeal that particular section, while preserving other vital protections included in the bill. In addition, I will be asking for input on this issue from teachers, parents and other stakeholders.

TO BAN OR NOT TO BAN—THAT IS THE QUESTION

In 2011, the Pinellas County School Board in Florida unanimously voted to ban teachers from communicating with students on either Facebook or Twitter. A policy of this type can have First Amendment ramifications as it can be interpreted—as above—as having a chilling effect on speech. It could also be viewed as a prior restraint on free speech. In the landmark case of *Near v. Minnesota*, 283 U.S. 697 (1931), the U.S. Supreme Court held that the First Amendment imposed a heavy presumption against the validity of a prior restraint on speech. Accordingly, any such bans must be very narrowly tailored and have specific justifications.

CYBERBULLYING—WHAT'S A SCHOOL ADMINISTRATOR TO DO?

With the advent of technology and social media such as Facebook, students now have the capacity to bully each other seven days a week, 24 hours a day. Often, the effects of cyberbullying carry over to the school campus, thus creating a material and substantial disruption under the U.S. Supreme Court's *Tinker* standard (as discussed above). One phenomenon that occurred on Facebook—the International "Kick a Ginger" Day—was sparked by the television series *South Park*. A student created the Facebook page, which set a specific date for students across the nation to kick students with red hair. In this particular instance, the *Tinker* standard was clearly met such that the student who created the web page could be disciplined as there was a material and substantial disruption and sufficient nexus. However, what happens when students are bullied online based on their race, color, national origin, sex, disability, sexual orientation, or religion? This behavior on the part of students can rise to the level of discriminatory harassment in violation of multiple federal civil rights laws, and a school district must be careful not to ignore it, or it could be in violation of federal law.

On October 26, 2010, the U.S. Department of Education, Office for Civil Rights sent a Dear Colleague letter to state departments of education and local school districts in which the assistant secretary wrote the following regarding school anti-bullying policies:

> I am writing to remind you, however, that some student misconduct that falls under a school's anti-bullying policy also may trigger responsibilities under one or more of the federal antidiscrimination laws enforced by the Department's Office for Civil Rights (OCR). As discussed in more detail below, by limiting its response to a specific application of its anti-bullying disciplinary policy, a school may fail to properly consider whether the student misconduct also results in discriminatory harassment.[5]

In Orange County, California, the American Civil Liberties Union sued the Newport-Mesa Unified School District and several school officials on behalf of a student, her parents, and the Orange County Equity Coalition, after the student alleged she was harassed and discriminated against on the basis of her perceived sexual orientation and that school officials permitted and fostered the dangerous development of an environment that was plainly hostile to female students, as well as lesbian, gay, bisexual, and transgender students (*Mary Doe v. Newport-Mesa Unified Sch. Dist.*, Plaintiffs' Complaint, para. 2). In January 2009, several male students at the high school posted a video on a social networking site in which they used homophobic slurs, directly addressed the plaintiff Mary Doe with sexually harassing and graphically explicit comments and threats of violence, and threatened to kill the plaintiff (Plaintiffs' Complaint, para. 3). Plaintiff Doe's parents met with school officials to alert them to the video, at which time things got worse and school administrators drastically altered her school schedule. The complaint included a declaration that the school district and its officials violated the equal protection clause of the Fourteenth Amendment, Title IX of the Education Amendments of 1972, several clauses of the California Constitution, and several sections of the California Education Code; and the complaint asked for an order requiring the district to address the hostile environment, adopt a formal complaint process, train school staff, train students on diversity, harassment, and discrimination, award damages, attorneys' fees, and costs. Ultimately, the case was settled when the school district agreed to provide mandatory training sessions for administrators, teachers and students that focused on the harmful impact of sexual discrimination and harassment, as well as on federal law and district complaint protocols to be followed whenever anyone experiences discrimination or harassment based on sex, sexual orientation and gender identity (ACLU/SC Settles Lawsuit Over Orange County High School that Tolerated Homophobia and Sexism, 9/9/09, http://www.aclu.org/lgbt-rights_womens-rights/aclusc-settles-lawsuit-over-orange-county-high-school-tolerated-homophobia).

Another issue touched upon in this section—which impacts policy decisions—is that of student publications. Decades ago, the ditto machine allowed for the development of "underground" student newspapers. Most school districts developed policies to address student publications. Now, it is important to review school district policies to ensure that they incorporate social media sites and other electronic publications within their scope. While a school district and school district officials cannot take action to restrict what is published in a purely student-created publication that has no nexus to the school district—unless it creates a material and substantial disruption at school—it typically can exercise editorial discretion in regard to student publications that are part of the curriculum. Once again, in any situation that arises where the school district wants to take action, it will need to have a specific policy in place at the outset in order to do so and will need to carefully analyze the facts to be certain that it is not violating the student's First Amendment or other constitutional rights.

Until the U.S. Supreme Court issues a landmark decision similar to *Tinker v. Des Moines* that deals with the issues of social media and cyberbullying, educators need to be careful in how they approach student discipline and regulation in cyberspace. The *Tinker* decision gives school administrators the right to discipline students when their actions materially impede the normal operations of the educational environment. However, this area of the law is still evolving, and some of the cases above show that the judiciary is occasionally just as confused as most administrators with regard to the correct course of action to take. As mentioned earlier, it is important for the educators to conduct a thorough investigation and to gather all of the facts in social media discipline situations. The specific facts of the case, which articulate how school resources were used to deal with the situation or how the school environment was affected, will be needed to establish the justification for disciplining students in situations where social media or electronic resources are involved. When in doubt, contact the district's legal counsel for advice or guidance.

NOTES

1. A copy of Senate Bill 54 can be found here: http://www.senate.mo.gov/11info/pdf-bill/tat/SB54.pdf

2. A copy of the complaint filed on behalf of the Missouri State Teachers' Association can be found here: www.msta.org/news/Petition_final.pdf

3. A copy of the lawsuit filed by the ACLU can be found here: www.courthousenews.com/2011/08/22/MoTeachCA.pdf

4. A copy of Judge Beetem's Order can be found here: www.msta.org/files/resources/publications/injunction.pdf

5. The full letter can be found here: http://www2.ed.gov/about/offices/list/ocr/letters/colleague-201010.pdf

APPENDIX: SAMPLE SOCIAL MEDIA POLICIES

Included in this section are some sample policies regarding various aspects of social media in schools.

- The Fairfax County (Virginia) Facebook Comments Policy is a good, concise policy for explaining how the district uses Facebook to solicit and respond to community comments and concerns.
- The Norton Public Schools (Massachusetts) Facebook and Social Media Policy identifies how staff should use social media when interacting with students and parents.
- The Forest Ridge (Illinois) School District #142 Policy 5:125 outlines similar criteria for how staff should use social media.
- The Maine School Administrative District #22 Policy on Use of Weblogs (blogs) is specific and detailed in what should or should not be done with school related blogs. It credits Harvard University's policy for the core ideas included in its policy.
- The Arapahoe High School and Littleton (Colorado) Public Schools Blogging Policy actually includes a sample of what it considers to be good blogging techniques and appropriate blogging behavior.
- The Kennent (Pennsylvania) Consolidated School District's acceptable use policy is one of the most comprehensive policies being used by a public school district. It covers all aspects of acceptable use and details of how infractions will be addressed.
- The St. Thomas Episcopal School (San Antonio, Texas) social media policy includes a nice purpose statement and then articulates the expected behavior for students, staff, and parents when using social media.
- The North Boone (Illinois) CUSD #200 procedures articulate how the district will implement its acceptable use policy and includes examples of the AUP signoff sheets used by both students and staff.

FAIRFAX COUNTY (VIRGINIA) FACEBOOK COMMENTS POLICY

Facebook Comments Policy

We welcome you and your comments to Fairfax County's Facebook Pages.

The purpose of this site is to present matters of public interest in Fairfax County, including its many residents, businesses and visitors. We encourage you to submit your questions, comments, and concerns, but please note this is a moderated online discussion site and not a public forum.

We recognize the web is a 24/7 medium, and your comments are welcome at any time. However, given the need to manage our staff resources (your tax dollars), we generally only monitor comments and postings during regular business hours.

Once posted, the Fairfax County reserves the right to delete submissions that contain:

1. Vulgar language
2. Personal attacks of any kind
3. Comments or content that promotes, fosters, or perpetuates discrimination on the basis of race, creed, color, age, religion, gender, marital status, genetics, status with regard to public assistance, national origin, physical or intellectual disability or sexual orientation
4. Spam or links to other sites
5. Clearly off topic
6. Advocate illegal activity
7. Promote particular services, products, or political organizations
8. Infringe on copyrights or trademarks
9. Personally identifiable medical information
10. Information that may compromise the safety, security or proceedings of public systems or any criminal or civil investigations.

Please note that the comments expressed on this site do not reflect the opinions and position of the Fairfax County government or its officers and employees. If you have any questions concerning the operation of this online moderated discussion site, please contact the Office of Public Affairs at publicaffairs@fairfaxcounty.gov.

Updated Nov. 23, 2011

NORTON PUBLIC SCHOOLS (MASSACHUSETTS) FACEBOOK AND SOCIAL NETWORKING POLICY

Official Facebook and Social Networking Policy

The Superintendent and the School Principals will annually remind current staff members and orient new staff members concerning the importance of maintaining proper decorum in the on-line, digital world and adhering to appropriate boundaries in the student/teacher relationship. The School Department's policy with regard to teacher interactions with students and families utilizing technology, such as electronic mail, social networking websites and cell phones is as follows:

1) Unacceptable Online Interactions With Students Using Facebook and Similar Internet Sites or Social Networks, or Via Cell Phone, Texting or Telephone.
   a. Staff members may not list current Norton Public School students or former Norton Public School students below the age of 18, as "friends" on private networking sites.
   b. All e-contacts with students should be through the district's computer and telephone system, except in emergency situations. Staff members will not give out their private cell phone or home phone numbers, or personal e-mails, without prior approval of the Principal. This policy does not apply to family relationships.
   c. Coaches and club/activity advisors will not give out their private cell phone or home phone numbers, or personal e-mails, without prior approval of the Principal. All contact and messages by coaches and club/activity advisors with team members shall be sent to all team members, except for messages concerning medical or academic privacy matters. Messages from coaches will be copied to the athletic director. The school principal will be copied on all contact and messages from coaches and club/activity advisors.
   d. The district will educate staff members on all capabilities of the district's EdLine system in order that staff will not feel a need to utilize their own personal resources.
2) Privacy of On-Line Content.
   Staff members are reminded that items placed on-line are never fully private and may affect how students, parents, administrators and peers perceive them. Posting items with sexual content and those exhibiting or advocating use of illegal drugs is poor judgment and may be deemed inappropriate.
3) Monitoring of On-Line Conduct.
   The School Department retains the right to monitor its internal technology systems. When inappropriate use of computers and

websites reaches the attention of administration, the School Principal will promptly bring this to the attention of the staff member
and the Superintendent. After investigation, and due process, disciplinary action for failure to exercise good judgment in on-line conduct, may be applied.

4) Teachers Shall Adhere to Existing Standards of Conduct in Connection With Electronic Communications with Students.

Teachers are already under an obligation to maintain appropriate
boundaries in their relationships with students (e.g., teachers should
avoid excessive attention to a student, communicate only on school-
related activities, maintain professionalism, etc). These same standards apply to electronic communications with students (e.g., social
networking, e-mail, "texting," or other cell phone communications).

FOREST RIDGE (ILLINOIS) SCHOOL DISTRICT 142, POLICY 5:125

General Personnel

Personal Technology and Social Media; Usage and Conduct

Definitions

Includes—Means "includes without limitation" or "includes, but is not limited to."

Social media—Media for social interaction, using highly accessible communication techniques through the use of web-based and mobile technologies to turn communication into interactive dialogue. This includes *Facebook*, *LinkedIn*, *MySpace*, *Twitter*, and *YouTube*.

Personal technology—Any device that is not owned or leased by the District or otherwise authorized for District use and: (1) transmits sounds, images, text, messages, videos, or electronic information, (2) electronically records, plays, or stores information, or (3) accesses the Internet, or private communication or information networks. This includes smartphones such as BlackBerry®, android®, iPhone®, and other devices, such as, iPads® and iPods®.

Usage and Conduct

All District employees who use personal technology and social media shall

1. Adhere to the high standards for appropriate school relationships in policy 5:120, *Ethics and Conduct* at all times, regardless of the ever-changing social media and personal technology platforms available. This includes District employees posting images or private information about themselves or others in a manner readily accessible to students and other employees that is inappropriate as defined by policy 5:20, *Workplace Harassment Prohibited*; 5:120, *Ethics and Conduct*; 6:235, *Access to Electronic Networks*; 7:20, *Harassment of Students Prohibited*; and the Ill. Code of Educator Ethics, 23 Ill.Admin.Code §22.20.

2. Choose a District-provided or supported method whenever possible to communicate with students and their parents/guardians.

3. Not interfere with or disrupt the educational or working environment, or the delivery of education or educational support services.

4. Comply with policy 5:130, *Responsibilities Concerning Internal Information*. This means that personal technology and social media may not be used to share, publish, or transmit information about

or images of students and/or District employees without proper approval. For District employees, proper approval may include implied consent under the circumstances. Refrain from using the District's logos without permission and follow Board policy 5:170, *Copyright*, and all District copyright compliance procedures. Use personal technology and social media for personal purposes only during non-work times or hours. Any duty-free use must occur during times and places that the use will not interfere with job duties or otherwise be disruptive to the school environment or its operation.

5. Assume all risks associated with the use of personal technology and social media at school or school-sponsored activities, including students' viewing of inappropriate Internet materials through the District employee's personal technology or social media. The Board expressly disclaims any responsibility for imposing content filters, blocking lists, or monitoring of its employees' personal technology and social media.

6. Be subject to remedial and any other appropriate disciplinary action for violations of this policy ranging from prohibiting the employee from possessing or using any personal technology or social media at school to dismissal and/or indemnification of the District for any losses, costs, or damages, including reasonable attorney fees, incurred by the District relating to, or arising out of, any violation of this policy.

The Superintendent shall:

1. Inform District employees about this policy during the in-service on educator ethics, teacher-student conduct, and school employee-student conduct required by Board policy 5:120, *Ethics and Conduct*.
2. Direct Building Principals to annually:
   a. Provide their building staff with a copy of this policy.
   b. Inform their building staff about the importance of maintaining high standards in their school relationships.
   c. Remind their building staff that those who violate this policy will be subject to remedial and any other appropriate disciplinary action up to and including dismissal.
3. Build awareness of this policy with students, parents, and the community.
4. Periodically review this policy and any procedures with District employee representatives and electronic network system administrator(s) and present proposed changes to the Board.

MAINE SCHOOL ADMINISTRATIVE DISTRICT #22 POLICY ON USE OF WEBLOGS

Weblogs Terms of Use

Welcome to Weblogs at MSAD #22!

We don't mean to turn you off from blogging by immediately inundating you with legal terms, but we need to make clear our respective rights and responsibilities related to this service.

By accessing, creating or contributing to any blogs hosted at http:// sad22.us/, and in consideration for the Services we provide to you, you agree to abide by these Terms. Please read them carefully before posting to or creating any blog.

Rights in the Content You Submit:

- All subject matter must be related to curriculum, instruction, school-authorized activities, professional development or it should relate to the school district or schools within the district.
- No unlawful use of copyrighted materials may be knowingly used, produced, or transmitted via school blogs.
- All material published to the MSAD 22 web server may be audited, suspended and removed from the web server without prior notice.

Conduct of posting:

Those of us who are coordinating this project believe deeply in free speech. Given our role in offering this service and our presence together as part of the extended community, however, we must reserve the right to remove certain content that you may post.

- Student or staff work may be published only as it relates to a class project or professional development.
- Staff may not publish personal websites on the web server.
- Staff is not to publish material that is offensive in nature.
- The web server is not to be used for the creation or distribution of any offensive or disruptive websites, including messages containing offensive comments about race, gender, age, sexual orientation, pornography, religious or political beliefs, national origin or disability.

You acknowledge that MSAD #22 does not pre-screen or regularly review posted content, but that it shall have the right to remove in its sole discretion any content that it considers to violate these Terms or the terms of any other MSAD #22 user agreements that may govern your use of the school networks.

Students:

Publishing personal information of our students is prohibited.

- Student names, work, and pictures may NOT be published unless a Parent or legal Guardian signs a signed permission form.
- Directory information such as names may be published without parent permission, but not with pictures or student work. Please use only first name and first initial to ID students. (Ex: Jeff Woodside = Jeff W.)
- Web page documents may not include a student's phone number, address, or complete names of any family members and/or friends.
- Web page documents may not include any information, which indicates the physical location of a student at a given time, other than attendance at a particular school or participation in activities.
- Web publishing of e-mail addresses is restricted to staff members only.

Modification of These Terms of Use

MSAD #22 reserves the right to change, at any time, at our sole discretion, the Terms under which these Services are offered. You are responsible for regularly reviewing these Terms. Your continued use of the Services constitutes your agreement to all such Terms.

Copyright Complaints

MSAD #22 respects the intellectual property of others, and requires that our users do the same. If you believe that your work has been copied and is accessible on this site in a way that constitutes copyright infringement, or that your intellectual property rights have been otherwise violated, please email Jeff Woodside for reporting copyright infringements.

MSAD #22 borrowed heavily from the Harvard.edu terms of use. Thank you Harvard for allowing MSAD #22 to remix your terms of use via the Creative Commons license.

Source: http://www.sad22.us/blogterms

ARAPAHOE HIGH SCHOOL AND LITTLETON (COLORADO) PUBLIC SCHOOLS BLOGGING POLICY

AHS Blogging Policy

This is a set of general guidelines for the use of weblogs ("blogs") at Arapahoe High School. Blogs are considered an extension of the classroom and therefore are subject to these guidelines as well as the rules and regulations of Arapahoe High School and Littleton Public Schools. The use of school computers is limited to assigned schoolwork; personal blogs that do not pertain to classwork at Arapahoe High School should not be accessed from school computers. These guidelines are not meant to be exhaustive and do not cover every contingency. If you are ever in doubt about the appropriateness of an item - ask a parent or teacher.

Safe and Responsible Blogging

The most basic guideline to remember when blogging is that the blog is an extension of your classroom. You should not write anything on a blog that you would not say or write in your classroom. Use common sense, but if you are ever in doubt ask a teacher or parent whether or not what you are considering posting is appropriate. If you are going to err, err on the safe side. Here are some specific items to consider:

1. The use of blogs is considered an extension of your classroom. Therefore, any speech that is considered inappropriate in the classroom is inappropriate on a blog. This includes, but is not limited to, profanity; racist, sexist or discriminatory remarks; personal attacks.
2. Blogs are used primarily as learning tools, either as extensions of conversations and thinking outside of regular class time, or as the basis for beginning new classroom discussions. Either way, be sure to follow all rules and suggestions that are offered by your teachers regarding appropriate posting in your class.
3. Blogs are about ideas—therefore, agree or disagree with the idea, not the person. Freedom of speech does not give you the right to be uncivil. Use constructive criticism and use evidence to support your position. Read others' posts carefully—often in the heat of the moment you may think that a person is saying one thing, when really they are not.
4. Try not to generalize. Sentences that start with words like "All" (e.g., "All teachers," "All administrators," "All liberals," "All conservatives") are typically going to be too general.
5. Blogs are public. Whatever you post on a blog can be read by anyone and everyone on the Internet. Even if you delete a post or

comment, it has often already been archived elsewhere on the web. Do not post anything that you wouldn't want your parents, your best friend, your worst enemy, or a future employer to read.

6. Blog safely. NEVER post personal information on the web (including, but not limited to, last names, personal details including address or phone numbers, or photographs). (Note: The advice to not use your last name is for your protection. Teachers may choose to use their last names for their posts/comments.) Do not, under any circumstances, agree to meet someone you have met over the Internet.

7. Because your login to the blogging site (e.g., Blogger) is typically linked to your profile, any personal blog you create in class is directly linked to your class blog and must follow these blogging guidelines. In addition to following the information above about not sharing too much personal information (in your profile or in any posts/comments you make), you need to realize that anywhere you use that login links back to your class blog. Therefore, *anywhere* that you use that login (posting to a separate personal blog, commenting on someone else's blog, etc.), you need to treat the same as a school blog and follow these guidelines. You should also monitor any comments you receive on your personal blog and - if they are inappropriate - delete them. If you would like to post or comment somewhere and not follow these guidelines, you need to create a separate login to the blogging site so that it does not connect back to your class blog. You may *not* use that login from school computers. We would still recommend you follow the portion of these guidelines that address your personal safety (e.g., not posting personal information, etc.)

8. Linking to web sites from your blog or blog comments in support of your argument is an excellent idea. But never link to something without reading the entire article to make sure it is appropriate for a school setting.

9. Use of quotations in a blog is acceptable. Make sure that you follow the proper formatting and cite the source of the quote.

10. Pictures may be inserted into a blog. Make sure that the image is appropriate for use in a school document and copyright laws are followed. Do not post any images that can identify yourself or others.

Successful Bloggers

The following are some traits of successful bloggers:

1. Their posts (or comments) are well written. This includes not only good content, but—because these are school-related blogs—also

follows writing conventions including spelling, grammar and punctuation.

2. Their posts (or comments) are responsive. They respond to other people's ideas—whether it is a post by a teacher, a comment by a student, or an idea elsewhere on the Internet. The power of blogs is in their connectedness—they are connected to a larger community of ideas. Participate in that community.

3. Their posts (or comments) include textual references to support their opinions. Adding quotes or links to other works strengthens their response.

4. They participate frequently. To be part of the dialogue, you have to participate fully and consistently.

5. They are respectful of others. It's okay to disagree; it's not okay to be disagreeable. Be respectful of others and their opinions, and be civil when you disagree.

Sample

Here is a sample* of what appropriate blogging looks like. (*This is actual work taken from an AHS classroom blog, with typos corrected.)
Drawing Electricity from the Sky

Examine Benjamin West's painting, Benjamin Franklin Drawing Electricity from the Sky (1805). You may access this painting via the following link: http://www.frankelec.com/west_fullsize.htm. You can also find the painting on page 87 of your yellow American Literature book. After spending a few moments with the painting, please respond to one or more of the following questions:

1. What do you think the artist is trying to achieve in this painting? Consider the sometimes clashing roles of science and religion and how they function in this painting.

2. What are your reactions to this painting?

3. What do you think Benjamin Franklin thought of this portrait of himself?

posted by Kristin | 9:17 AM

20 Comments:

Robn said . . .
1) The artist behind "Benjamin Franklin Drawing Electricity from the Sky" wanted to juxtapose religion and science in a similar environment. However, he was probably looking for more similarities than differences. That is, science and religion have always been thought of as mutually exclusive,

but Benjamin West brought them together to show that they cannot exist without each other. Benjamin Franklin is depicted as drawing science (electricity) from the heavens (God). The two are intertwined, for science seeks to explain the ways of the universe as designed by a creator, and the creator uses the natural laws of science to govern his kingdom.
12:33 PM

Robn said . . .
2) I really like the way Benjamin West brought science and religion together into a mutual package/relationship. It calls for more harmony and balance in society, instead of the polarized world we live in today.
12:35 PM

Robn said . . .
3) Initially, Franklin may have resented the connection between himself and religion; being a dissenting agnostic himself. However, Franklin, who holds himself in high regard, would appreciate the intonation that he serves as a transitive between science and religion for all people. He also knew that religious people would hold him in higher regard if he was portrayed not as blasphemer, but as a servant of God seeking to know the ways of the heavens.
12:40 PM

JocelynH said . . .
In the painting of Benjamin Franklin, he looks like he is trying to figure out what electricity is conducted from, in this case the metal key, and how it relates to science. In the background, there are children that look like something that Michelangelo would draw on the ceiling in which it represents the heavens from above. He looks like he is showing that there is a greater connection to science and to religion than there is or there should be a bigger connection.

In this painting, my first reaction was that I just saw Benjamin Franklin holding the key and thought back to what I had learned in elementary school. We all learned some time in our life that Mr. Franklin was the one who discovered that metal had a connection some how to lightning and that's how electricity was conducted, but what we didn't realize is its connection to religion. After analyzing the painting at a closer look, I saw the children in the background and it simply symbolized that religion was somehow related to his religion.

After Benjamin Franklin saw the portrait of himself, I think he probably would have liked it and it proved to people the connection with science and religion at a greater glance. He might've also had a strong reaction to what it shows and how "crazy" he is to try and conduct electricity with lightning weather.

12:56 PM

Elizabeth B. said . . .
1) I think that the artist is trying to show that he believes that science and religion should mix because even though they are very different, they coexist with each other. Religion cannot be 100% proven, but Science is all about facts and concepts that can be proven. Usually religion does not agree with science such as people evolving from apes not the seven days view that come religions have. Maybe the artist is trying to show that the two help explain each other and that they need each other to coexist for man to be able to explain the unknown.
1:32 PM

JeffN said . . .
1) Generally, science and religion have a very difficult time coexisting with one another. Take the idea of evolution and creationism. Only evolution can be taught in schools due to not only the Constitution of the United States but also because of their contrasting ideas. The picture, however, depicts the idea of the invention of electricity having something to do with the religion that Ben Franklin followed. This painting could potentially be saying that even though there is a separation of church and state and that even though the ideas of religion and science are on two entirely different ends of the spectrum, there is a possibility that the two do have something in common, share a common bond that could potentially affect life in the future.
4:12 PM

JacobW said . . .
I believe that the artist Benjamin West wanted to show that electricity was discovered through an act of spiritual not material enlightenment. He might have supposed that the means by which Benjamin Franklin stumbled upon his revelation where far too coincidental to present any other cause except a genuine miracle. The roles of science and religion coincide in the painting because the artist believed it was God who gave the discovery to Benjamin Franklin and the rest of humanity.

I admire the way the artist skillfully fused the two aspects of religion and science into one accumulative amalgam, but I do not find this relationship to be far fetched. However, I believe that the artist was giving Benjamin Franklin far too much credit. The painting depicts him splashed in holy rays of righteous sunshine, and assisted by the profits of the Almighty Himself, as if Benjamin Franklin were an electrocuted profit reaching towards the towering heavens with eyes thirsting for the betterment of mankind; all the while enthralled in rapture, clothed in splendor, and beset upon a moral foundation of stone.

Benjamin Franklin would have looked at the picture and laughed at the fact that our nations love for his acclaimed heroism was ever taken to such an extreme.
4:27 PM

BrittanyL said...
Wow, Jacob, those are some powerful statements about the holiness Franklin seems to posses in this painting. I would have to agree with you that the artist does make him look like a divine god. I also think that Franklin would have been offended by this portrait because he does not believe in angels or any other religion; he said himself he was an atheist. He would not appreciate that it looks like he discovered electricity with the help of angels and not on his own.
4:42 PM

LindsayD said...
This made milk come out of my nose! I find this painting to be more humorous than powerful and awesome. Benjamin Franklin did invent, discover, and improve on many aspects of daily life including his own self-improvement. Really this painting makes science and religion come as a whole under Benjamin Franklin as "lord of the universe" it seems. The painter did an excellent job, and Benjamin Franklin may secretly have liked it but wouldn't have admitted it with his Quaker buddies around.
4:46 PM

Raychel H said...
I think the artist was trying to convey a point that what Benjamin Franklin did was truly a miracle. Also that he had angels working with him and helping him achieve such a great thing. Whether it be accidental or completely on purpose, Benjamin Franklin DID discover electricity and the painter wanted the world to see his opinion on this event.
    I think this is a very interesting view of the discovery of electricity, I never really thought too much about it before.
    I think that Benjamin Franklin's reaction would have been somewhat humorous, although I'm sure he liked being portrayed as such an important person, he probably didn't feel that a reaction like this was necessary.
6:24 PM

KerstinM said...
1) I believe that the artist is trying to achieve the fact that what some may invent, without a little help from God would never have come true. Maybe the lightning storm that helped create the possibility of electricity was made by God. Without it electricity would not have been discovered on that

stormy night. Or would it? If you look at Franklin's left hand in it is a piece of paper. Assuming this paper is his thinking behind the idea of electricity, it is depicted in the painting because it shows that with his thought process he was able to create an idea that changed the human race and how we live forever. If one idea written out on a small piece of paper can change human race forever what can a big piece of paper do?
7:00 PM

Cayleigh B said...
In this painting, it seems that the artist is trying to portray that what Benjamin Franklin did was not necessarily an act of genius, it was more a miracle. If you look at how the light comes down on Benjamin, it only illuminates his head. The rest of his body is dark. The angel, standing beside him however, is fully illuminated. This could be taken that Benjamin Franklin did not really discover electricity, it merely just fell into his hands. It was all just a miracle, a coincidence.
7:04 PM

KerryL said...
The painting is depicting the way the artist himself views Franklin and his inventions. Not only did the painting show that Franklin shouldn't be the only one credited for his invention of electricity, it showed that the children and a higher power created the experiment and benefited from electricity. The picture took me a while to view and see all of the different perspectives that the artist was trying to portray. Franklin probably thought that this was a crazy painter with odd ideas about how his incredible invention came to be.
7:40 PM

KaiaN said...
Personally, I thought this painting was very annoying. Benjamin Franklin is put on a pedestal like a god while the angels are helping him pull electricity out of the sky. Where is the electricity coming from- God? If so, why does this painting make Ben look so amazing? He didn't MAKE it. I think the artist is trying to portray Ben as admirable, and I'm sure Ben loved that he looked so good.
7:41 PM

Katy L said...
In this painting I believe that Benjamin West is trying to show us that Ben Franklin was very strong in his faith. I also think the painting is trying to portray the idea that although science and religion beliefs are very different, they may relate somehow.

My reaction to this painting is that Ben Franklin did not discover electricity by himself, but God and the angels helped bless him with knowledge.
7:45 PM

KatieC said...
I think that this painting is quite funny and maybe even a little ridiculous. It's making it seem like Ben Franklin had done something that could relate to the power of God. Quite flattering I must say. Pulling electricity from heaven? I guess I can understand why this painting was done; it was because the artist obviously was or is a fan of Franklin, and his "invention," however I still think it's a bit much to compare the discovery of electricity to a supposed "miracle from heaven."
7:50 PM

DanielC said...
I think that Ben Franklin must have thought he was some sort of instrument in the hands of God. That's cool by me. I think its a little prideful if convinced himself of that. For all I know though, maybe that was his destiny, kind of deal. Ben can be credited with discovering electricity I guess. But it still took many more years and other men to learn how to harness it. I think the painting is misleading because it suggests that Ben gets all the glory.
7:45 AM

MeganJ said...
Quite personally I believe this painting is a little ridiculous. It is as if the artist is trying to make Ben resemble some sort of a god. He certainly discovered electricity, but he himself did not MAKE it. I believe this portrait could be interpreted in several different ways. Take for instance, it could be humbling—the way it shows the dwarfs and angels assisting him. In a way showing that he himself did not do all the work in discovering electricity. Yet I do not believe that the painting was meant to be interpreted that way, especially if one takes into consideration the smug look that is upon Ben's face. The way I view the portrait is I resent the way the little dwarfs and angels in the background appear to be his slaves. I believe that Ben would have appreciated this painting, especially after reading the assigned short story about him, he seemed to think of himself very highly.
11:10 AM

amandag said...
In my opinion I think that the artist of this painting views Ben Franklin as a median for a higher power to reach humanity. Franklin, in this painting, was willing to reach for this opportunity. It's as if the angels have been holding this string up ... just waiting for some human to jump at the opportunity

to "make this invention." I think that Franklin was a very knowledgeable man, but I think that he gives himself too much credit. I believe that this artist is also trying to show that Ben Franklin shouldn't give himself as much credit as he does.

http://arapahoe.littletonpublicschools.net/forStudents/AHSBloggingPolicy/tabid/1486/Default.aspx

KENNETT SQUARE (PENNSYLVANIA) SCHOOL DISTRICT

816. Acceptable use of the Computers, Network, Internet, Electronic Communications, and Information Systems

1. Purpose
2. Definitions
3. Authority
4. Responsibility
5. Delegation of Responsibility
6. Regulations
   a. Access to CIS Systems
   b. Parental Notification and Responsibility
   c. School District Limitation of Liability
   d. Prohibitions
   e. Content Regulations
   f. Due Process
   g. Search and Seizure
   h. Copyright Infringement and Plagiarism
   i. Selection of Material
   j. School District Web Site
   k. Blogging
   l. Safety and Privacy
   m. Consequences for Inappropriate, Unauthorized, and Illegal Use
7. Downloadable CIS Acknowledgment and Consent Forms

Purpose

The Kennett Consolidated School District ("School District") provides employees, students, and guests ("users") with access to the School District's electronic communication systems and network, which includes Internet access, whether wired or wireless or by any other means. Guests include but are not limited to visitors, workshop attendees, volunteers, independent contractors, adult education staff, students, and Board members.

Computers, network, Internet, electronic communications, and information systems (collectively "CIS systems") provide vast, diverse, and unique resources. The Board of School Directors will provide access to the School District's CIS systems for users if there is a specific School District–related purpose to access information and research, to collaborate to facilitate learning and teaching, and to foster the educational purpose and mission of the School District.

For users, the School District's CIS systems must be used for education-related purposes and performance of School District job duties. Incidental personal use of school computers is permitted for employees so long as such use does not interfere with the employee's job duties and performance, with system operations, or with other system users. Personal use must comply with this Policy and all other applicable School District Policies, procedures and rules contained in this Policy, as well as Internet service provider ("ISP") terms, local, state, and federal laws, and must not damage the School District's CIS systems. Students may only use the CIS systems for educational purposes. At the same time, personal technology devices brought onto the School District's property or at School District events or connected to the School District's network that the School District reasonably believes contain School District information or contain information that violates a School District Policy or contain information/data that the School District reasonably believes involves a criminal activity may be legally accessed to insure compliance with this Policy, other School District Policies, and to comply with the law. Users may not use their personal computers to connect to the School District's intranet, Internet, or any other CIS System unless approved by the Technology Manager and/or designee.

The School District intends to protect its CIS systems strictly against numerous outside and internal risks and vulnerabilities. Users are important and critical players in protecting these School District assets and in lessening the risks that can destroy these important and critical assets. Consequently, users are required to comply fully with this Policy and to report immediately any violations or suspicious activities to the building principals or the Superintendent. Conduct otherwise will result in actions further described in Section 13 - Consequences for Inappropriate, Unauthorized, and Illegal Use, found in the last Section of this Policy and provided in relevant School District Policies.

Definitions

1. (Reference: 18 U.S.C. § 2256(8)) *Child Pornography*—Under Federal law, any visual depiction, including any photograph, film, video, picture, or computer or computer-generated image or picture, whether made or produced by electronic, mechanical, or other means, of sexually explicit conduct, where:
   a. The production of such visual depiction involves the use of a minor engaging in sexually explicit conduct;
   b. Such visual depiction is a digital image, computer image, or computer-generated image that is or is indistinguishable from that of a minor engaging in sexually explicit conduct; or
   c. Such visual depiction has been created, adapted, or modified to appear that an identifiable minor is engaging in sexually explicit conduct.
      (Reference: 18 Pa.C.S. § 6312) Under Pennsylvania law, any book, magazine, pamphlet, slide, photograph, film, videotape,

computer depiction, or other material depicting a child under the age of 18 years engaging in a prohibited sexual act or in the simulation of such act.

2. *Computer*—Includes any School District owned, leased, licensed, or user-owned personal hardware, software, or other technology used on School District premises or at School District events or connected to the School District network containing School District programs or School District or student data (including images, files, and other information) attached or connected to, installed in, or otherwise used in connection with a computer. Computer includes but is not limited to the School District and users: desktop, notebook, power book, tablet PC or laptop computers, printers, facsimile machine, cables, modems, and other peripherals; specialized electronic equipment used for students' special educational purposes; Global Positioning System (GPS) equipment; personal digital assistants (PDAs); iPods, MP3 players; cell phones, with or without Internet access and/or recording and/or camera/video and other capabilities and configurations, telephones, mobile phones, or wireless devices, two-way radios/telephones; beepers; paging devices, laser pointers and attachments, and any other such technology developed. Students are not permitted to attach personally owned computers and devices to the School District's network (whether wired or wireless) without expressed written approval from the Technology Manager, who will assume the responsibility to supervise the student(s) and such use.

3. *Electronic Communications Systems*—Any messaging, collaboration, publishing, broadcast, or distribution system that depends on electronic communications resources to create, send, forward, reply to, transmit, store, hold, copy, download, display, view, read, or print electronic records for purposes of communication across electronic communications network systems between or among individuals or groups that is either explicitly denoted as a system for electronic communications or is implicitly used for such purposes. Further, an electronic communications system means any wire, radio, electromagnetic, photo-optical, or photo-electronic facilities for the transmission of wire or electronic communications and any computer facilities or related electronic equipment for the electronic storage of such communications. Examples include, without limitation, the Internet, intranet, electronic mail services, GPS, PDAs, facsimile machines, cell phones with or without Internet access and/or electronic mail and/or recording devices, cameras/video, and other capabilities and configurations.

4. *Educational Purpose*—Includes use of the CIS systems for classroom activities, professional or career development, and to support the School District's curriculum, Policy and mission statement.

5. (Reference: 20 U.S.C. § 6801, 47 U.S.C. § 254(h)) *Harmful to Minors*—Under Federal law, any picture, image, graphic image file, or other visual depictions that:
   a. taken as a whole, with respect to minors, appeals to the prurient interest in nudity, sex, or excretion;
   b. depicts, describes, or represents in a patently offensive way with respect to what is suitable for minors, an actual or simulated sexual act or sexual content, actual or simulated normal or perverted sexual acts, or lewd exhibition of the genitals, and
   c. taken as a whole lacks serious literary, artistic, political, educational, or scientific value as to minors.
      (Reference: 18 Pa.C.S.A. § 5903(e)(6)) Under Pennsylvania law, any depiction or representation, in whatever form, of nudity, sexual conduct, sexual excitement, or sadomasochistic abuse, when it:
   d. predominantly appeals to the prurient, shameful, or morbid interest of minors; and
   e. is patently offensive to prevailing standards in the adult community as a whole with respect to what is suitable for minors; and
   f. taken as a whole, lacks serious literary, artistic, political, educational, or scientific value for minors.
6. *Incidental Personal Use*—Incidental personal use of school computers is permitted for employees so long as such use does not interfere with the employee's job duties and performance, with system operations, or with other system users. Personal use must comply with this Policy and all other applicable the School District's procedures and rules contained in this Policy, as well as ISP terms, local, state, and federal laws, and must not damage the School District's CIS systems.
7. (Reference: 20 U.S.C. § 6777(e), 47 U.S.C. § 254(h)) *Minor*—For purposes of compliance with the Children's Internet Protection Act ("CIPA"), an individual who has not yet attained the age of seventeen (17). For other purposes, minor shall mean the age of minority as defined in the relevant law.
8. (Reference: 18 U.S.C. § 1460) *Obscene*—Under Federal law, analysis of the material meets the following elements:
   a. whether the average person, applying contemporary community standards, would find that the material, taken as a whole, appeals to the prurient interest;
   b. whether the work depicts or describes, in a patently offensive way, sexual conduct specifically designed by the applicable state or federal law to be obscene; and
   c. whether the work, taken as a whole, lacks serious literary, artistic, political, educational, or scientific value.

(Reference: 18 Pa.C.S. § 5903) Under Pennsylvania law, analysis of the material meets the following elements:

d. the average person, applying contemporary community standards, would find that the material, taken as a whole, appeals to the prurient interest;

e. the subject matter depicts or describes in a patently offensive way, sexual conduct described in the law to be obscene; and

f. the subject matter, taken as a whole, lacks serious literary, artistic, political, educational, or scientific value.

9. (Reference: 18 U.S.C.§ 2246, 18 Pa.C.S.§ 5903) *Sexual Act and Sexual Contact*—As defined at 18 U.S.C. § 2246(2), and at 18 U.S.C. § 2246(3), 18 Pa.C.S.A. § 5903.

10. (Reference: 20 U.S.C.§ 6801, 47 U.S.C.§ 254, 47 U.S.C.§ 254(h)) *Technology Protection Measure(s)*—A specific technology that blocks or filters Internet access to visual depictions that are obscene, child pornography or harmful to minors.

11. (Reference: 18U.S.C.§ 1460(b), 18 U.S.C.§ 2256) *Visual Depictions*—Undeveloped film and videotape and data stored on computer disk or by electronic means which is capable of conversion into a visual image but does not include mere words.

Authority

1. Access to the School District's CIS systems through school resources is a privilege, not a right. These, as well as the user accounts and information, are the property of the School District, which reserves the right to deny access to prevent further unauthorized, inappropriate, or illegal activity and may revoke those privileges and/or administer appropriate disciplinary action. The School District will cooperate to the extent legally required with ISP, local, state, and federal officials in any investigation concerning or related to the misuse of the CIS systems.

2. It is often necessary to access user accounts in order to perform routine maintenance and security tasks. System administrators have the right to access by interception and the stored communication of user accounts for any reason in order to uphold this Policy and to maintain the system. Users have no privacy expectation in the contents of their personal files or any of their use of the School District's CIS systems. The School District reserves the right to monitor, track, log, and access CIS systems use and to monitor and allocate fileserver space.

3. The School District reserves the right to restrict access to any Internet sites or functions it may deem inappropriate through general policy, software blocking, or online server blocking. Specifically,

the School District operates and enforces technology protection measure(s) that block or filter online activities of minors on its computers used and accessible to adults and students so as to filter or block inappropriate matter on the Internet. Inappropriate matter includes, but is not limited to, visual, graphic, text, and any other form of obscene, sexually explicit, child pornographic, or other material that is harmful to minors, hateful, illegal, defamatory, lewd, vulgar, profane, rude, inflammatory, threatening, harassing, discriminatory (as it pertains to race, color, religion, national origin, gender, marital status, age, sexual orientation, political beliefs, receipt of financial aid, or disability), violent, bullying, terroristic, and advocates the destruction of property. Measures designed to restrict adults' and minors' access to material harmful to minors may be disabled to enable an adult or student to access bona fide research, not within the prohibitions of this Policy, or for another lawful purpose. No person may have access to material that is illegal under federal or state law. Expedited review and resolution of a claim that the Policy is denying a student or adult to access material will be enforced by an administrator, supervisor, or their designee upon the receipt of written consent from a parent or guardian of a student and upon the written request from an adult.

4. The School District has the right, but not the duty, to monitor, track, log, access, and/or report all aspects of its computer information, technology, and related systems of all users and of any user's personal computers, network, Internet, electronic communication systems, and media that they bring onto School District property or to School District events that were connected to the School District network and which contained School District programs or School District or student data (including images, files, and other information), all pursuant to the law, in order to insure compliance with this Policy and other School District Policies, to protect the School District's resources, and to comply with the law.

5. The School District reserves the right to restrict or limit usage of lower priority CIS systems and computer uses when network and computing requirements exceed available capacity according to the following priorities:
   a. *Highest*—uses that directly support the education of the students.
   b. *Medium*—uses that indirectly benefit the education of the students.
   c. *Lowest*—uses that include reasonable and limited educationally-related interpersonal communications.

d. *Forbidden*—all activities in violation of this Policy.
6. The School District additionally reserves the right to:
   a. Determine which CIS systems' services will be provided through School District resources.
   b. Determine the types of files that may be stored on School District file servers and computers.
   c. View and monitor network traffic, file server space, processor, and system utilization and all applications provided through the network and communications systems, including e-mail, and other electronic communications.
   d. Remove excess e-mail or files taking up an inordinate amount of fileserver disk space after a reasonable time.
   e. Revoke user privileges, remove user accounts, or refer to legal authorities when violation of this and any other applicable School District Policies occur or state or federal law is violated, including but not limited to those governing network use, copyright, security, privacy, employment, data breaches, and destruction of School District resources and equipment.

Responsibility

1. Due to the nature of the Internet as a global network connecting thousands of computers around the world, inappropriate materials, including those which may be defamatory, discriminatory (as it pertains to race, color, religion, national origin, gender, marital status, age, sexual orientation, political beliefs, receipt of financial aid, or disability), inaccurate, obscene, sexually explicit, lewd, vulgar, rude, harassing, violent, inflammatory, threatening, terroristic, hateful, bullying, profane, pornographic, offensive, or illegal, can be accessed through the network and electronic communications systems. Because of the nature of the technology that allows the Internet to operate, the School District cannot completely block access to these resources. Accessing these and similar types of resources may be considered an unacceptable use of school resources and will result in actions explained further in Section 13, Consequences for Inappropriate, Unauthorized, and Illegal Use, found in the last Section of this Policy and as provided in relevant School District Policies.
2. Users must be capable and able to use the School District's CIS systems and software relevant to their responsibilities. In addition, users must practice proper etiquette, School District ethics, and agree to the requirements of this Policy.

Delegation of Responsibility

1. The Technology Manager and/or designee will serve as the co-ordinator to oversee the School District's CIS systems and will work with other regional or state organizations as necessary to educate users, approve activities, provide leadership for proper training for all users in the use of the CIS systems and the requirements of this Policy, establish a system to insure adequate supervision of the CIS systems, maintain executed user agreements, and interpret and enforce this Policy.
2. The Technology Manager and/or designee will establish a process for setting-up individual and class accounts, set quotas for disk usage on the system, establish a document retention and destruction Policy and schedule to include electronically stored information in accordance with Board Policy, and establish the School District virus protection process.
3. Unless otherwise denied for cause, student access to the CIS systems resources shall be through supervision by the professional staff. Administrators, teachers, and staff have the responsibility to work together to help students develop the skills and judgment required to make effective and appropriate use of the resources. All users have the responsibility to respect the rights of all other users within the School District and School District CIS systems, and to abide by the rules established by the School District, its ISP, local, state, and federal laws.

Regulations

1. Access to the CIS Systems
   a. CIS systems user accounts will be used only by authorized owners of the accounts for authorized purposes.
   b. An account will be made available according to a procedure developed by appropriate School District authorities.
   c. CIS System. The School District's Acceptable Use of the Computers, Network, Internet, Electronic Communications, and Information Systems Policy, as well as other relevant School District Policies, will govern use of the School District's CIS systems for users.
   d. Types of Services include, but are not limited to:
      i. *World Wide Web*. School District employees, students, and guests will have access to the Web through the School District's CIS systems as needed.
      ii. *E-Mail*. School District employees may be assigned individual e-mail accounts for work related use, as needed.

iii. *Guest Accounts.* Guests may receive an individual account with the approval of the Technology Manager and/or designee if there is a specific School District-related purpose requiring such access. Use of the CIS systems by a guest must be specifically limited to the School District-related purpose and comply with this Policy and all other School District Policies, procedures, and rules, as well as Internet Service Provider ("ISP") terms, local, state, and federal laws and may not damage the School District's CIS systems. An agreement between the School District and a guest and a parental signature will be required if the guest is a minor.

iv. *Blogs.* Employees may be permitted to have School District-sponsored blogs after they receive training and the approval of the School District. All Bloggers must follow the rules provided in this Policy, the School District's Blogging Policy, and other applicable Policies, regulations, and rules of the School District.

v. *Web 2.0 Second Generation Web-based Services.* Certain School District authorized second generation web-based services, such as social networking sites, wikis, podcasts, RSS feeds, social software, folksonomies, and collaboration tools that emphasize online educational collaboration and sharing among users, may be permitted by the School District; however, such use must be approved by the Technology Manager or designee, followed by training authorized by the School District. Users must comply with this Policy as well as any other relevant Policies, regulations, and rules during such use.

e. Access to all data on, taken from, or compiled using School District computers is subject to inspection and discipline. Users have no right to expect that School District information placed on users' personal computers, networks, Internet, and electronic communications systems is beyond the access of the School District. The School District reserves the legal right to access users' personal technology devices brought onto the School District's property or to School District events or connected to the School District's network when the School District reasonably believes they contain School District information or contain information that violates a School District Policy or contains information/data that the School District reasonably believes involves a criminal activity.

2. Parental Notification and Responsibility

The School District will notify the parents about the School District CIS systems and the Policies governing their use. This Policy contains restrictions on accessing inappropriate material. There is a wide range of material available on the Internet, some of which may not be fitting with the particular values of the families of the students.

It is not practically possible for the School District to monitor and enforce a wide range of social values in student use of the Internet. Further, the School District recognizes that parents bear primary responsibility for transmitting their particular set of family values to their children. The School District will encourage parents to specify to their child(ren) what material is and is not acceptable for their child(ren) to access through the School's District's CIS system. Parents are responsible for monitoring their children's use of the School District's CIS systems when they are accessing the systems.

3. School District Limitation of Liability

The School District makes no warranties of any kind, either expressed or implied, that the functions or the services provided by or through the School District's CIS systems will be error-free or without defect. The School District does not warrant the effectiveness of Internet filtering. The electronic information available to users does not imply endorsement of the content by the School District nor is the School District responsible for the accuracy or quality of the information obtained through or stored on the CIS systems. The School District shall not be responsible for any damage users may suffer, including but not limited to, information that may be lost, damaged, delayed, misdelivered, or unavailable when using the computers, network, and electronic communications systems. The School District shall not be responsible for material that is retrieved through the Internet or the consequences that may result from them. The School District shall not be responsible for any unauthorized financial obligations, charges, or fees resulting from access to the School District's CIS systems. In no event shall the School District be liable to the user for any damages, whether direct, indirect, special, or consequential, arising out the use of the CIS systems.

4. Prohibitions

The use of the School District's CIS systems for illegal, inappropriate, unacceptable, or unethical purposes by users is prohibited. Such activities engaged in by users are strictly prohibited and illustrated below. The School District reserves the right to determine if any activity not appearing in the list below constitutes an acceptable or unacceptable use of the CIS systems.

These prohibitions are in effect any time School District resources are accessed, whether on School District property, when using mobile commuting equipment, telecommunication facilities in unprotected areas or environments, directly from home, or indirectly through another ISP, and if relevant, when an employee or student uses their own equipment.

Students may possess their personal computers as defined by this Policy, but they must keep them out of sight and may not use them on School District premises and property (including but not limited to buses and other vehicles) or through connection to the School District CIS systems, unless expressed permission has been granted by a teacher or administrator, who will then assume the responsibility to supervise the student in its use, or unless an IEP team determines otherwise, in which case, an employee will supervise the student in its use. Thus, users are prohibited from using cell phones with or without Internet access and/or recording, and/or camera/video and other capabilities and configurations. Cameras and the like may not be used to take images of others, transfer them, or place them on web sites without the consent of Technology Manager. Students who are performing volunteer fire company, ambulance, or rescue squad functions or who need such a computer because of their medical condition or the medical condition of a member of the family, with notice and the approval of the school administrator, may qualify for an exemption of this prohibition.

a. General Prohibitions

Users are prohibited from using School District CIS systems to:

i.   Communicate about non-work or non-school related communications.

ii. Send, receive, view, download, access, or transmit material that is harmful to minors, indecent, obscene, pornographic, child pornographic, and terroristic. Neither may users advocate the destruction of property.

iii. Send, receive, view, download, access, or transmit inappropriate matter and material likely to be offensive or objectionable to recipients including but not limited to that which may be defamatory, inaccurate, obscene, sexually explicit, lewd, hateful, harassing, discriminatory (as it pertains to race, color, religion, national origin, gender, marital status, age, sexual orientation, political beliefs, receipt of financial aid, or disability), violent, vulgar, rude, inflammatory, threatening, profane, pornographic, offensive, terroristic, and/or illegal.

iv. Cyberbully another individual or entity.

v.   Access or transmit gambling pools for money, including but not limited to basketball and football, or any other betting or games of chance.

vi. Participate in discussion or news groups that cover inappropriate and/or objectionable topics or materials, including those that conform to the definition of inappro-priate matter in this Policy.

vii. Send terroristic threats, hateful mail, harassing communi-cations, discriminatory remarks, and offensive or inflam-matory communications.

viii. Participate in unauthorized Internet Relay Chats, instant messaging communications, and Internet voice communi-cations (on-line, real-time conversations) that are not for school-related purposes or required for employees to per-form their job duties.

ix. Facilitate any illegal activity.

x. Communicate through e-mail for non-educational pur-poses or activities. The use of e-mail to mass mail non-educational or non-work related information is expressly prohibited (for example, the use of the "everyone" distri-bution list, building level distribution lists, or other e-mail distributions lists to offer personal items for sale is prohibited).

xi. Engage in commercial, for-profit, or any business pur-poses (except where such activities are otherwise permit-ted or authorized under applicable School District Policies); conduct unauthorized fund raising or advertis-ing on behalf of the School District and non-school School District organizations; resale of School District computer resources to individuals or organizations; or use the School District's name in any unauthorized manner that would reflect negatively on the School District, its employees, or students. Commercial purposes is defined as offering or providing goods or services or purchasing goods or services for personal use. School District acquis-ition policies will be followed for School District purchase of goods or supplies through the School District system.

xii. Engage in political lobbying.

xiii. Install, distribute, reproduce, or use copyrighted software on School District computers or copy School District soft-ware to unauthorized computer systems, intentionally infringing upon the intellectual property rights of others or violating a copyright.

xiv. Install computer hardware, peripheral devices, network hardware, or system hardware. The authority to install hardware or devices on School District computers is restricted to the Technology Manager or designee.

xv. Encrypt messages using encryption software that is not authorized by the School District from any access point on School District equipment or School District property. Users must use School District approved encryption to protect the confidentiality of sensitive or critical information in the School District's approved manner.

xvi. Access, interfere, possess, or distribute confidential or private information without permission of the School District's administration. An example includes accessing other students' accounts to obtain their grades.

xvii. Violate the privacy or security of electronic information.

xviii. Send any School District information to another party, except in the ordinary course of business as necessary or appropriate for the advancement of the School District's business or educational interest.

xix. Send unsolicited commercial electronic mail messages, also known as spam.

xx. Post personal or professional web pages without administrative approval.

xxi. Post anonymous messages.

xxii. Use the name of the "Kennett Consolidated School District" in any form in web blogs, on School District Internet pages or websites not owned or related to the School District, or in forums/discussion boards to express or imply the position of the Kennett Consolidated School District without the expressed, written permission of the Superintendent. When such permission is granted, the posting must state that the statement does not represent the position of the School District.

xxiii. Bypass or attempt to bypass Internet filtering software by any method including but not limited to the use of anonymizers/proxies or any websites that mask the content the user is accessing or attempting to access.

xxiv. Advocate illegal drug use, whether expressed or through a latent pro-drug message. This does not include a restriction on political or social commentary on issues, such as the wisdom on the war on drugs or medicinal use.

xxv. Attempt to or obtain personal information under false pretenses with the intent to defraud another person.

b. Access and Security Prohibitions

Users must immediately notify the Technology Manager and/or designee if they have identified a possible security problem. Users must read, understand, provide signed acknowledgement form(s), and comply with this Policy that includes network, Internet usage, electronic communications, telecommunications, non-disclosure, and physical and information security policies.

The following activities related to access to the School District's CIS systems, and information are prohibited:

    i.   Misrepresentation (including forgery) of the identity of a sender or source of communication.

    ii.   Acquiring or attempting to acquire passwords of another. Users will be held responsible for the result of any misuse of users' names or passwords while the users' systems access were left unattended and accessible to others, whether intentional or through negligence.

    iii.   Using or attempting to use computer accounts of others. These actions are illegal, even with consent or if only for the purpose of "browsing."

    iv.   Altering a communication originally received from another person or computer with the intent to deceive.

    v.   Using School District resources to engage in any illegal act which may threaten the health, safety, or welfare of any person or persons, such as arranging for a drug sale or the purchase of alcohol, engaging in criminal activity, or being involved in a terroristic threat against any person or property.

    vi.   Disabling or circumventing any School District security program or device, for example but not limited to anti-spyware, anti-spam software, and virus protection software or procedures.

    vii.   Transmitting electronic communications anonymously or under an alias unless authorized by the School District.

    viii.   Users must protect and secure all electronic resources and information, data, and records of the School District from theft and inadvertent disclosure to unauthorized individuals or entities when they are under the supervision and control of the School District and when they are not under the supervision and control of the School District, for example but not limited to working at home, on vacation, or elsewhere. If any user becomes aware of the release of School District information, data, or records, the release must be sent to the Technology Manager immediately. See the Board's Data Breach Policy No. 817 for further information.

c. Operational Prohibitions

The following operational activities and behaviors are prohibited:

    i.   Interference with or disruption of the CIS systems, network accounts, services, or equipment of others, including but not limited to, the propagation of computer "worms" and "viruses", Trojan Horse, and trapdoor program code, the sending of electronic chain mail, distasteful jokes, and the inappropriate sending of "broadcast" messages to large numbers of individuals or hosts. The user may not hack or crack the network or others' computers, whether by parasiteware or spyware designed to steal information or viruses and worms or other hardware or software designed to damage the CIS systems or any component of the network, or strip or harvest information, or completely take over a person's computer, or to "look around".

   ii. Altering or attempting to alter files, system security software or the systems without authorization.

  iii. Unauthorized scanning of the CIS systems for security vulnerabilities.

  iv. Attempting to alter any School District computing or networking components (including but not limited to file-servers, bridges, routers, or hubs) without authorization or beyond one's level of authorization.

   v. Unauthorized wiring, including attempts to create unauthorized network connections, or any unauthorized extension or re-transmission of any computer, electronic communications systems, or network services, whether wired, wireless, cable, or by other means.

  vi. Connecting unauthorized hardware and devices to the CIS systems.

 vii. Loading, downloading, or using unauthorized games, programs, files, or other electronic media, including but not limited to downloading music files.

viii. Intentionally damaging or destroying the integrity of the School District's electronic information.

  ix. Intentionally destroying the School District's computer hardware or software.

   x. Intentionally disrupting the use of the CIS systems.

  xi. Damaging the School District's CIS systems' networking equipment through the users' negligence or deliberate act.

 xii. Failing to comply with requests from appropriate teachers or School District administrators to discontinue activities that threaten the operation or integrity of the CIS systems.

5. Content Regulations

Information electronically published on the School District's CIS system shall be subject to the following regulations:

  a. Published documents, including but not limited to audio and video clips or conferences, may not include a student's phone number, street address, or box number, name (other than first name), or the names of other family members without parental consent.

b. Documents, web pages, electronic communications, or video-conferences may not include personally identifiable information that indicates the physical location of a student at a given time without parental consent.

c. Documents, web pages, electronic communications, or video-conferences may not contain objectionable materials or point directly or indirectly to objectionable materials.

d. Documents, web pages, and electronic communications must conform to all School District Policies and guidelines, including copyright laws.

e. Documents to be published on the Internet must be edited and approved according to School District procedures before publication.

6. Due Process

a. The School District will cooperate with the School District's ISP rules, local, state, and federal officials to the extent legally required in investigations concerning or relating to any illegal activities conducted through the School District's CIS systems.

b. If students or employees possess due process rights for discipline resulting from the violation of this Policy, they will be provided such rights.

c. The School District may terminate the account privileges by providing notice to the user.

7. Search and Seizure

a. Users' violations of this Policy, any other School District Policy, or the law may be discovered by routine maintenance and monitoring of the School District system, or any method stated in this Policy, or pursuant to any legal means.

b. The School District reserves the right to monitor, track, log, and access any electronic communications including but not limited to Internet access and e-mails at any time for any reason. Users should not have the expectation of privacy in their use of the School District's CIS systems and other School District technology, even if they use the CIS system for personal reasons. Further, the School District reserves the legal right, but not the obligation, to access any personal technology device of students and employees brought onto the School District's property or to School District events, or connected to the School District network, containing School District programs or School District or student data (including images, files, and other information) to insure compliance with this Policy and other School District Policies, to protect the School District's resources, and to obtain information/data that the School District reasonably believes involves criminal activity.

   c. Everything that users place in their personal files should be written as if a third party will review it.

8. Copyright Infringement and Plagiarism

   a. Federal laws, cases, and regulations pertaining to copyright will govern the use of material accessed through the School District resources. Users will make a standard practice of requesting permission from the holder of the work and complying with license agreements. Employees will instruct users to respect copyrights, request permission when appropriate, and comply with license agreements. Employees will respect and comply as well.

   b. Violations of copyright law can be a felony, and the law allows a court to hold individuals personally responsible for infringing the law. The School District does not permit illegal acts pertaining to the copyright law. Therefore, any user violating the copyright law does so at his/her own risk and assumes all liability.

   c. Violations of copyright law include but are not limited to the making of unauthorized copies of any copyrighted material (such as commercial software, text, graphic images, audio and video recording), distributing copyrighted materials over computer networks, and deep-linking and framing into the content of others' web sites. Further, the illegal installation of copyrighted software or files for use on the School District's computers is expressly prohibited. This includes all forms of licensed software—shrink-wrap, clickwrap, browsewrap, and electronic software downloaded from the Internet.

   d. School District guidelines on plagiarism will govern use of material accessed through the School District's CIS systems. Users will not plagiarize works that they find. Teachers will instruct students in appropriate research and citation practices.

9. Selection of Material

   a. School District Policies on the selection of materials will govern use of the School District's CIS systems.

   b. When using the Internet for class activities, teachers will select material that is appropriate in light of the age of the students and that is relevant to the course objectives. Teachers will preview the materials and web sites they require or recommend students access to determine the appropriateness of the material contained on or accessed through the web site. Teachers will provide guidelines and lists of resources to assist their students in channeling their research activities effectively and properly. Teachers will assist their students in developing the critical thinking skills necessary to ascertain the truthfulness of information, distinguish fact from opinion, and engage in discussions about controversial issues while demonstrating tolerance and respect for those who hold divergent views.

10. School District Web Site

The School District will establish and maintain a Web Site and will develop and modify its Web pages that will present information about the School District under the direction of the Technology Manager and/or designee. Publishers must comply with this Policy and the Board's Policies.

11. Blogging

a. If an employee, student, or guest creates a blog with their own resources, the employee, student, or guest may not violate the privacy rights of employees and students; may not use School District personal and private information/data, images, and copyrighted material in their blog; and may not disrupt the School District.

b. Conduct otherwise will result in actions further described in Section 13 of this Policy and provided in relevant School District Policies.

12. Safety and Privacy

a. To the extent legally required, users of the School District's CIS systems will be protected from harassment or commercially unsolicited electronic communication. Any user who receives threatening or unwelcome communications must immediately send or take them to the Technology Manager and/or designee.

b. Users will not post personal contact information about themselves or other people on the CIS systems. The user may not steal another's identity in any way; may not use spyware, cookies; and may not use School District or personnel technology or resources in any way to invade one's privacy. Additionally, the user may not disclose, use, or disseminate confidential and personal information about students or employees (examples include but are not limited to using a PDA, iPod, MP3; cell phone with camera/video and Internet access to take pictures of anything including but not limited to persons, places, and documents relevant to the School District, saving, storing, and sending the image with or without text, or disclosing them by any means, including but not limited to print and electronic matter; revealing student grades, social security numbers, home addresses, telephone numbers, school addresses, work addresses, credit card numbers, health and financial information, evaluations, psychological reports, educational records, reports, and resumes or other information relevant to seeking employment at the School District unless legitimately authorized to do so).

c. Student users will agree not to meet with someone they have met online unless they have parental consent.

13. Consequences for Inappropriate, Unauthorized, and Illegal Use

    a. General rules for behavior, ethics, and communications apply when using the CIS systems and information, in addition to the stipulations of this Policy. Users must be aware that violations of this Policy or other Policies or for unlawful use of the CIS systems may result in loss of CIS access and a variety of other disciplinary actions including but not limited to warnings, usage restrictions, loss of privileges, position reassignment, oral or written reprimands, suspensions (with or without pay for employees), dismissals, expulsions, and/or legal proceedings on a case-by-case basis. This Policy incorporates all other relevant School District Policies such as but not limited to the student and professional employee discipline policies, copyright policy, property policy, curriculum policies, terroristic threat policy, and harassment policies.

    b. The user is responsible for damages to the network, equipment, electronic communications systems, and software resulting from deliberate and willful acts. The user will also be responsible for incidental or unintended damage resulting from willful or deliberate violations of this Policy.

    c. Violations as described in this Policy may be reported to the School District and to appropriate legal authorities, whether the ISP, local, state, or federal law enforcement. The School District will cooperate to the extent legally required with authorities in all such investigations.

    d. Vandalism will result in cancellation of access to the School District's CIS systems and resources and is subject to discipline.

ST. THOMAS EPISCOPAL SCHOOL (SAN ANTONIO, TEXAS)
Social Media Policy

Purpose

St. Thomas Episcopal School understands the importance of teachers, students and parents engaging, collaborating, learning, and sharing in the fast-moving world of the Internet and "social media"—such services as "Facebook," "Twitter," "Shutterfly," Wikipedia, "blogs," and many other online tools through which people connect and share information. With this in mind,

St. Thomas Episcopal School has developed the following guidelines to provide direction for instructional employees, students and the school community when participating in online social media activities. Whether or not an employee chooses to participate in a blog, wikipedia, discussion forum, online social network or any other form of online publishing or discussion it is his or her own decision. However, to the extent that employees, faculty, parents and members of the school community represent St. Thomas Episcopal School to each other and to the wider community, participation in such social media should be done responsibly with a mind toward how both the location where one chooses to participate and the content one posts reflect on that person individually and on the School. Moreover, issues concerning the proper respect for the privacy of our students, confidentiality of sensitive information and respect for copyrights and trademarks are all important to understand before participating in an online social environment.

The St. Thomas Episcopal School social media guidelines encourage employees and students to participate in social computing and strive to create an atmosphere of trust and individual accountability, keeping in mind that information produced by St. Thomas Episcopal School, our faculty, staff, students and their parents is a reflection on the entire School community and is subject to our Acceptable Use Policy, the School's Mission and the obligation to protect the children entrusted to us. By accessing, creating or contributing to Facebook, Twitter, blogs, discussion fora, wikis, podcasts or other social media for classroom or school use, you agree to abide by these guidelines. Please read them carefully before making use of such social media. If you have any doubts or concerns about how these guidelines apply to you or your situation, or how they might apply to some new form of social media in the future, please err on the side of caution and direct your questions and concerns to the Director of the School before you make use of such media. In the online world, an ounce of prevention is worth far more than a pound of cure.

General Guidelines

Consult the employee manual and/or parent and student handbook. Be aware that all existing policies and behavior guidelines extend to School-related activities in the online environment as well as on School premises.

Use good judgment. Think about the type of image that you want to convey on behalf of the School when you're posting to social networks and social media sites. Remember that what you post will be viewed and archived permanently online once you hit the "publish" button. On sites where you publicize your professional affiliation, make sure that your profile adheres to established criteria.

Provide value. Think about what you have to offer the community, whether it's thoughtful, relevant blog posts, newsy tweets, or homework help, and focus on providing that consistently. Look for opportunities on these social sites to offer recommendations or services to engage patrons and provide value to your community. Don't be an Internet "troll" by posting or passing along mass email forwards and urban legends (funny stories, videos, non-school photos and other "SPAM").

Accept responsibility. If you're wrong about something, admit it and move on. It's not the end of the world to have made a mistake, and in the long run it's better to be honest about it and apologize than to deny it or cover it up. People on the Internet are still people.

Copyright and Fair Use

- Respect copyright and fair use guidelines. See http://www.copyright.gov/fls/fl102.html
- Hyperlinking to outside sources is recommended. Be sure not to plagiarize and give credit where it is due. If you are re-posting photos, videos, poems, music, text, artwork or other copyrightable material, take the extra step of identifying the creator of the materials to the extent reasonably possible.
- When hyperlinking to other sites and media, be sure that the content to which you are hyperlinking is appropriate and consistent with these guidelines.
- Be aware that photographs taken by professional photographers cannot be scanned and used on the internet without the photographer's permission—even if they are photos of you and for which you paid. Most photographers will charge a little extra for "digital rights" to photos.

Profiles and Identity

- Remember your association and responsibility with St. Thomas Episcopal School in online social environments. If you identify yourself as a School employee, ensure your profile and related content is consistent with how you wish to present yourself with colleagues, parents, and students and consistent with the image, purpose and Mission of the School. Remember how you represent yourself online should be comparable to how you represent yourself in person.

- No identifying personal information, such as full names, addresses or phone numbers should appear on blogs or wikis or other social media.
- Be cautious how you setup your profile, bio, avatar, etc. The same guidelines apply to this information as well as the substantive content you post.
- When uploading digital pictures or avatars that represent yourself make sure you select a school appropriate image. Also remember not to utilize protected images.

Social Bookmarking

- Be aware that others can view the sites that you bookmark.
- Be aware of words used to *tag* or describe the bookmark.
- Be aware of URL shortening services and verify the landing site they point to before submitting a link as a bookmark.
- Attempt to link directly to a page or resource if possible as you do not control what appears on landing pages in the future.

Faculty and Staff Guidelines

Blogs, Wikis, Podcasts, Digital Images & Video
Personal Responsibility

- St. Thomas Episcopal School employees are personally responsible for the content they publish online. Be mindful that what you publish will be public for a long time—protect your privacy and that of the school, our students and their families. Once materials have been published online, they may be out of your control.
- Your online behavior should reflect the same standards of honesty, respect, and consideration that you use face-to-face and should be carried out consistent with the standards applied on school premises and in furtherance of the School's Mission.
- When posting to a blog, discussion forum, or Twitter or Facebook account, be sure you make it clear that the information is representative of your views and opinions and not necessarily the views and opinions of St. Thomas Episcopal School. Remember that blogs, wikis, discussion groups, and podcasts are an extension of your classroom. What is inappropriate in your classroom should be deemed inappropriate online.
- The lines between public and private, personal and professional are blurred in the online world. By virtue of identifying yourself online as affiliated with St. Thomas Episcopal School, you are now connected to colleagues, students, parents and the School community.

You should ensure that content associated with you is consistent with your work at the School and School's Mission.

- Don't participate in spreading false or unsubstantiated rumors or false information.
- Strive to speak the truth—and when you don't know, sometimes saying nothing is the best choice.
- When contributing online do not post confidential student information.
- Before posting videos and photographs of students to any online forum, including Facebook, Shutterfly, a blog or any other media, notify the Director in advance of posting them, letting him or her know the content of what you intend to post, where you intend to post it, and the identity of any St. Thomas staff, faculty or students depicted in the media. Photographs, videos and other digital content identifying St. Thomas students or their families should not be posted online without prior approval from the Director.
- Such materials should ONLY be posted to social media that provides reasonable protection against general public access and has tools in place to limit access only to identified or invited persons.

Use of student time for social media should have an articulated and defined instructional purpose consistent with the School's Mission.

Disclaimers

- St. Thomas Episcopal School employees must include disclaimers within their personal blogs and other media in which they either identify themselves or are likely to be identified as affiliated with the School that the views are their own and do not reflect on St. Thomas Episcopal School. For example, "The postings on this site are my own and don't necessarily represent St. Thomas Episcopal School positions, strategies, or opinions."
- This standard disclaimer does not by itself exempt St. Thomas Episcopal School employees from a special or personal responsibility when posting online.
- Where online media are open to content and participation (such as comments) from students and parents, teachers are encouraged to carefully review and moderate such comments or disable their use.

Instant Messaging

- School employees are required to get authorization to have instant messaging programs downloaded on their school computers.
- School employees also recognize this same authorization is required for access to instant messaging programs that are available through web interfaces with no download.

- Avatar images and profile information should follow the same guidelines as the above *Profiles and Identity* section.
- A written request must be submitted to the Director for approval.
- When submitting a request to the Director please provide a statement identifying the program and explaining your instructional purposes for using the program.

Requests for Social Media Sites

St. Thomas Episcopal School understands that technology is constantly changing and that many sites have pedagogical significance for teacher and student use.

- If you would like to request that another online site be accessible to use for teaching and learning, please submit a request to the Director for review, indentifying the online tools you wish to use, and your instructional purpose in using them.
- Requests will be reviewed by the Director and the School Board, if necessary, and these social media guidelines will be updated periodically throughout the school year as needed to keep up with emerging technologies and challenges in the online environment.
- A description should be provided of the intended use of the site and what tools on the site match your needed criteria.
- A link to the sites privacy policy should be included if possible, and printed and attached to your request if reasonably feasible.

Student Guidelines

Due to the wealth of new social media tools available to students, student products and documents have the potential to reach audiences far beyond the classroom. This translates into a greater level of responsibility and accountability for everyone. Below are guidelines students in St. Thomas Episcopal School should adhere to when using Web tools in the classroom or in any way related to classroom or School activities.

Also understand that as a St. Thomas student you represent the School even when you are not posting to social media during classtime, and you should follow these guidelines anytime you post material that could identify you or your relationship to the School.

1. Be aware of what you post online. Social media venues are very public. What you contribute leaves a digital footprint for all to see. Do not post anything you wouldn't want friends, enemies, parents, teachers, or a future employer to see.
2. Follow the school's code of conduct when writing online. It is acceptable to disagree with someone else's opinions, however, do

it in a respectful way. Make sure that criticism is constructive and not hurtful. What is inappropriate in the classroom is inappropriate online.

3. Be safe online. Never give out personal information, including, but not limited to, last names, phone numbers, addresses, exact birthdates, and pictures. Do not share your password with anyone besides your teachers and parents.

4. Linking to other websites to support your thoughts and ideas is recommended. However, be sure to read the entire article prior to linking to ensure that all information is appropriate for a school setting.

5. Do your own work! Do not use other people's intellectual property without their permission. Be aware that it is a violation of copyright law to copy and paste other's thoughts. It is good practice to hyperlink to your sources.

6. Be aware that pictures, videos, songs, and audio clips may also be protected under copyright laws. Verify you have permission to use the images, videos, songs or other clips.

7. How you represent yourself online is an extension of yourself. Do not misrepresent yourself by using someone else's identity.

8. Blog and wiki posts should be well written. Follow writing conventions including proper grammar, capitalization, and punctuation. If you edit someone else's work be sure it is in the spirit of improving the writing.

9. If you run across inappropriate material that makes you feel uncomfortable, or is not respectful, tell your teacher right away.

10. Students who do not abide by these terms and conditions may lose their opportunity to take part in the project and/or access to future use of online tools.

Parent Guidelines

Classroom blogs and other social media are powerful tools that open up communication between students, parents, and teachers. This kind of communication and collaboration can have a huge impact on learning. St. Thomas Episcopal School encourages parents to participate in such projects when appropriate, but requests that Parents act responsibly and respectfully at all times, understanding that their conduct not only reflects on the School community, but will be a model for our students as well.

Parents should adhere to the following guidelines:
Parents should expect communication from teachers prior to their child's involvement in any project using online social media applications, i.e., blogs, wikis, podcast, discussion forums, etc.

1. Parents will be asked to sign a release form for students when teachers set up social media activities for classroom use.

2. Parents will not attempt to destroy or harm any information online.
3. Parents will not use classroom social media sites for any illegal activity, including violation of data privacy laws.
4. Parents are highly encouraged to read and/or participate in social media projects.
5. Parents should not distribute any information that might be deemed personal about other students participating in the social media project.
6. Parents should not upload or include any information that does not also meet the student guidelines above.

Source: http://www.stthomaskids.com/socialmedia.pdf

NORTH BOONE COMMUNITY UNIT SCHOOL DISTRICT 200

Administrative Procedure—Acceptable Use of Electronic Resources

All use of electronic resources shall be consistent with the District's goal of promoting educational excellence by facilitating resource sharing, innovation, and communication. These procedures do not attempt to state all required or proscribed behavior by users. However, some specific examples are provided. The failure of any user to follow these procedures will result in the loss of privileges, disciplinary action, and/or appropriate legal action.

Definitions

Includes—Means "includes without limitation" or "includes, but is not limited to."

Social media—Media for social interaction, using highly accessible communication techniques through the use of web-based and mobile technologies to turn communication into interactive dialogue. This includes *Facebook*, *LinkedIn*, *MySpace*, *Twitter*, and *YouTube*.

Personal technology—Any device that is not owned or leased by the District or otherwise authorized for District use and: (1) transmits sounds, images, text, messages, videos, or electronic information, (2) electronically records, plays, or stores information, or (3) accesses the Internet, or private communication or information networks. This includes smartphones, tablet computers and other personal electronics.

Terms and Conditions

1. Acceptable Use—Access to the District's electronic resources must be: (a) for the purpose of education or research, and be consistent with the educational objectives of the District, or (b) for legitimate business use.
2. Privileges—The use of the District's electronic resources is a privilege, not a right, and inappropriate use will result in a cancellation of those privileges. The system administrator will make all decisions regarding whether or not a user has violated these procedures and may deny, revoke, or suspend access at any time; his or her decision is final.
3. Unacceptable Use—The user is responsible for his or her actions and activities involving the network. Some examples of unacceptable uses include, but are not limited to:

    a. Using the network for any illegal activity, including violation of copyright or other contracts, or transmitting any material in violation of any U.S. or State law;

    b. Unauthorized downloading of software, regardless of whether it is copyrighted or de-virused;

    c. Downloading copyrighted material for other than personal use;

    d. Using the network for private financial or commercial gain;

    e. Wastefully using resources, such as file space;

    f. Hacking or gaining unauthorized access to files, resources, or entities;

    g. Invading the privacy of individuals, which includes the unauthorized disclosure, dissemination, and use of information about anyone that is of a personal nature;

    h. Using another user's account or password;

    i. Posting material authorized or created by another without his/her consent;

    j. Posting anonymous messages;

    k. Using the network for commercial or private advertising;

    l. Accessing, submitting, posting, publishing, or displaying any defamatory, inaccurate, abusive, obscene, profane, sexually oriented, threatening, racially offensive, harassing, or illegal material; and

    m. Using the network while access privileges are suspended or revoked.

4. Network Etiquette—The user is expected to abide by the generally accepted rules of network etiquette. These include, but are not limited to, the following:

    a. Be polite. Do not become abusive in messages to others.

    b. Use appropriate language. Do not swear, or use vulgarities or any other inappropriate language.

    c. Do not reveal personal information, including the addresses or telephone numbers, of students or colleagues.

    d. Recognize that electronic mail (E-mail) is not private. People who operate the system have access to all mail. Messages relating to or in support of illegal activities may be reported to the authorities.

    e. Do not use the network in any way that would disrupt its use by other users.

    f. Consider all communications and information accessible via the network to be private property.

5. No Warranties—The District makes no warranties of any kind, whether expressed or implied, for the service it is providing. The District will not be responsible for any damages the user suffers. This includes loss of data resulting from delays, non-deliveries,

missed-deliveries, or service interruptions caused by its negligence or the user's errors or omissions. Use of any information obtained via the Internet is at the user's own risk. The District specifically denies any responsibility for the accuracy or quality of information obtained through its services.

6. Indemnification—The user agrees to indemnify the School District for any losses, costs, or damages, including reasonable attorney fees, incurred by the District relating to, or arising out of, any violation of these procedures.

7. Security—Network security is a high priority. If the user can identify a security problem on the Internet, the user must notify the system administrator or Building Principal. Do not demonstrate the problem to other users. Keep your account and password confidential. Do not use another individual's account without written permission from that individual. Attempts to log-on to the Internet as a system administrator will result in cancellation of user privileges. Any user identified as a security risk may be denied access to the network.

8. Vandalism—Vandalism will result in cancellation of privileges and other disciplinary action. Vandalism is defined as any malicious attempt to harm or destroy data of another user, the Internet, or any other network. This includes, but is not limited to, the uploading or creation of computer viruses.

9. Telephone Charges - The District assumes no responsibility for any unauthorized charges or fees, including telephone charges, long-distance charges, per-minute surcharges, and/or equipment or line costs.

10. Copyright Web Publishing Rules - Copyright law and District policy prohibit the re-publishing of text or graphics found on the Web or on District Web sites or file servers without explicit written permission.

   a. For each re-publication (on a Web site or file server) of a graphic or a text file that was produced externally, there must be a notice at the bottom of the page crediting the original producer and noting how and when permission was granted. If possible, the notice should also include the Web address of the original source.

   b. Students and staff engaged in producing Web pages must provide library media specialists with e-mail or hard copy permissions before the Web pages are published. Printed evidence of the status of "public domain" documents must be provided.

   c. The absence of a copyright notice may not be interpreted as permission to copy the materials. Only the copyright owner may provide the permission. The manager of the Web site displaying the material may not be considered a source of permission.

   d. The "fair use" rules governing student reports in classrooms are less stringent and permit limited use of graphics and text.

e. Student work may only be published if there is written permission from both the parent/guardian and student.

11. Use of Electronic Mail

a. The District's electronic mail system, and its constituent software, hardware, and data files, are owned and controlled by the School District. The School District provides e-mail to aid students and staff members in fulfilling their duties and responsibilities, and as an education tool.

b. The District reserves the right to access and disclose the contents of any account on its system, without prior notice or permission from the account's user. Unauthorized access by any student or staff member to an electronic mail account is strictly prohibited.

c. Each person should use the same degree of care in drafting an electronic mail message as would be put into a written memorandum or document. Nothing should be transmitted in an e-mail message that would be inappropriate in a letter or memorandum.

d. Electronic messages transmitted via the School District's Internet gateway carry with them an identification of the user's Internet "domain." This domain name is a registered domain name and identifies the author as being with the School District. Great care should be taken, therefore, in the composition of such messages and how such messages might reflect on the name and reputation of this School District. Users will be held personally responsible for the content of any and all electronic mail messages transmitted to external recipients.

e. Any message received from an unknown sender via the Internet should either be immediately deleted or forwarded to the system administrator. Downloading any file attached to any Internet-based message is prohibited unless the user is certain of that message's authenticity and the nature of the file so transmitted.

f. Use of the School District's electronic mail system constitutes consent to these regulations.

12. Use of Social Networks and Web 2.0 Resources

All District employees and student who use personal technology and social media shall:

a. Adhere to the high standards for appropriate school relationships in policy 5:120, *Ethics and Conduct* at all times, regardless of the ever-changing social media and personal technology platforms available. This includes District employees posting images or private information about themselves or others in a manner readily accessible to students and other employees that is inappropriate as defined by policy 5:20, *Workplace Harassment Prohibited*; 5:120, *Ethics and Conduct*; 7:20, *Harassment of Students Prohibited*; and the Ill. Code of Educator Ethics, 23 Ill.Admin.Code §22.20.

b. Use only District-provided or approved methods to communicate with students and their parents/guardians.

c. Not interfere with or disrupt the educational or working environment, or the delivery of education or educational support services.

d. Comply with policy 5:130, *Responsibilities Concerning Internal Information*. This means that personal technology and social media may not be used to share, publish, or transmit information about or images of students and/or District employees without proper approval. For District employees, proper approval may include implied consent under the circumstances.

e. Refrain from using the District's logos without permission and follow Board policy 5:170, *Copyright*, and all District copyright compliance procedures.

f. Use personal technology and social media for personal purposes only during non-work times or hours. Any duty-free use must occur during times and places that the use will not interfere with job duties or otherwise be disruptive to the school environment or its operation.

g. Assume all risks associated with the use of personal technology and social media at school or school-sponsored activities, including students' viewing of inappropriate Internet materials through the District employee's personal technology or social media. The Board expressly disclaims any responsibility for imposing content filters, blocking lists, or monitoring of its employees' personal technology and social media.

Internet Safety

1. Internet access is limited to only those "acceptable uses" as detailed in these procedures. Internet safety is almost assured if users will not engage in "unacceptable uses," as detailed in these procedures, and otherwise follow these procedures.

2. Staff members shall supervise students while students are using District Internet access to ensure that the students abide by the Terms and Conditions for Internet access contained in these procedures.

3. Each District computer with Internet access has a filtering device that blocks entry to visual depictions that are: (1) obscene, (2) pornographic, or (3) harmful or inappropriate for students, as defined by the Children's Internet Protection Act and as determined by the Superintendent or designee.

4. The system administrator and Building Principals shall monitor student Internet access.

Authorization for Use of Electronic Resources

Student's Name (Please print): _____

School: _____

Basic Computer Use

Every student will be given access to the district's electronic resources. It is expected that students will follow the general rules of student conduct that are outlined in the student handbook when using any of the district's electronic resources.

Off-Campus Computers

While home-based student web sites and other uses of home-based computers are regarded as a benefit to a student's computer literacy, the student needs to be aware of the following:

Using a home-based or other off-campus computer such that the use results in material and/or substantial disruption to the school and/or a true threat will constitute grounds to investigate whether the use violates applicable law or district rules. Should such misuse be determined, the school will implement appropriate consequences as defined in the Acceptable Use Policy and the student discipline code.

As computer use is a privilege, such violations may result in suspension, expulsion, or other discipline, as noted, based upon the seriousness of the offense's impact or the threat's ability to have caused material and/or substantial disruption were it carried out.

Internet and Electronic Resource Access

The North Boone CUSD #200 provides access to the Internet for educational use, and is in compliance with the Children's Internet Protection Act (CIPA) of 2001. In order to use these services, each student and their parent/guardian must read and sign the following:

For Parent/Guardian(s)

I (We) understand that access to the Internet via the North Boone CUSD #200 network is for educational purposes only. I (We) also recognize that it is impossible to eliminate controversial material, and that it is impossible for the District to restrict access to all controversial materials. I (We) will hold harmless the District, its employees, agents, or Board members, for any harm caused by material or software obtained via the Internet. I (We) accept full responsibility for supervision if and when my child's use is not in a school setting. I have read the information provided in the following section ("For the Student") and understand that a violation of these rules may result in the loss of Internet access or computer privileges, or disciplinary action in accordance with the rules set forth in the student handbook and District policy.

For the Student

As a student in the North Boone CUSD #200, I understand that access to the Internet via the District's network is a privilege, not a right, and may be revoked if I choose to use my Internet access in a manner that violates the rules set forth in the student handbook and district policy. Furthermore, I understand that I am expected to use my Internet access in a responsible manner, which includes, but is not limited to the following:

- Not accessing/downloading games or other non-educational materials
- Not attempting to gain access to unauthorized resources or entities
- Not invading the privacy of individuals
- Not using another user's account or password

Signature of Parent(s)/Guardian(s): _____

                                                                    Date

Signature of Student: _____

                    (5th Grade or Above)   Date

Authorization for Use of Electronic Resources

Name (Please Print): _____

Date: _____

Basic Computer Use

Every employee of the North Boone CUSD #200 will be given appropriate access to the district's electronic resources. It is expected that individuals will follow the rules of conduct that are outlined in the appropriate staff handbook(s) and District policy and procedures when using the district's electronic resources or when representing the district in any electronic or virtual environment.

Electronic Resource Access

The North Boone CUSD #200 provides access to electronic resources for educational use, and maintains compliance with the Children's Internet Protection Act (CIPA) of 2001. In order to use these services, you must read and sign the following:

> I understand that access to the district's electronic resources is provided to assist me in carrying out my official job duties. As an employee of the District I understand that my electronic activity is subject to review as stated in the Children's Internet Protection Act (CIPA) of 2001 and other applicable statutes and policies.

> Furthermore, I understand that the District cannot couch for the accuracy of any information or the reliability of any file that is made available to me on the Internet. I will hold harmless the District, its employees, agents, or Board members, for any harm caused by material or software via the Internet.

> As a District employee, I understand that access to electronic resources on any level (data sources, social networks, e-mail, etc.) via the District's resources is a privilege, not a right, and may be revoked if I choose to use my access in a manner that violates the rules set forth in District policy or administrative procedure. Furthermore, I understand that I am expected to use my access in a responsible manner, which includes, but is not limited to the following:

> - Not intentionally accessing materials that are inappropriate for students
> - Not excessively accessing personal material during work hours

- Not attempting to gain access to unauthorized resources or entities
- Not invading the privacy of individuals
- Not posting anonymous messages
- Not using the network for private or commercial gain or advertising
- Not using social networks to make inappropriate contact with students or other staff
- Discourage students from violating the terms set forth in the Acceptable Use of Electronic Resources and similar policies

Employee Signature: _____

GLOSSARY

AFK: way from Keyboard; e.g., taking a break, using the restroom, etc.

Aggregator: See Feed aggregator

Avatar: A virtual representation of a user. Used in virtual worlds and some other social media networks.

Backchanneling (also Back channeling): The process of carrying on secondary "sidebar" conversations via instant messenger, text, e-mail, and other written media while someone presents at the front of the room.

Bandwidth: The amount of data connectivity that a network can transport at one time. Some social media, particularly those with audio and video components take up significant bandwidth and may be controlled or limited by the network administrator as to the percentage of the usable bandwidth that can be used by those types of media. This is generally done so more traditional traffic, like e-mail, web pages, grade book information, etc., isn't impacted by social media.

Blog: A contraction of Web log. A blog is a website that serves as a publicly accessible journal for an individual or a group. Blogs often reflect the personality of the author. School blogs may replace informational newsletters.

Bookmark (also Favorite): A link to a web address saved electronically in a browser to facilitate quick access to the web page without having to remember the URL.

BYOD: Bring Your Own Device—Normally meant for workshops or sessions where participants are required to bring their own laptop, tablet, or other smart device to the session.

BYOL: Bring Your Own Laptop—Normally meant for workshops or sessions where participants are required to bring their own laptop.

BYOT: Bring Your Own Technology—Normally referring to school districts that allow students to bring their own 1:1 device as opposed to having the school or district provide them.

Channel (also web channel): A data stream tied to a specific content provider. At a minimum it has a title, link, and description.

Chat: Generally a text-based method for instant real-time communications. Chat sites allow for both public and private chat. Some chat sites allow users to create private chat rooms for a user and her or his friends. Most social media networks include some level of chat services.

Cheat (also game cheat): Normally a key combination or sequence that gives the player an advantage in the game. For example, you may have a cheat code to give your character infinite health, walk through walls, or even "god mode" in which your character can't die. Codes are initially used by developers to test specific aspects and functions in a game and cheat modes are often left in the finished game product. Students are often used to using these "cheats" in outside-of-school activities, so they are more likely to look for "cheats" in academic situations.

Curate: Gather materials for dissemination, in a social media context, via the Internet or the web. However, it is also being used by disk jockeys "gathering" or curating music, etc.

Curator: Derived from the traditional use of the term for a museum curator who develops museum collections, blog or wiki curators develop virtual collections.

Creative Commons: A nonprofit organization that works to enable copyright holders to grant some rights for use to the public. Many Wikipedia images are available due to Creative Commons licensing.

Cyberbaiting: Occurs when students irritate or "bait" a teacher until the teacher becomes so frustrated that she or he yells or has a breakdown. Students record the outburst and later post the audio or video online. This differs from "cyber bait," which refers to online scams.

Digital media: (1) News from a television network, magazine, or newspaper that is presented in a web format, sometimes expanded to include any web-based news service including blogs, etc. (2) Any information saved in a digital format, particularly audio, images, or video.

Directory: A listing (complete or partial) of users or subscribers to a given social media service. Facebook includes the listings alphabetically as well as by popularity. Some directory listings can be dynamic based on the user's relationship to the listings.

Event Calendar: A dynamic shared calendar that allows users to subscribe to or post events. Many social media sites allow users to share multiple calendars.

Feed (also news feed or web feed): A means to provide users with frequently updated content usually through a blog or other news service. Users can subscribe to these feeds to be notified of new content.

Feed aggregator (also aggregator or feed reader): Combines web feeds such as news headlines, blogs, podcasts, and video logs into a single location for ease of access.

Friending: The process of linking accounts together in a social media network. Users "friend" individuals in Facebook and "like" organizational pages. In Google+, these links are called circles and organized into friends, family, acquaintances, and following.

Forum: A type of message board, this is a discussion site on which people can hold conversations in the form of posted messages. They differ from chat rooms in that messages are archived, at least for a short time. Depending on the access level of a user or the forum setup, a posted message might need to be approved by a moderator before it becomes visible to all users. Such moderated forums require messages by anonymous or unsubscribed users to be validated by a moderator.

Groups: A like-minded mix of users who all subscribe or otherwise join an online organization. Yahoo Groups is potentially the largest provider of groups, providing e-mail, polls, file sharing, and calendaring for group members. Some groups can be joined without moderation. Others require moderator or group owner approval.

Hashtag # for Twitter: Allows you to follow a subject on Twitter as opposed to following individuals. The # symbol, called a hashtag, is used to mark keyword or topic in a tweet. Any Twitter user can categorize or follow topics with hashtags. For more information on hashtags, visit http://hashtags.org.

IIRC: If I Remember Correctly: Often used in e-mail and chat, in which the user doesn't want to or have time to thoroughly research a response.

IM: Short for instant messaging, this is a real-time, text-based chat communication between two or more people. Advanced instant messaging clients sometimes allow live voice and linking to other video, etc.

IRL: In Real Life—Meaning outside of the social network or the Internet/computer, in general.

LMS: Learning Management System—A system including resources that deliver, track, and manage online learning. Some LMSs are open sourced, but many are fee-based systems.

Mashup: A site or service that combines two or more services. The primary purpose of most web mashups is to consolidate information with a single easy-to-use interface.

Mention: In the context of Twitter, a tweet containing another user's Twitter username, preceded by the @ symbol—e.g., "Hello @NBCUSD200."

MMORPG: Massively Multiplayer Online Role Playing Games (MMORPGs), also known as Massively Multiplayer Online Environment (MMOs).

New media: Defined as media formats developed in the late twentieth century. These generally refer to blogs, video journals, and other web-based interactive media as compared with traditional broadcast media (radio and television) and print media (newspapers and magazines).

Ning: A service that allows users to create their own personalized social network. AASL used a Ning to share information about the 2011 AASL Conference (http://aasl11.ning.com). Ning is named for the Chinese word for peace.

OER: Open Education Resource—Materials that are designed to be shared for teaching and learning and are available for free through open licenses, which allow for uses of these materials that would not be easily permitted under traditional copyright. Many OER providers use social media channels to distribute and publicize their materials.

Steven Baule

North Boone CUSD 200

Phone: 815-765-3322
Mobile: 815-520-4851
email: baules@nbcusd.org
Skype: steve.baule

Change Picture

Edit Profile

WORK INFO
Location: Poplar Grove, IL
Position: North Boone CUSD 200

Biography:
Even a monkey can do my job....or so I am often told (My appologies to this particular white cheeked gibbon)

Expertise:
Instructional Technology (in theory - again, depending who you speak with)

Education:
Ph.D.: Loyola University of Chicago, Ed.D.: Northern Illinois University, MLS: University of Iowa, BA: Loras College

Groups / Associations:
AASA, ICE, CMH

MY WEBSITES
LinkedIn
Twitter
My public blog
My public website

IASA profile page

Open source: Generally software that is available without charge for anyone to share, use, distribute, or modify. This is in contrast with proprietary software, which is copyrighted and generally not available for distribution without the approval of the producer. Many social media platforms are trying to use open source products in their development.

PLE: Personal Learning Environment—A Web 2.0 collaborative environment that lets the users share their learning and information gathering while also allowing them to bring order and meaning to the disparate parts of their experiences.

PLN: Personal Learning Network—A collection of resources that support ongoing learning, including mentors, colleagues, social networks, and other digital and traditional resources.

Podcast: An audio file, sometimes including video that is syndicated, subscribed to, and downloaded automatically when new content is added. Podcasts of meetings or even class sessions are then available for review on iPads and many other devices.

Profile Page: The main page of a social network for an individual, which lists basic information about the person usually including interests, background, and other demographic information. The image in this section shows a sample profile page from the IASA social network.

Rager: Someone who posts rants, rage, or other divisive or confrontational information in order to elicit some type of response.

Replacement player: An alternative service one can use when the more popular service is overloaded, slow, or simply lagging in development. For instance, Plurk would be a replacement player for Twitter.

RSS: Real Simple Syndication, or RDF Site Summary: A family of feed formats used to publish frequently updated works such as blogs, news feeds, or video channels, in a standardized format.

RSS feeds: A convenient way to gather and review content from blogs or other news sources. Subscribers select sites and blogs and subscribe to an online "aggregator" service to keep track of all their news feeds through one service.

SLUrl: (1) A location marker in Second Life. (2) A URL that has a second, potentially unintended meaning. An example is www.carsexpress.com, meant to represent Cars Express, but potentially also viewed as "car sex press." Another representative example is www.choosespain.com, meant to be Choose Spain, but is "chooses pain" as well.

Social bookmarking: See Tagging.

Social media: Media for social interactions using accessible and scalable publishing techniques. YouTube is an exceptional example.

Social networking: Participation in a dedicated site to communicate with other members of the site, by posting messages, photographs, calendars, etc.

Tagging: process that allows users to comment on or add subject headings to favorite web resources or other content and share them with others. This also allows other users to more easily find similar content. The social bookmark sites allow users to easily see what others tagged.

Toon: A character or avatar in a virtual world, most often used in regard to characters used in MMORPGs.

Troll: Someone who posts inflammatory or out-of-context messages to a blog, forum, or other social network

Web 2.0: The current interactive web in comparison with Web 1.0, which debuted with the http browsers in 1994 and provided static, not interactive content.

Web 3.0: The future or next generation of web tools, which are implied to bring greater fusion and holistic clarity to the current array of tools.

Wiki: A series of web pages that can be edited and maintained by multiple users, typically as a long-term knowledge repository or database. Originally intended to be a simple shared database engine, it is usually devoted to a specific subject or field of interest. Wikipedia is one of the most well-known examples. Wiki is the Hawaiian word for fast or quick.

BIBLIOGRAPHY

Ainslie, D. (2010). How to Be Professional in the Digital World. http://djainslietech
.com/2010/08/22/being-professional-in-a-digital-world.

Atkinson, C. (2009). *The Backchannel: How Audiences Are Using Twitter and
Social Media and Changing Presentations Forever.* Berkeley, CA: New Riders.

Byrne, R. (2010). Resources to Help Schools Understand Social Media. www
.freetech4teachers.com 2010/12/resources-to-help-schools-understand.html.

Carr, N. (2011). Facing Facebook. *American School Board Journal.* February.

Coombs, K. A., & Griffey, J. (2008). *Library Blogging.* Worthington, OH: Linworth
Books.

Davis M. R. (2011). "Safe" Social Networking Tailors for K–12 Schools. *Education
Week.* June 15

Domenech. D. (2010). What's the Purpose: Transforming or Tinkering? School
Administrator. April.

EdWeb.net (2010). A Survey of K–12 Educators on Social Networking and Content-
Sharing Tools. http://www.edweb.net/fimages/op/K12Survey.pdf.

Ferenstein, G. (2011). 4 Web-Based Meeting Schedulers Reviewed. Mashable. http://
mashable.com/2010/04/07/meeting-schedulers.

Ferriter, B. (2009). Learning with Blogs and Wikis, *Educational Leadership.*
February.

Holcomb, L., Brady, K., and Smith, B. (2010). The Emergency of "Educational Networking": Can Non-commercial, Education-Based Social Networking Sites
Really Address the Privacy and Safety Concerns of *Educators, Journal of Online Learning and Teaching.* http://jolt.merlot.org/vol6no2/holcomb_0610
.htm.

Howard, T., & Metzner, R. (2011). How Social Media Can Aid during a Crisis.
eSchool News. June.

Jackson, C. (2009). Your Students Love Social Media . . . and So Can You. *Teaching Tolerance*. Spring.

Jaksec, C. M. (2011). *Texting's Effects on School Crisis Announcements*. *The School Administrator*. September.

Jordan, K. (2012). 2012 Social Media Demographics: An Infographic. www .sitepronews.com/2012/04/01/2012-social-media-demographics-an-infographic.

Kennedy, M. (2011). Facing the Future: Social Media Sites such as Facebook and Twitter Are Becoming an Important Tool for Schools and Universities. *American School and University*. October.

Knorr, C. (2011). Caught Cheating: New Ways Kids Are Breaking the Rules. www .commonsensemedia.org/advice-for-parents/caught-cheating-new-ways-kids -are-breaking-rules.

Koenig, D. (2011). Social Media in the School House. *Teaching Tolerance*. Spring.

Lawson, M. (2005). Berner-Lee on the Read/Write Web. British Broadcasting Corporation. http://news.bbc.co.uk/2/hi/technology/4132752.stm.

Lenhart, A., et al. (2010). Teens and Mobile Phones. Pew Internet and American Life Project. http://pewinternet.org/Reports/2010/Teens-and-Mobile-Phones/ Introduction/Introduction.aspx.

NSBA. (2007). Creating and Connecting: Research and Guidelines on Online Social—and Educational—Networking. Alexandria, VA: National School Board Association. www.nsba.org/Services/TLN/BenefitsofMembership/ Publications/Creating-and-Connecting.pdf.

News One (2011). Shocking States on Cheating from Kindergarten through College. http://newsone.com/the-education-zone/newsonestaff2/cheating-kids-school -college.

Pingdom (2010). Study: Ages of Social Network Users. http://royal.pingdom.com/ 2010/02/16/study-ages-of-social-network-users.

Quillen, I. (2011). Getting beyond the hype over Skype. *Education Week Digital Directions*. Winter.

Schwartz, Janes, & Reed (2008). *A Principal's Guide to Internet Policies & Electronic Communication, IASB Education Law*. October.

Stover, D. (2010). The Top 10 Legal Issues. *American School Board Journal*. October.

Tapscott, D. (2008). *Grown Up Digital: How the Net Generation is Changing Your World*. New York: McGraw-Hill.

TeachPaperless (2009). Social Media and Cheating. http://teachpaperless.blogspot .com/2009/04/social-media-and-cheating.html.

Tech and Learning (2011). Web 2.0 Survey Shows More Use and Positive Results. *Tech and Learning*. May.

U.S. Air Force (2008). Air Force Blog Assessment. Ballstown, VA: USAF Public Affairs Agency.

U.S. Department of Education, Office of Educational Technology (2010). *Transforming American Education: Learning Powered by Technology*. Washington, DC: U.S. Department of Education. www.ed.gov/sites/default/files/netp2010 .pdf.

YALSA (2010). *Teens and Social Networking in School and Public Libraries: A Toolkit for Librarians and Library Workers*. Chicago: American Library Association.

Young, J. (2010). After Frustrations in Second Life, Colleges Look to New Virtual Worlds. *Chronicle of Higher Education*. February 10. http://chronicle.com/article/After-Frustrations-in-Second/64137.

Zwang, J. (2011, July). Facebook App Tracks Students' Cafeteria Purchases. *eSchool News*. July 27. http://www.eschoolnews.com/2011/07/27/facebook-app-tracks-student-cafeteria-purchases.

Zwang, J. (2011, September). Teen's Social Media Use Inspires Others. *eSchool News*. September.

Zyowsky, J. E. (2011) Tweeting in Schools. *The School Administrator*. March.

LEGAL REFERENCES

Asia Global Crossing, Ltd., 322 B.R. 247, 257 (S.D.N.Y. 2005).

Barnett v. Tipton County Board of Education, 601 F.Supp.2d 980 (W.D.Tenn. 2009).

Bethel Sch. Dist. No. 403 v. Fraser, 478 U.S. 675 (1986).

Beussink v. Woodland R-IV School District, 30 F.Supp.2d 1175 (E.D.Mo. 1998).

Chicago v. Morales, 527 U.S. 41, 56, 144 L.Ed.2d 67 (1999).

City of Madison Joint School Dist. v. Wisconsin Employment Relations Comm'n, 429 U.S. 167 (1976).

Coy v. Board of Education of North Canton City Schools, 205 F.Supp.2d 791 (N.D.Ohio 2002).

Doninger v. Niehoff, 527 F.3d 31 (2nd Cir. 2008); 642 F.3d 334 (2nd Cir. 2011).

Emmett v. Kent School District, 92 F.Supp.2d 1088 (W.D.Wash. 2000).

Evans v. Bayer, 684 F.Supp.2d 1365 (S.D.Fla. 2010).

Flaherty v. Keystone Oaks School District, 247 F.Supp.2d 698 (W.D.Pa. 2003).

Frisby v. Schultz, 487 U.S. 474, 480 (1988).

Garcetti v. Ceballos, 547 U.S. 410 (2006).

Hague v. CIO, 307 U.S. 496, 515 (1939).

Hustler Magazine, Inc. v. Falwell, 485 U.S. 46, 57, 99 L.Ed.2d 41 (1988).

International Society for Krishna Consciousness, 505 U.S. 672, 678 (1992).

J.C. v. Beverly Hills Unified School District, 711 F.Supp.2d 1094 (C.D.Cal. 2010).

J.S. ex rel. Snyder v. Blue Mountain School Dist. 593 F.3d 286 (3rd Cir. Feb. 4, 2010).

Killion v. Franklin Regional School District, 136 F.Supp.2d 446 (W.D.Pa. 2001).

Kolender v. Lawson, 461 U.S. 352, 357, 75 L.Ed.2d 903 (1983).

Kowalski v. Berkeley County Schools, 652 F.3d 565 (4th Cir. 2011).

Latour v. Riverside Beaver School District, 2005.

Layshock v. Hermitage School Dist. 593 F.3d 249 (3rd Cir. Feb. 4, 2010).

Mahaffey v. Aldrich, 236 F.Supp.2d 779 (E.D.Mich. 2002).

Perry Education Association v. Perry Local Educators' Association, 460 U.S. 37, 45 (1983).

Pickering v. Board of Education, 391 U.S. 563 (1968).

Scott v. Beth Israel Medical Center, 847 N.Y.S.2d 436, 441 (N.Y.Sup. 2007).

Stored Communications Act, 18 U.S.C. § 2701.

Tinker v. Des Moines Indep. Community Sch. Dist., 393 U.S. 503 (1969).

T.V. v. Smith-Green Community School Corporation, 2011 WL 3501698 (N.D.Ind. Aug. 10, 2011).

U.S. v. Bailey, 272 F.Supp.2d 822 (D.Neb. 2003).
Virginia v. Black, 538 U.S. 343, 359 (2003).
Widmar v. Vincent, 454 U.S. 263 (1981).
Wisniewski v. Board of Education of the Weedsport Central School District, 494
     F.3d 34 (2nd Cir. 2007), cert. denied, 552 U.S. 1296 (2008).

INDEX

About the Authors

STEVEN M. BAULE is currently the Superintendent of North Boone CUSD 200 in Poplar Grove, Illinois. He was named one of the Top Ten Technology Savvy Superintendents in 2010 by *eSchool News*. Previously he was superintendent in CUSD 201 in Westmont, Illinois. Previously, Baule served as a high school principal and assistant superintendent for information technology. Baule was the executive director of the New Trier Township Technology Cooperative, which provides wide-area-networking, e-mail, and Internet services to New Trier and its six elementary sender districts. Dr. Baule was previously a high school administrator, a middle school library media specialist, and a classroom teacher. Dr. Baule has presented on technology-related topics to a wide range of educators and librarians. Dr. Baule has also served as an adjunct faculty member in educational administration, instructional technology, and library and information science programs at a number of universities, including Loyola University of Chicago, Northern Illinois University, and the University of Wisconsin. Baule received his BA from Loras College, his MLS from the University of Iowa, a doctorate in instructional technology from Northern Illinois University, and a doctorate in educational leadership from Loyola University of Chicago. He has written several books on historical and educational topics, including *Technology Planning for Effective Teaching and Learning* and *Facilities Planning for School Library Media and Technology Centers*.

JULIE E. LEWIS is a partner with Klein, Thorpe & Jenkins, Ltd., in Chicago, Illinois, where she concentrates her practice in school and municipal law. She has served as General Counsel for a large metropolitan school system in Georgia; as Deputy General Counsel for the Georgia Department of Education; and as an attorney with the Weatherly Law Firm, a firm that specializes in the representation and defense of school agencies exclusively in the area of educating children with disabilities under the Individuals with Disabilities Education Act, Section 504 of the Rehabilitation Act of 1973, the Americans with Disabilities Act, and the No Child Left Behind Act. Ms. Lewis has also served as Senior Staff Attorney for the National School Boards Association in Alexandria, Virginia, and as Legal Counsel and Legislative Specialist for the American Association of School Administrators in Arlington, Virginia. She authored the School Board Governance chapter in *The Yearbook of Education Law*, published by the Education Law Association, and coauthored the book *Caregiver Alliance for At-Risk and Dangerous Youth and Safe Schools, Safe Communities*. She is a member of the Oxford Round Table on Educational Policy, where she copresented a paper entitled "Providing Children an Education to Participate in a Democracy." She graduated with honors from Northwestern University and received her JD from Loyola University Chicago School of Law.